Y0-BVN-657

FINDING OUT

BOOKS BY LEO BOGART

Commercial Culture
Preserving the Press
Press and Public
Cool Words, Cold War
Polls and the Awareness of Public Opinion
Current Controversies in Marketing Research (editor)
Project Clear
Strategy in Advertising
The Age of Television

FINDING OUT

Personal Adventures in Social Research—
Discovering What People Think, Say, and Do

LEO BOGART

IVAN R. DEE   CHICAGO   2003

HM
571
.B64
2003
WEST

FINDING OUT. Copyright © 2003 by Leo Bogart. All rights reserved, including the right to reproduce this book or portions thereof in any form. For information, address: Ivan R. Dee, Publisher, 1332 North Halsted Street, Chicago 60622. Manufactured in the United States of America and printed on acid-free paper.

Library of Congress Cataloging-in-Publication Data:
Bogart, Leo.
    Finding out : personal adventures in social research : what people think, say and do / Leo Bogart.
        p. cm.
    Includes bibliographical references and index.
    ISBN 1-56663-482-2 (alk. paper)
    1. Sociology—Research—Case studies. 2. Sociology—Research—Anecdotes. 3. Social surveys—Case studies. I. Title.

HM571 .B64 2003
301'.072—dc21   2002071644

For Michele and Greg

to explain what I was doing the rest of the time

CONTENTS

Preface

Investigating the public's opinions, preferences, and behavior has become a multi-billion-dollar industry* since I first became engaged in it more than half a century ago. It has not only grown enormously; it has changed character, becoming more publicized, specialized, bureaucratized, and mechanized.

The heart of the research process is the encounter with an individual who has something to say. The art of research is to get that something articulated and to ponder its meaning. As I write these words, the telephone rings. A recorded message asks me to take part in a survey. My number has been called automatically through a process known as random-digit dialing. A disembodied voice asks me a series of questions to which I respond by pressing numbers on my telephone keypad. A computer instantly tabulates the answers, calculates measures of statistical significance, and transforms the numbers into charts ready for presentation. The complex thoughts and emotions evoked in me by the subject of the survey have been lost in this abstract compilation.

*There are varying estimates of annual expenditures on survey research in the United States, which account for about half the world's total. They range between $5 billion and $10 billion for commercial survey research. Government studies amount to another $3 billion, and research by academic and nonprofit institutions, most of it government-funded, adds another $2 billion to $3 billion.

This book relates some of my personal experiences in finding out the answers to questions posed by clients and employers or generated by my own curiosity and interests. How these answers are communicated reflects the motivations of the researchers. Ordinarily a research report is framed as an impersonal statement of facts and commentary. When properly prepared, it describes the methods used to gather the data, and then it presents, analyzes, and interprets the findings. If the research is intended to guide managers or policymakers, the report often ends with conclusions and recommendations, which are—or should be—clearly distinguished from the presentation of the data.

But researchers whose work is not purely scholarly or academic find it difficult to avoid moving from dispassionate investigation to active intervention in the decision-making process of the organization that employs them. Grave problems of propriety and professionalism sometimes arise from this ambiguity of role.

No research report is antiseptic, whatever the integrity of its authors or their zeal for objectivity. Every study occurs in a social context. It is shaped by the project director's relation to the client, to a supervisor, to colleagues and subordinates. Research designs are developed under constraints of budget and time, and these are also reflected in the thoroughness and acuity of the finished reports.

Only a small fraction of all public opinion surveys are designed to clarify fundamental questions in social science. Another small fraction is accounted for by the opinion polls that most people think of as "research," especially in the now endless course of presidential election campaigns. Most research, by far, is conducted for marketing purposes, and most of that, in turn, is dedicated to repetitious and massive quantitative tracking of trends in consumer purchases or media audiences.

A long professional journey has led me through an improbable medley of places and problems. As an applied sociologist, I have had the good fortune to work in some distinctive institutions at critical times in their histories: an international oil company, a packaged-goods company, a large advertising agency, and the newspaper business. Some of my studies were done out of personal curiosity, others on assignment; still others were extracted at my initiative from research done on assignment. They used an assortment of methods, and they fell under two main themes: the clash of cultures and the effects of mass communications. Where I summarize or quote from them here, I have added comments and anecdotes that cast light on research practices and personalities during the second half of the twentieth century.

This book seeks to place an assortment of my studies within their human settings. It is a memoir of a professional career, not an autobiography. But it is impossible to separate my recollections of research colleagues from those of others—lovable and not—whom I have encountered along the way.

This book owes much to the comments and encouragement of its publisher, Ivan Dee, and of my wife, Agnes Bogart.

L. B.

New York City
July 2002

FINDING OUT

527147
693604
411082
354755
102986

AN ACADEMIC APPRENTICESHIP

■ My first encounter with survey research came about through an early dedication to journalism. In 1936, as a high school newspaper editor in Brooklyn, I attended a meeting of the Inter-Scholastic Press Association at the Columbia University School of Journalism. George Gallup was conducting a poll on the impending presidential election (Franklin Roosevelt versus Alf Landon), and he patiently explained the principle of sampling, asking us to imagine a jar filled with an equal number of blue and red balls. If we drew just one ball from the jar, he explained, we couldn't tell what the real proportions were, but the more we drew, the closer we would come to the truth. The election that year demonstrated the validity of his methods and killed the *Literary Digest*, which had predicted a Landon victory on the basis of postcards received from its mostly Republican readers.

Gallup's lecture was not the main inspiration for my adult interests. I was fascinated by the things people did and perplexed by what they did to each other. I wanted to find explanations and tell stories. Why shouldn't this go beyond straightforward reporting of what I observed?

The dividing line between journalism and sociology is not easily drawn. Robert W. Park, the principal figure of the Chicago school of sociology, began his career as a newspaper reporter. As

3

a social science, sociology aspires to move beyond a simple description of social relationships; it wants to discover their underlying rules and principles. The social psychologist Gordon
Allport distinguished between studies that are "idiographic"
case histories and those that are "nomothetic," or law-giving,
and thus aspire to scientific status. The idiographic tradition,
dealing in the examination of specific cases, comes closest to
purely journalistic inquiry and is therefore generally placed
lower than social theory in the profession's prestige hierarchy.
Presumably what distinguishes scholarly research from journalistic reportage is the selection of questions to be investigated.
The reporter wants drama; the scholar tests hypotheses grounded
in what we know or assume about people's motivations, actions,
and reactions.

My first venture into social research came in the course of
growing up during the dreary and harrowing years of the Great
Depression and fascism's rise. In New York this was a period of
great anxiety and political passions, expressed by hundreds of
organizations on the extreme right and left through rallies, dem-
onstrations, street-corner speeches, and mimeographed leaflets.

I was swept up in this flow of energy, sometimes as a participant (as editor of the Brooklyn College student newspaper, the
Vanguard, which, as its name suggests, originated as an ideological expression) but more often as an observer. I sat in meetings
organized by Father Coughlin's fascist-minded Christian Front,
by a host of Communist front organizations, and by miscellaneous eccentrics—proselytizers for Esperanto, proponents of
Henry George's Single Tax, black converts to Judaism. I was not
yet familiar with the sociological term "participant observation,"
but, unsystematically, that was what I was attempting to do.

One organization that fascinated me was led by a black man
who went by the name of Father Divine. Some twenty or thirty
years earlier, as George Baker, "The Messenger," he had belonged
to a small religious sect which preached that God was present in
everyone. More successful than his main rival, Daddy Grace, Father Divine had built an extensive network of "Peace Missions."

One, conveniently located in mid-Manhattan, offered a delicious chicken dinner, accompanied by mashed potatoes and gravy, for twenty-five cents. (A generous serving of apple pie a la mode was five cents extra.) But at Father Divine's Harlem headquarters, the weekly Saturday night banquet was free of charge.

I had been stirred by the fiery rhetoric of black ministers preaching to their small flocks in dilapidated storefront chapels, but the scale of Father Divine's evangelism was a revelation. On Saturday nights his great hall in Harlem was jammed with worshipers. A select group sat with him on the dais. The banquet followed a set sequence: loaves of sliced white bread were passed around and rapidly consumed during the long preliminaries taken up by Father's homilies and the songs of the Rosebuds, his white-clad young female choir. Father's adjutant, a soberly dressed middle-aged white man, kept a sharp eye on the proceedings. When the meal arrived, the potatoes and other starchy items were served first, so that any diners who had not gorged themselves on bread would quickly fill their stomachs, leaving scant room for the roast turkey. (The prevailing etiquette discouraged leftovers.)

In classic oratorical style, Father began his speeches in a low, even voice and worked himself up into a frenzy of denunciation and exhortation. The congregants responded enthusiastically, even ecstatically. The shocking ability of this individual to manipulate the audience reminded me of the Nazi's Nuremberg rallies I had seen in the movie newsreels. Could this firsthand exposure to the behavior of the incited crowd offer insight into the psychological mechanisms at work in the phenomenon of fascism?

FATHER DIVINE (1941)

The visitor at any Peace Mission meeting is immediately struck by similarities to the fascist model. There is a deliberate evocation of mob hysteria. The audience is carefully prepared for

the appearance of the leader, who is greeted by
pandemonium. All previous proceedings come to an
abrupt end. The believers make a ritual of their
adulation and their organized responses.

The movement's organization and doctrines bear
close resemblance to those of numerous evangelical
religious sects that have flourished for many years
in the South and in Northern black communities.
Many of their characteristics have specifically
African origins (the ecstatically emotional quality
of the proceedings: steady drum beats, dancing,
chanting, epileptiform seizure, wild outcries).

As in the established fascist systems, "Heaven"
uses the mechanism of identification with a
superior being (the mystic leader or god) to give
the individual a sure place in the scheme of
things. This involves the dual concept of
renouncing oneself (a heroic act) and of
participating in the guiding power. "Father Divine
is the Dean of the Universe. . . . FATHER tells the
world just how to act; what to talk about and the
thoughts to think."

Divine's extrapersonal power is striking, given
his personal limitations: he is not merely a member
of an oppressed group, he is an almost ridiculously
short man. He constantly asserts his patriotic
devotion, assuring his followers that they are
"True Americans." The most obscure white visitor is
pushed onto the rostrum where he will be most
visible.

Fascism cultivates the imaginative and
irrational; its powerful propaganda gives it the
illusion of a functioning fairyland. Similarly,
Father's disciples are described in their
publications as "happy and satisfied . . . , not even
caring, less more knowing that war exists!"

"Heaven," with its atmosphere of tremendous joy
and love and warmth, evokes the image of a womb.
Thus the words of "the Holy Spirit": Here, in the
Ark of Safety, here with ALMIGHTY GOD, the MAKER and
the CREATOR! You know it is wonderful! It is hard to
comprehend and hard to realize, but it is a
reality."

Not only does Divine, as God, enjoy eternal life; every one of his disciples will also live forever. (A follower who gets sick or dies shows that his faith is incomplete.) Fascism cultivates the notion of a corporate immortality: the Race, the State, the Party—extensions of the individual participant—will continue into eternity. Just as fascism endows its leaders with infallibility, "Father can never fail." Neither can Hitler. If the leader errs, he would be mortal.

Immortality implies a renunciation of the former, mortal, personality, and rebirth in a higher form. (Father Divine's followers change their names on entering his "Kingdom" and give up all previous relationships.) This "New Birth Under God," this "New Order" of things, provides freedom from ordinary human mores and from guilt as well.

Immortality involves desexualization. Father's virginity is continually stressed in speech and song; sexual activity is totally forbidden to all followers.

Like the fascist dictators, Father Divine continually demands sacrifices of the faithful. They give all their income and property up to him; their personal lives are limited strictly to his "Kingdom." But God (as Father) also sacrifices. The bountiful blessings that "flow free" from him, the colossal banquets of stale dainties where his wondering disciples eat of him ("Here is my body") in holy communion, the good weather he graciously bestows on festive occasions—these are but symbols of his willingness to give of himself. (Similarly, Hitler: "My own life and my own health are of no importance. . . . Workers, you must look upon me as your guarantor!")

There is heavy sexual symbolism in the wholesale "union" of the people with the fascist leader. Similarly, "Unite! Unite! Unite!" is Father's constant admonition. In the nation he urges "more perfect union"; he demands that the three Americas unite (by having the United States purchase Central and South America); he tells his followers to live in unity with him and among themselves. ("Unity" is also one of Hitler's key words.) The theme of loving Father, of "knowing" and "feeling" him, predominates in the exhortations. At a Peace Mission meeting, one of the Rosebuds, a young white woman in a tight-fitting, low-cut black dress, arises to sing a popular sexy love song with the words changed slightly so that the lover is only Father. "Ain't he sweet?" shout the enraptured Angels, in whom Father has promised to "impregnate equality."

"God has a body like you and me," carol the worshiping Rosebuds. Directly analogous is Hitler's constant emphasis that he is just one of the boys: "I was born a son of the people. . . . Who was I before the Great War? An unknown, nameless individual. What was I during the war? A quite inconspicuous soldier."

"Peace" is a slogan that particularly fits the needs and purposes of the Peace Mission movement. Its members want rest and freedom from their cares. But Father has built upon this essential element, making it an attribute of the order and symmetry that derive from his power. "Peace" now becomes a dynamic concept; its proponents are "Crusaders." (In an ecstatic frenzy during one of Father's speeches, a young man seated near me at the banquet table sprang up violently, smashed his fist through the air with a gesture of prodigious power, and crashed it mightily on the table, hissing, "Peace!")

Father brilliantly refutes those who suggest that he stop the war if he is God, by asking why the God of these doubters does not do likewise. "Everybody needs FATHER!" says Father. "Everybody needs ME, the HOPE of the REDEMPTION of all humanity, and all must take cognizance of my message with or without MY Body! If not, they will be failures!"

As in fascist regimes, the photographic likeness of the leader is a totemic image for his followers. (For years, The New Day, Divine's house organ, has carried only pictures of him, in various attitudes, on its front cover. These include one

priceless bird's-eye view of his bald head.) Most
important of all in creating the illusion of
divinity is the personal attitude of the leader
himself. Father Divine, like Mussolini and Hitler,
presents a Godlike attitude of aloofness, of
sublime self-assurance, and of cynical contempt for
human failings. In a hysterical paroxysm, a woman
screaming "God!" rushes wildly through a dense mob,
hurdles a tall barrier, and flings herself
frantically on the floor before Father Divine. She
must have hurt herself badly, but he continues
implacably to dish out the feast.

One can understand that fierce blind faith
rationally, intellectually; one can be affected by
its sheer physiological appeals, yet there is
something that defies one to say, "I know just how
they feel."

It was not lack of empathy that led me to this conclusion. Rather,
I had to acknowledge the limitations of reason to comprehend
unreason. Father Divine was someone I could see and listen to at
first hand. When I drew my parallel between him and the European dictators, fascism was an abstraction viewed from afar.
Four years in the army brought me to face it directly. To change
the world one had to understand it. This brought me to social research as a vocation.

When I arrived at the University of Chicago in 1946, a freshly
placed plaque at a former laboratory site on the campus com-
memorated the first achievement of controlled nuclear fission.
But the physicists who had produced the atomic bomb were
deeply troubled by its consequences. Each issue of the *Bulletin
of the Atomic Scientists* carried on its cover the image of a clock,
with the minute hand approaching midnight. When international crises mounted, as Stalin moved to extend his empire, the
hand came closer to 12; it was set back when tensions abated.

The nuclear threat to human survival was one of the large

themes heatedly discussed in Edward Shils's graduate seminar. Red-haired and freckled, ever animated, Shils sprayed forth sparkling ideas like bullets from a Gatling gun. He divided his time between Chicago and Cambridge. When he was in England, his wife, Ruth, kept watch over his formidable library and edited the *Bulletin*. One of its founders, the atomic scientist Leo Szilard, came to dinner and, drink in hand, took a book down from the shelf to inspect it. Ruth was shocked. "Leo, that's a bad book!" "Sometimes one must read a bad book," he grunted dispiritedly.

At Chicago, several fellow graduate students worked as interviewers on projects run by Social Research, Inc. (SRI), a firm co-founded by one of my professors, W. Lloyd Warner, and run by his fellow social anthropologist, Burleigh Gardner.* Gardner had written (unprecedentedly, with a black colleague) an important study of racial segregation.[1] In contrast to Warner, who radiated opinionated energy, Gardner presented the deceptively phlegmatic appearance of a small-town Southern justice of the peace.

Warner had moved from field research on the kinship structure of Australian aborigines to the examination of social class structure in Newburyport, Massachusetts. He defined social status as the level of an individual's prestige rather than in Marxist terms. Warner had entertainingly described the lifestyles and even the personality traits of each of seven social classes, which ranged in his scheme from "upper-upper" to "lower-lower." The "middle majority" represented the primary market for most consumer goods. SRI applied Warner's theories to the study of consumer behavior for clients like Sears, Roebuck and the *Chicago Tribune*. His students and associates used the scheme to illuminate the public's habits in radio listening, magazine reading, and product purchasing. The budding sociologists who augmented their income with part-time work on these studies had mixed

---

*The psychologist William Henry was the company's other principal. Warner and Gardner employed such eminent colleagues as Sidney Levy and Lee Rainwater, who successfully mined data originally gathered for purely commercial purposes to produce research monographs of scholarly interest.

feelings. The activity fascinated them, but at the same time they felt it was demeaning to use the lessons of social science for crass commercial purposes.

The sociology faculty was varied in its styles and outlooks. Its notable elder was Ernest W. Burgess, a former collaborator of Robert Park's, renowned for his investigations of Chicago's neighborhoods. A bachelor, gentle and watchful as a bunny rabbit, he was reported to be conducting research on the "fallen women" of the city's central Loop. Herbert Blumer, a massive former football player, lectured his classes on the follies and evils of public opinion polling. "What is an attitude?" he asked his classes in a tone of extreme exasperation. "What *is* it?"

The graduate students in this first postwar group were extraordinary, dominated by veterans supported by the GI Bill. Those with families were housed in converted military barracks while others found even more spartan accommodations in the rooming houses of Hyde Park. Social life gravitated to Sixty-third Street, which, under the thundering El, harbored an astonishing array of liquor stores and bars in which miraculous jazz could be heard for the price of a beer. Inside the entrance to each of these establishments a "B-girl" alluringly offered a roll of the dice. In the evening, live bands alternated with jukebox jazz. Racial change had not yet transformed this area of Chicago.

Many of my fellow graduate students had transferred their interests to sociology in the course of the war. I classified them as physics majors and English lit majors. In the former category I would have put Otis Dudley Duncan, an early practitioner of the multivariate statistical analysis that became widespread in the computer era. In the latter category was Erving Goffman, who formulated frame theory, which subtly systematized the study of interpersonal relationships.

My army buddy Robert Strotz had found me a place in his rooming house on Kimbark Avenue. Strotz thought and spoke with deliberation and keen precision. Slight and blond, he commanded authority, his manner switching abruptly from deep earnestness to knowing giggles. (He was later the editor of

Ekonometrika and chancellor of Northwestern University.) He and his brother Loren had assembled a cluster of old friends at our undistinguished address. One was Vasile ("Louie") Ratiu, a student of Romance languages who pursued an unusual time schedule, alternately studying and prowling at night and sleeping through most of the day. When he came home in the early hours, he would bring a quart bottle of beer and wake up Loren with the words "Loren, here is your beer." Loren would sit up in bed, chugalug his beer, and go back to sleep.

Like Strotz, another resident of the establishment, Oscar William Perlmutter, had been a member of my army cryptoanalytic training group. Willy had been recruited for flying duty with the Eighth Air Force in England, had survived his missions, and had turned up in Chicago with his bride, Eila, whom he had met in basic training. They were a most dissimilar pair. Eila, a Finnish girl from Minnesota, had flaxen hair, a broad face, and a tiny pug nose. Willy might have stepped out of one of Rembrandt's portraits of rabbis from the Amsterdam ghetto. He had a long head, already balding, a long chin, and a long nose. He was indeed a rabbinical sage—wise, learned, and sweet-tempered; he had attended Brooklyn yeshivas as a child and was a graduate of Yeshiva University.

Willy's Orthodox Jewish parents had not taken kindly to his marriage. When they learned of it they cut off all contact and held a wake (sat *shiva*) for him as though he were dead. Many years later the rupture was healed in a strange way. Willy had managed to establish contact with his younger brother, who had actually rented a post office box so that he could receive mail from Willy without alerting the parents. The younger brother continued to work on them, pleading for a reestablishment of relations, and finally persuaded the father reluctantly to agree to accept a visit from his banished son. At the last minute the father decided not to go through with the reunion and called Western Union to send the message, "Do not come. Mother and Dad." But the operator had misunderstood his heavy Yiddish accent, and the last three words came through in the telegram as "Mother is dead." Willy took the next train out to New York.

Eila kept house in the tiny room they occupied and in which Willy researched and wrote his doctoral dissertation on the foreign policy of Dean Acheson. Although Eila called Willy "Daddy" in a whiny tone that contrasted with his soft and considered way of speaking, the couple was never able to produce a child. When they confronted this fact, Willy was teaching at Xavier College in Chicago, a small institution run by Catholic nuns with whom he got along wonderfully, ascending to the rank of provost and then vice president. The sisters arranged for this Jewish/Protestant couple to adopt an American Indian infant, whom the Perlmutters named Francis Xavier, and who eventually grew to towering height. Then they decided that one child was not enough and went back to the nuns, who had no infants available but asked whether the Perlmutters would be interested in an eight-year-old boy. They decided they would. There was a catch: the child was disturbed. Well, they decided they could handle this. Another catch: the boy was attached to his nine-year-old brother, who was also a problem case. They decided they could handle that too, and miraculously they did. In 1958 Willy was running an international student exchange program from an elegant office near the Étoile in Paris, and he, Eila, and the children were living in a small trailer and tent in a trailer camp in the Bois de Boulogne. The Perlmutters had just adopted twin infants born to refugees from the 1956 Hungarian revolt. When I last saw them in Albany, where Willy was vice president of the State University of New York, they were settled in a more suitably bourgeois house, and Willy's mother was taking care of the twins. (He died not long afterward.)

I moved from the rooming house to an attic apartment in a spacious Woodlawn residence owned by the laboratory research vice president of the Armour meatpacking company. He supple-

mented his income by renting out rooms, mostly to students of
optometry who addressed each other deferentially as "doctor."
Armour was an inescapable presence on the South Side of
Chicago. The smell of the stockyards was occasionally dis-
cernible on Mies van der Rohe's brand new campus of the Illinois Institute of Technology (formerly the Armour Institute).
There I faced the challenging task of teaching undergraduate veterans who were for the most part older than I was. (One demanded a revision of his final grade on the grounds that his
father was a policeman.)

My new residence was guarded by two ferocious Doberman
pinschers who barked and snarled convincingly at all of us ten-
ants. When I was visited by an FBI agent, checking on the true
Americanism of an acquaintance, the beasts sat growling quietly
but intimidatingly on either side of me. This may have been the
shortest FBI interview in history.

I shared the attic with Don Michael, who brought an astonishing and indefatigable enthusiasm to everything he did. Don
had been a physics major at Harvard and was deeply concerned about the consequences of atomic energy. He would say
earnestly, "We're walking on the edge of the precipice every
minute," and sustained a mood of great urgency throughout his
lifetime. In an age when the social sciences were increasingly
specialized, he was a generalist in the grand tradition of the giants who were not afraid to look at humanity as a whole and to
consider the great issues that confront it. His abiding concern
with technology's impact on society led him to ponder the questions of how to reduce tensions and build trust in international
affairs, and to a pioneering examination of how computers
would change the world. He was an active environmentalist long
before the term was invented. He was a fierce believer in the necessity of social planning and regarded the conquest of ignorance
as mankind's first priority.

Don grasped the significance of the Soviet space satellite
Sputnik immediately when it was launched in 1957. At a meeting where he argued strongly for the need to research the social

implications of space travel, I sat in the audience next to Harry Alpert, a social psychologist who headed the social science division of the National Science Foundation. I asked him whether this wouldn't be a great project for the NSF. Alpert, who was not usually unpleasant, tightened his lips smugly and wagged his head from side to side. He had no time for such far-out ideas. After President Kennedy announced the project to land men on the moon, Michael organized a session of the American Psychological Association in which he asked me to speculate on the same topic.

SPACE (1961)

In the perspective of history, the times in which we live may be compared with those of the generation that preceded Columbus. The geographers and navigators of the early Renaissance conjectured about the earth's roundness and pondered the old tales of a lost continent. Columbus's expedition was carefully planned on the basis of every available scrap of scientific information and the most advanced technical knowledge of the time. Yet the most farsighted seer of the age could not have foreseen how the discovery of America might lead to the growth of rivalrous national monarchies, the accretion of capital, the stimulation of commerce and industry, shifts and growth in population, an uprooting of faith, vast transformations in cultural styles, and many other fantastic developments.

How far ahead should we look when we consider the events that will follow from man's first landing on the moon? A mere five hundred years after the first European sight of the West Indies, we are no longer able to trace history back to that day. We take it for granted. The cold war, urban decay, the crescendo of population, and the other assorted problems of contemporary society bear no relation, we like to think, to the fact that Columbus discovered America. For there it was,

America, and if it hadn't been Columbus in 1492 it
would have been someone else a few years earlier or
later. It is inconceivable to us, given the facts
of technical progress, that Europeans should not in
due time have come to America, or that being there,
their civilization should not have been profoundly
altered by the vast resources that challenged both
the most sublime and most base elements of human
nature.

And five hundred years from now, who will be
able to trace back any particular set of
consequences to man's first landing on the moon?
After all, this landing will be only the first step
in a continuing series of explorations of celestial
bodies which are "there," as America was "there,"
inevitably to be discovered and exploited, and
inevitably to transform their discoverers.

Like Don, who spent most of his career at the University of
Michigan, most of my friends at Chicago remained in academic
life. The bearlike Gregory Prentice Stone had been suddenly
shipped from a university-based military program to a wearying
war as an infantryman in the Battle of the Bulge. He was amused
by his interviews with Sears customers for SRI, but his real love
was the theory of the Chicago philosopher George Herbert Mead.
(Mead's notions of the I and the Me offered an explanation of
how people acquire an identity and how they relate to each
other.) Stone founded the Society for the Study of Symbolic Interaction and drank significant and ever-increasing quantities of
vodka. Robert Habenstein, who had ridden the rails as a hobo
during the worst depression years, chose to study the growing
popularity of cremation as an example of a progressive social
movement. Eventually he became the court sociologist of the Funeral Directors association.

On Sunday afternoons I had a standing invitation to the apartment of Abba Lerner, who had just taken a professorship at the

then-new Roosevelt College (now Roosevelt University). Lerner made a mark as an economic theorist in spite of the amazing lucidity of his writing style. His academic career had been erratic, probably because of his personal eccentricities. He went tieless and wore sandals and baggy clothes in defiance of conventional professorial proprieties. An unruly fringe of long hair semicircled his bald head. He had grown up in London's East End, received his early education in Jewish religious schools, and gone on to become a favored student of Harold Laski at the London School of Economics. As an avocation he fashioned fanciful sculptures out of wire coat hangers.

Lerner collected a variegated assortment of people to his Sunday salons. The sofas and chairs in his large living room were augmented with folding chairs squeezed along every inch of the walls. All in attendance were required to be seated, without any standing-around preliminaries, and participate in a single hour-long conversation, which Lerner moderated with great skill. At the end we were free to move about. Once, in a brash, graduate-student way, I asked the unprepossessing man beside me what his "field" was. He replied that he was a salesman, and he meant it. He was the president of Roosevelt College.

Wherever he traveled, Lerner would prevail upon an acquaintance to host a party to which he could invite his local contacts and re-create his Chicago salon. At LSE he had befriended a variety of student radicals, including some in the movement for Indian independence. Among these was H. L. Krishna Menon, who later became India's fiery first ambassador to the United Nations. Menon's demeanor was that of an angry hawk. When Lerner brought him to a cocktail gathering in New York, the hostess, attempting light conversation, asked the wasp-tongued Menon what India was doing about its "overpopulation problem." Menon brought his ever-simmering rage to a furious boil. "Overpopulation? Overpopulation? Perhaps it is you who are *under*populated!"

527147
693604
411082
354755
102986

CONFRONTING THE UNIMAGINABLE

■ I had turned to sociology for answers to the perplexing and agonizing questions posed daily in the newspaper headlines ever since I was old enough to read them. My master's thesis was begun little more than a year after the liberation of the German death camps. I had not seen those camps myself, though I had come to Chicago straight from four years in the army, which included the trek from Omaha Beach to Berchtesgaden. In the early fall of 1944, in the newly liberated Dutch town of Maastricht, a Jewish woman who had remained hidden during the German occupation took a photo of her young daughter out of her purse and asked me when I thought she would come back from Poland. I did not tell her that she never would. Because I *knew*. My grandmother, an uncle, and innumerable other relatives were among the victims. The horror and insanity of what the Nazis had done affected me deeply. How general was this feeling?

Being Jewish was something I had taken for granted since childhood, but my family did not observe the rituals of Judaism. I had encountered anti-Semitism in innumerable ways, most directly in the restrictions ("Ang. Sax. Prot.") almost universal in employment ads when I entered the job market, most virulently in the hate literature and stump speeches of native fascists. Their voices had been hushed, but not stilled, during the war years. I heard them again when I returned from the army.

The Germans' destruction of Europe's Jews has been the subject of a continuing body of scholarly books, of a number of museums, and of widely seen films and television programs. Survivors' memoirs and recorded reminiscences are on the historical record. But works of fiction (like Vasily Grossman's *Life and Fate*) that seek to evoke the harrowing experiences of the doomed have never achieved an appropriate scale and intensity. Even the literary genius of a Dante or a Milton, envisioning the horrors of hell, might falter in the face of murders executed so methodically by a state apparatus in which hundreds of thousands, if not millions, of individuals played a part, with varying degrees of zeal and enthusiasm.

Much of the historical research has been done by American scholars like Raul Hilberg[1] and Lucy Dawidowicz,[2] publishing decades after the events. American historians have also focused attention on the shortcomings and unfulfilled responsibilities of American institutions during the years of World War II: anti-Semitism at high levels in the State Department;[3] Franklin Roosevelt's political anxieties about a popular anti-Semitic backlash that might injure the war effort if it were identified with saving the Jews; the indifference of the press to news reports of mass murders and death camps.[4]

These studies all start with the same agonizing questions: Why? How could such events have taken place without an outcry, without public threats against the perpetrators, without attempts to destroy the murder factories, without public awareness and indignation? Why couldn't the Allies have prevented or stopped them?

In the study I began in 1946, I did not raise such questions, let alone try to answer them. My research was not informed by hindsight, since it was begun in the immediate aftermath of the Jewish catastrophe itself. ("Catastrophe" is the noun I used; the term "Holocaust" had not yet been applied.) I set out to answer the query of how genocide had affected Jews in the United States—their feelings, values, opinions, self-conceptions, and actions.

The topic seemed inordinately ambitious for a master's thesis, but one of my professors, Louis Wirth, encouraged me to take it on. (His own doctoral dissertation had been on "The Ghetto."[5]) I submitted my proposal to Wirth at a faculty-student tea, since he was unapproachable in his office, where he hid behind immense piles of papers, reports, and other documents that he was constantly shuffling. Wirth had himself arrived in the United States from Germany at the age of fourteen, but his English was flawless. He was an inspiring and witty lecturer, offering a somewhat cynical touch to his erudition. (His lecture notes were on white 3 x 5 cards, with the jokes on blue ones; he was said to remove and shuffle them after each course was completed.) Wirth offered no advice while I developed my project, and his only comment on the final manuscript was, "The methodology is certainly eclectic!" He didn't ask me to change a word. Nor did Burgess, the department chairman, who weighed the large bulk of my completed thesis in his hands, and without opening it, muttered abstractedly, "Could be a doctor's!"

My methodology certainly *was* eclectic. I quickly discovered that I could not address the subject of how American Jews had reacted to the catastrophe without also looking into the wider and murkier subject of how they thought of themselves and their place in the world. I approached this in an avowedly secular manner and therefore scanted the spiritual and theological elements of Jewish religious tradition, which might have provided valuable insights into the phenomena I was trying to probe.

I examined the limited statistical data that were on the public record, conducted a one-man field survey with one hundred interviews, collected personal documents in the fashion (I hoped) of Robert Park and W. I. Thomas, and culled the literature produced by American Jewish authors during the Nazi years.

More than fifty years later I review the results with a sense of shock at my own obtuseness and insensitivity. With the wartime events so recently behind me, how could I have failed to ask the most obvious questions that would occur to a sociologist in 2002? "How did you first become aware that the Jews of Europe were being killed? Did you believe these reports, and if not, why not? How did you feel when you first learned what was happening? Do you recall discussing the subject with anyone, and if so, with whom, and under what circumstances? Did you do anything about it, like giving money, joining organizations, going to meetings, writing letters to the editor or to public officials? Now that it's all over, is there anything else you think you might have done or should have done? Is there anything else you think someone should have done, and if so, who and what?"

I did not ask these obvious questions, neither of the hundred strangers I interviewed in Chicago nor of the seventeen friends who wrote essays on my assignment. To understand why I did not is to confront a central problem in the study of history. Each generation reinterprets the past according to its own requirements, but in the process it loses what may appear essential to eyewitnesses of the past. That is why the ABC-TV "Holocaust" extravaganza was phony, for all its meticulous attention to detail in such matters as the cut of German uniforms, and why Claude Lanzmann's melancholy documentary, *Shoah*, recording only the words and expressions of elderly survivors, was authentic and disturbing. An extraordinarily gifted novelist—Balzac writing of the French counterrevolutionaries in *Les Chouans*, or Tolstoy describing Napoleon's brooding egotism on the battlefield—can re-create the essence of events he has not himself lived through. We sense the inherent truth of their reflections but cannot be certain of it. Instead we must look to the chroniclers, be they novelists or journalists, to give us a sense of what it was really like to be in a certain place and time. But this type of depiction was almost absent from American literature in the immediate postwar years. At the time, I wrote: "The murder of Europe's Jews has won relatively little direct attention, among writers generally, and among Jewish writers. Perhaps it is too early for such an observation to have validity. It is possible that later students, examining the literature of our period with more acuteness and perspective, will detect a greater sensitivity and a more social passion that the knowledge of Buchenwald and Belsen has helped to forge."

In soliciting the opinions of both friends and strangers for this study, I did not ask the questions that (with more than fifty years' hindsight) I should have asked, precisely because the answers then seemed to me so self-evident. Although now it is often assumed that no one at the time knew about the slaughter of the Jews, everyone of my acquaintance knew the facts. We didn't know details about the gas chambers, the incinerators, the assembly-line disposition of dental fillings, hair, and property, and we didn't know that the annihilation was nearly complete by the time the war ended. But we were well aware that the murders were under way.

After all, they had begun in 1933. But even before the burning of the Reichstag, Hitler was a familiar and dreaded figure for Jews in America. If rabbis compared him with Haman, it was to position him in a long line of persecutors who had afflicted the Jews since biblical times. Persecution was endemic to the condition of being a Jew.

Even so unique an act as the attempted extermination of an entire people cannot be isolated from its larger historical matrix. The disaster of European Jewry consisted of a great many incidents that received varying degrees of publicity at the time. The persecution of German Jews came as the latest link in a chain of ordeals that reached back into antiquity. The periodic anguish of pogroms was part of the Jewish heritage. The outrages of the Nazis seemed at the outset far less egregious than the horrendous oppression before and during World War I in tsarist Russia and in postwar Poland. Verbal abuse and physical attacks, the confiscation of Jewish property, even the herding of Jews from throughout German-occupied Europe into the Lublin reservation—all could be interpreted as the extensions of an already familiar pattern. But the initiation of the conveyor-belt murders gave the whole scheme a different quality. The Nazi program of planned annihilation was a phenomenon of an entirely new order.

In the mid-1980s, at the annual meeting of journalism educators, a professor presented a paper on the treatment of the Holocaust by the American press. He asked, ingenuously, "Who could have known these events were taking place?" I raised my hand but no one paid attention, especially not the speaker, who went ahead blithely pursuing the thesis that no one could have known what was happening.

There are no neat correlations between a given "cause" in history and an "effect" on opinion or belief. American Jews were acutely conscious of the concentration camps, the Nuremberg Laws, and the revival of German military power. They knew of the vicious preachings of *Mein Kampf* and the grotesque cartoons of *Der Stürmer.* Many had personal contact with the growing stream of refugees from Germany. All saw the haunting photographs of Jews humiliated at the time of the *Kristallnacht,* photographs that no newspaper reader or viewer of movie newsreels could avoid.*

The flow of information was continuous, from the time the Germans invaded Poland and the first Jews were rounded up for "resettlement." Stories of massacres, forced prostitution, and torture found their way into the press, generally as unconfirmed reports buried as tiny items on inside pages. (A six-paragraph story on the middle of page 7 of the *New York Times* of June 30, 1942, is headlined, "1,000,000 Jews Slain by Nazis, Report Says.") Obscurely placed as these stories were, the Jewish press and Jewish organizations amplified them to their own constituents. The agony of Europe's Jews was the subject of sermons, meetings, and petitions. On March 1, 1943, a "Stop Hitler Now" rally drew

---

*Recent revelations that British intelligence knew about the systematic murders as soon as they began were found "not surprising" by Lucile Lichtblau, who reported in a letter to the *New York Times* that "My grandparents, who lived in a two-family house in Paterson, N.J., lacking cryptography tools and intelligence reports, knew of it even earlier [as did] virtually everyone of their acquaintance. . . . It was passed by word of mouth and smuggled letters."

thousands to Madison Square Garden.[6] America's entry into the war had provided a channel through which Jewish concerns could be vented. To win the war was to save the Jews. What other way was there to save them?

It is easy to pass judgment on such reasoning in retrospect; I do not defend it. The only purpose of the preceding observations is to explain why awareness of the European Jewish catastrophe did not come to anyone as a sudden revelation on a specific date that might be recalled in answer to a question on an opinion survey. Awareness was a process that emerged from childhood ingestion of five thousand years of Jewish history and an accretion of terrible new information almost day by day throughout World War II. When I planned this study in 1946 or wrote it up in 1947–1948, it was simply inconceivable that any American Jew would have been unaware that the Germans were killing the Jews of Europe. Only the scale and methods were unfamiliar, and knowledge was tempered with hope, to the very end.

So perhaps, apart from assuming that the answers were well known, I didn't ask the obvious questions because they were still too painful to probe. I assumed that the evidence I wanted would come indirectly—that if I asked my respondents to define their feelings as Jews, they would give vent to their sense of identity with the victims of the Germans. But as I discovered, this did not happen. Whatever was hidden did not rush forth; in fact it remains hidden to this day.

Why was the grief of American Jews not more intense, their empathy stronger, their resolve more passionate? The study concluded that they felt powerless, except as contributors to the greater war effort. They had no confidence that there were means at hand, as long as the war went on, through which they could alter the fate of their brethren. When the war ended and the lines of communication were open again, the Zionist cause offered a rallying point, if only for a minority. With the establishment of the state of Israel in 1948, American Jews eventually came to find a focus for emotions and energies that could find no outlet while the catastrophe was in progress. American Jews are today almost unanimous in their support of Israel, but this attachment has taken years to evolve, and was far from evident at the time of my study.

If the research suggested that American Jews at the time were preoccupied with their own problems, their response to the events in Europe must be seen not as indifference but as an extension of what many must have perceived as Jewish misfortune that they experienced at closer hand. It was well understood that when the Nazis started out, they had not looked very different from the native American fascists who were much in evidence. In the years 1933–1945 anti-Semitism was rampant in the United States, with demagogues like Father Coughlin and the Reverend Gerald L. K. Smith echoing Hitler's diatribes. The German-American Bund was parading about, and in 1941 Nazi propaganda films were being played in Yorkville, on Manhattan's Upper East Side. In 1944, in the midst of the war against fascism, two of three polled Americans agreed that "the Jews have too much power." Jews faced active discrimination in employment, education, residence, and social life. Such irritations seem minor compared to the horrors of Europe, but they were real and psychologically injurious.

Like American society itself, America's Jewish population has undergone a remarkable transformation in the past fifty years. As barriers of educational discrimination came down (partly because of the GI Bill), Jews surged into the professions, and their incomes moved into the front rank among American ethnic and religious groups. They became suburbanized, more geographically scattered. New immigrants from Israel, Hungary, Iran, and the former Soviet Union altered the ethnic mix within the Jewish population itself. Partly as a response to racial changes in urban public school systems (and a consequent growth in religious schools), the trend away from Orthodoxy reversed. At the same time, however, intermarriage with non-Jews grew (it is now at the 50 percent level), raising serious questions as to whether American Jews are a vanishing species. The outlook and values of Jews changed. While terrorism in the Middle

East brought new anxieties, the injuries and injustices of the past were ancient history for generations that had not experienced them directly.

The destruction of Europe's Jews and of Yiddish as an active language severed the connections that had nourished traditions in an earlier era. As Jews entered the mainstream of American life, they no longer even qualified for minority status in a society now dedicated to the improvement and empowerment of minorities. The Jewish working class, suffused with the romantic socialist idealism of tsarist times, survives only in old people's homes in Brighton Beach and Miami Beach.

Fifty-five years ago the people I talked to were in a state of transition between the world of the immigrant ghetto and the new world of Manhasset and Beverly Hills. That gives their testimony a touch of nostalgia, apart from the light it sheds on the response of Jews in the United States to the European Jewish catastrophe. That response can only be understood in the light of the fact that in 1947 most American Jews were first-generation immigrants and their children, faced with the challenge of adapting to a culture dramatically different from that of Eastern Europe.

THE RESPONSE OF U.S. JEWS TO THE EUROPEAN JEWISH CATASTROPHE (1948)

Has the persecution and murder of Europe's Jews made American Jews a more cohesive group? How has it changed the way they see themselves? One answer to these questions might be in the record of their voluntary associations.

In a predominantly Jewish neighborhood in a city of ethnic enclaves, the usual types of group activity are in evidence: a merchants' association in the shopping district, a local of the painters' union, a dramatic society in the high school, a district Democratic party club, a chapter of the American Legion. The individual members of these groups act within them primarily as movie fans,

bridge players, or veterans. Yet these roles are
subtly altered when all or virtually all the
members of the group are Jewish. Organizations
composed of Jews but with no Jewish purpose have
been an important element in American Jewish life,
because they create and strengthen a sense of group
solidarity.

An individual might be unconscious of this,
like the thirty-two-year-old woman who told me,
"Why, yes, all the girls in the club are Jewish,
but it just happened to be that way. We were all
in school at the same time and our families knew
each other, so it just happened that way."

In the case of organizations with a
specifically Jewish description or mission, a
marked contrast exists between well-defined
official programs and members' contradictory,
inconsistent, and ambivalent opinions. Voluntary
associations are based on their members' real
needs, which find expression in statements of
principle or ideology. In large organizations,
members' loyalties shift from such generalities to
the more immediate personal connections with others
in their local unit. The leadership of even the
most democratic association exerts strong power
over its members' opinions because it provides
clearly formulated and consistent policy positions
to which they can adhere. Some associations (like
the activist Zionist youth groups) exact a high
degree of ideological commitment and zeal. Others
(like the B'nai B'rith), play a political role but
attract their members for primarily nonpolitical
reasons.

Before America's entry into the war, the Nazi
persecutions seem to have stimulated participation
in organized Jewish life, while the years in which
the European Jews were being systematically
murdered did not show a rise in this activity.[7]

During the depression years between 1935 and
1941, when the persecution of the German Jews
captured worldwide attention, the membership of
nonpolitical Jewish organizations declined while

membership in political organizations doubled.
(Membership in American voluntary associations was
static during this period.) During the war, Jewish
nonpolitical organizations showed only half the
great membership increases of all American
associations, and Jewish political organizations
grew even more slowly. While enrollment in Jewish
religious schools grew markedly during the war,
contributions to the major Jewish charities rose at
about the same rate as did American philanthropies
in general. When the war ended, contributions to
Jewish charities, particularly overseas causes,
grew rapidly.

While the major national Jewish organizations
have all taken a stand on Zionism, mainly in its
favor, ordinary people rarely think in terms of
clearly framed organizational ideology. Public
opinion is an amorphous and unstructured
combination of sentiments and loyalties. Persons
who support the same program may do so for
conflicting reasons.

At the time of my interviews (May-July 1947),
the fate of Jewish "displaced persons" in Europe
was dramatically publicized by several unsuccessful
efforts to run the British blockade and by violent
actions on the part of the Palestinian underground
movement.

Questions that probed the subject of Jewish
identity elicited few references to the Germans'
machinery of extermination. Over half of those
interviewed had a personal connection with the
events in Europe. One in five had known of
relatives in Europe before the war but had made no
effort to discover what had happened to them.

> Attorney's wife, twenty-six: "We've just never
> gotten in touch with them. One is a brother and
> the other is a sister. But the sister is only a
> half-sister. They never came to America and
> they just got lost in the shuffle."

Many were unaware of the extent of the atrocities.

Twenty-two-year-old female bookkeeper: "Does it run in the millions? No, it doesn't run into the millions. Well, maybe it's close to a million. No, it couldn't be that many!"

An individual's level of Jewish identity is not significantly related to personal contact with the fate of Europe's Jews, to personal exposure to anti-Semitism (less common among women than among men), or to participation in Jewish organizations. This suggests that the persecution and murder of Europe's Jews has not had much direct effect upon beliefs. Three of four respondents say their answers to a series of questions on Jewish identity would have been the same in 1941.

Secretary, forty-five [speaking of Eastern European Jews]: "Their way of life over there was what brought on a lot of trouble. They were a little too rabid."

Salesman, forty-six: "We as Jews should mind our own business as much as possible and not try to make ourselves rambunctious. We should keep a reserved place. It's about all we can do."

Remarks like these reflect a number of elements: a rejection of Old World attributes, self-hatred (an inversion of aggressive impulses), resentment of Eastern European Jews by those of Western origin—a resentment that is sometimes reciprocated.

The interviews reveal a fundamental uncertainty as to what being Jewish really means.

Wife of a shoe dealer, thirty-five: "Jew is besides being a religion it isn't anything that he can change. He's just a Jew and that's all there is to it. It's more than that. It's something that's born in them."

Contractor's widow, fifty-nine: "I don't know what we are. We're just human beings like everyone else."

The Jewish underground movement in Palestine came up spontaneously in almost all the interviews. At that time the lines of battle were drawn not merely between Jews and British and Jews and Arabs, but among Jews themselves. Opinions on this subject are not significantly related to personal feelings of loyalty to the Jewish group or to views on the status of Jews in America. Nor do they relate to personal experience with anti-Semitism or contact with the plight of Europe's Jews. They are also unrelated to gender, age, nativity, or social status. Evidently it is individual temperament that prompts support or rejection of violence.

Pharmacist, forty-three: "I don't think it will do them a lot of good to keep up activities of this sort. On the other hand, I don't think it will do much good if they keep still. It won't do much good either way."

Stenographer, twenty-eight: "If there were some opportunity for them in their own country to get along with their neighbors I imagine that's something they'd rather do than go where they don't know too much about it."

The most striking conclusion to be drawn from the interviews is that the murder of Europe's Jews has not strongly affected American Jews' existing patterns of thought, feeling, and Jewish identity.

This conclusion is buttressed by personal statements that I obtained from youthful acquaintances, on the subject, "How I feel about being a Jew." (I suggested some themes but avoided any direct reference to what had happened during the war.)

Student and housewife, twenty-three: "I have no allegiance to the Jewish race nor do I feel personally outraged at the knowledge of Jewish persecution. I feel no special indignance [sic] at instances of anti-Semitism. My indignance seems to be generalized at all types of persecution and intolerances."

In a number of other statements, the refusal to identify with the Jewish group is just as emphatic, but the rejection reveals a deep emotional struggle.

Editor of a trade publication, twenty-eight: "Jewish religion is more deplorable, in my opinion, than many others. In a nutshell, I find it hypocritical, materialistic, reactionary, devoid, for the most part, of any spiritual value whatever. . . . Being Jewish has little intrinsic significance to me."

Shopkeeper, twenty-five: "I didn't like Jewishy Jews. Their vulgar habits and talk made my skin crawl and still do. . . . Yet I know I was born a Jew and will always call myself one. I am uncomfortably a Jew and I know it. I don't like it. Yet, considering my dignity as a human being, I would never do anything to disown my heritage."

He refers to "the persecution of the Jews in Germany" (a prewar term), suggesting that he had repressed his awareness of the systematic mass murder that followed throughout Europe.

Graduate student in physics, twenty-six: "I have no more intellectual sympathy for the Jews than I have for any persecuted or mistreated people. My only identification with the Jews is a fear that what is happening to them in Europe could easily happen to me and my friends sometime during our lives."

Graduate student in social science, twenty-five: "There is present in me, and I think in almost every American Jew, a resentment that he is a Jew, and a consequent dislike for other Jews. I

go out of my way to avoid offending people, by
perhaps profuse courtesy . . . because I feel that
as a Jew I am under observation continually by
the Protestants toward whom I still feel a
sneaking inferiority."

As strong a variety as there is among my
informants, all sense hostility in the surrounding
Gentile world, a hostility made more poignant by
their own identification with the dominant American
values. In the absence of any positive emotional
attachment to Jewish tradition and religious
practice, Jewishness is a burden, an identification
worn out of duty but which they seek to make as
inconspicuous as possible. What does arouse feeling
is the recollection of Jewish experiences, enjoyed
with family or friends, that arouse "atavistic
stirrings, even longing," and the invocation of
those symbols that represent active threats to them
as individuals (the Nazis, the British military in
Palestine) and that evoked "pity and solidarity-
yearning."

> Sociologist, twenty-six: "It has been difficult
> for me to respond to the problems of European
> Jews on a Jewish level. I found what response I
> did experience—particularly emotional response—
> oriented to the condition of human rather than
> peculiarly Jewish suffering."

> Journalist, twenty-eight: "I accept Jewishness
> as I accept being a member of *Homo Sapiens*
> rather than a member of any other tribe of
> animal life."

Both the interviews and the personal documents indicate that
many American Jews were concerned at this time with the
preservation of Jewish culture, quite apart from the depth of their
personal adherence to the religious faith. This concern demanded a special interest in the affairs of Jews abroad. Before the

war, ties with the strongly self-conscious Jewish community in Eastern Europe were maintained through visits, correspondence, motion pictures, theatrical troupes, books, and periodicals. These links, cut during the war, were displaced afterward to the Jews of Palestine. But since these were so many fewer than with those who had been killed, the connections were no longer personal.

The United States had become the center of world Jewish population and resources. But the destruction of European Jewry had drastically reduced the non-American influence on America's Jews, leaving them with few direct experiences of European ways. With the passing of the prewar immigrants, following generations would be still farther removed from such recollections. At the time I predicted that as Jews became indistinguishable from the general population, religious rather than secular cultural institutions would become central to their identity and that the religious institutions would conform to prevailing American standards. But if the general trend was away from traditional religious practices and few cultural peculiarities or loyalties remained, the most significant ties to the Jewish group

> may well be forged, in the future, as in the past, by the pressure of discrimination. . . . A unity forged under such pressure is hardly propitious either for maintaining a positive culture or for attaining a stable group life. . . . To remain vital, [Jewish] culture would have to be sustained by continuing creative contributions; otherwise it would have a merely antiquarian interest. . . . Little of the intellectual or creative talent of American Jewry is seeking or finding expression through Jewish channels. Though some sensitive individuals have been deeply moved by the European disaster, this emotion has rarely been transferred into either artistic or political endeavor.

The foregoing predictions did not anticipate a number of important developments: (1) The emergence of Israel and its continuing battles, which generated passionate support from American

Jews; (2) the accelerating growth of Jewish-Christian intermarriage; (3) new waves of Jewish immigration; (4) the rise of ultra-
Orthodox sects, strongly resistant to cultural assimilation.

The masses of American Jews did not interpret the European
murders as a direct threat to their own security. Although they
all—more or less perfectly—knew what the Germans had done,
and though they were deeply affected by what had happened,
comparatively few felt an acute personal involvement through
family ties. Many may have deliberately avoided reading, thinking, or pondering upon the European events that had such a potential to disturb them. They were far more ready to take an
interest in the condition of the surviving Jews of Europe than to
reflect on the occurrences of the immediate past. The people interviewed in Chicago were more concerned with the immediate
issue of terrorism in Palestine than with what had happened during the war. Their hostile feelings were more often directed at the
British, who were barring Jewish refugees, than at the Nazis.

David P. Boder, a psychologist who gathered and recorded a
large set of interviews with "displaced persons" in 1945, found
American Jewish audiences restive when he lectured on the firsthand accounts of the deportations and slaughter. Instead they demanded, "Tell us of the future, not of what's past and done
with."[8]

The reluctance of American Jews to think about the European massacres has several possible explanations: (1) Guilt. A
sense that something more could have been done to prevent
what happened. (2) Incredulity. An inability to conceive of mon-
strosities on such a scale in terms of everyday human experience. (3) Impotence. Contemporary Palestine held interest
because it was the scene of a *struggle*, while the ruined and
empty ghettos carried the memory of defeat. (4) Fear. Of all the
world's countries, the United States had offered its Jews the
greatest measure of security and peace, and they had responded
with passionate loyalty. This security, this assuredness of be-
longing, had permitted them, in the space of one or two generations, to slough off most of the unique customs that their

ancestors had preserved through centuries. For them to reflect intently upon the fate of their co-religionists in Europe might give rise to feelings of doubt and uncertainty about the stability of their own condition. But the masses of American Jews may have found it necessary to repress any doubts about their own future status, if only to maintain mental balance and get on with normal daily life. Neither the degree of their own personal contact with European events nor their encounters with anti-Semitism altered their outlook on the subject of Jewish nationalism.

Empathy requires a comprehensible subject and an element of drama. The most historically significant events of the twentieth century occurred on a scale that surpasses human imagination and that is difficult for mass media to convey. In an era when individuals have less and less control over their own destinies, it is natural for war and desolation to be seen as the products of inexorable, impersonal forces and therefore regarded with false complacency. Nations could arm themselves for nuclear warfare not only because their technicians had the necessary knowledge but because their citizens could not comprehend its devastating consequences.

This study of American Jews' reaction to a great human catastrophe reveals that, even for a group closely involved with the victims by kinship, history, and custom, many people are unable to identify fully with calamities of which they are not an immediate, living part. Such disengagement may provide parables for moralists, but it should trouble those who seek to understand the human condition.

527147
69**3**604
411082
354755
102986

THE LURE OF MASS MEDIA

■ My study of response to the European Jewish catastrophe was prompted by a strong sense of the subject's urgency and a realization that the historical moment to study it would soon be past. My doctoral dissertation, about readers of the comics, was to show that, even in academia, the choice of a research topic may hinge on chance. In May 1948 I returned from Chicago to New York as an A.B.D. (All But Dissertation), in search of a teaching job. Leaving resumés with every college and university in the area, I called on Harvey Zorbaugh, the sociology chairman at New York University's School of Education and author of a classic study of Chicago's Near North Side (*The Gold Coast and the Slum*,[1] his own dissertation at the University of Chicago).

Zorbaugh was extroverted and cordial, qualities abetting a strong entrepreneurial streak that took him beyond the academic cloister. He had been consulting for Metropolitan Sunday Comics, an advertising sales cooperative of big newspapers, which had just completed (in 1947) a national survey of comics reading habits and preferences. Would I be interested in analyzing the results and comparing them with those of a similar study done a few years earlier? He offered $300. Apart from this irresistible monetary incentive, the subject resonated with a long-standing fascination I had with the press and with what were colloquially known in New York not as "the funnies" but as "the jokes."

My attraction to the mass media came early in life. We acquired a radio—probably a hand-me-down from one of my father's friends—much later than other families of my childhood acquaintances. It had an impressive large horn of a loudspeaker, like that of an old-fashioned phonograph (which we never possessed), and worked erratically, with a great deal of static. An array of large black bakelite dials had to be twirled continually to achieve the best reception.

As a small boy I acquired the makings of a crystal radio set, which I put together, using a salvaged earphone. Not many readers of this book have owned a crystal radio, or perhaps even know what it is. Its heart is a small lump of quartz, whose surface is scratched by a small bent wire called a cat's whisker. No batteries, no wall socket; it is powered by the radio waves it picks up from a wire antenna. My crystal radio could receive only a single local station. I listened in bed at night to distant voices and music that sounded softly in my ear. Radio enveloped me in a delicious intimacy; it was as personal as a telephone conversation between close friends, and it brought the whole world into my orbit. The best radio disc jockeys of today, with their soft, low-key comments on the musical recordings they play, still strive for this kind of close personal relationship with the listener—one person speaking in the ear of another.

Later at some point I acquired a soldering iron and experimented with the assembly of more elaborate radios, using discarded and salvaged condensers, rheostats, earphones, and other components. These devices had a disconcerting tendency to short out.

Radio was already well beyond the conversational stage. Amplifiers became progressively more powerful, culminating in the assertive boom-boxes of the 1970s. Radio's function as the main instrument of family entertainment was replaced by television. The advent of the transistor allowed it to resume its more intimate character. The advent of digital radio on the Internet has reinforced this transformation.

When our original superheterodyne set died, my father reluctantly purchased a new one, encased in a small ogival wooden box with only two knobs, for tuning and volume. I bent over it each evening to listen to such favorite daily serials as "The Rise of the Goldbergs," "Amos 'n' Andy" and "Lum 'n' Abner," whose hillbilly twangs my parents found both unintelligible and distasteful. These programs moved at a tortuous pace, their desultory conversations punctuated with long and portentous pauses.

An exception in this genre was "Buck Rogers," which entrapped my imagination with its visits to remote planets and asteroids, mostly inhabited by singularly malevolent creatures who spoke perfect English. "Buck Rogers" was already familiar to me from the comics pages of Bernarr MacFadden's *New York Evening Graphic*, renowned for its green-tinted newsprint and its photomontage reenactments of crime scenes. The sinister powers who opposed Buck and his girlfriend Wilma were Killer Kane and his consort, Ardala. When I was taken to hear one of these broadcasts, I was shocked to discover that the voices of the evil pair belonged to two pleasant-looking blond actors, while the heroes were dark and scowling. The bellowing voice that proclaimed the start of the broadcast, "Buck Rogers in the Twenty-fifth *Cen*-tury!!!" belonged to Paul Douglas, whose career on stage and in film took off from there. Watching this broadcast, with the sound-effects man rattling something like pots and pans to simulate the careening of rockets in outer space, was a disillusioning experience which made me aware of mass media's power to manipulate fantasy.

That was my second visit to a radio studio; earlier I had seen a broadcast by The Happiness Boys, Billy Jones and Ernie Hare, who, with their accompanying orchestra, were brought to a grateful public by Hellmann's Mayonnaise. The link between happiness and commerce was already well established in this pioneer period of broadcasting, and I was in no position to question it.

In the 1920s I had already been taken to the movies to see Jackie Coogan and Charlie Chaplin. (My mother fantasied that I too might well be suited to the career of a child star.) By the 1930s sound had come, a terrifying growling sound that I found disturbing. Our second-floor apartment overlooked the back alley of the Manor Theater, through which youngsters more enterprising than myself would sometimes sneak into an afternoon performance. I was permitted to go alone to the Saturday matinees, which included an A picture, a B picture, and sometimes a Western thrown in as a third feature. There were also coming attractions, several cartoons, a newsreel, and, best of all, an episode of a serial, invariably ending with the mad scientist about to send the heroine to a horrific end. A white-coated matron patrolled the rowdy children's section, vainly seeking to control feral outcries, pugilistics, and improvised projectiles.

At the age of ten or eleven I became a sales agent for the *Saturday Evening Post*, lured by the promise of fabulous prizes for outstanding sales accomplishments that I never achieved. The young man who recruited me from his car as I walked with my mother dropped off a pile of magazines at my door each week and periodically came around to collect his money. I was able to solicit subscriptions from my barber, from some friends of my parents, and from two or three other regulars who could afford the heavy financial commitment.

Curtis Publishing offered a dazzling array of premiums for its juvenile vendors, displayed in booklets that spurred them on to superior heights of performance. But I never qualified for any of the bicycles, air rifles, radios, and other enticements. The magazine sold for a nickel, of which I kept one cent, and I never had more than five or six regular subscribers, so the few pennies I turned over to my mother each week never made much of a contribution to the family's fortunes. I undoubtedly wore out much more in shoe leather, since my delivery route extended over sev-

eral widely scattered miles. I diligently stood at the subway station at rush hour week after week, shouting "*Saturday Evening
Post* five cents!" but never sold a single copy. In that depression-
bowed community of immigrant workers, the *Post*'s wholesome
small-town Midwestern version of America simply did not res-
onate. For me, however, the *Post* opened a window into the nation's larger society. This was the *Post* of Norman Rockwell and
E. C. Leyendecker covers, of stories by John P. Marquand,
Clarence Buddington Kelland, and Arthur Train. Nordhoff and
Hall's *Mutiny on the Bounty* was being serialized. On the days
when my bundle arrived at the front door, I rushed to absorb its
literary treasures. Reading the *Post* was the main motivation for
trying to sell it.

Comics were seldom present in my home when I was a child. My
lifelong addiction to the *New York Times* was derived from my
father. In the depression years, when every nickel counted, he
faithfully collected a daily copy that someone had discarded in
the subway. On a lucky day he might also find a *World*, a
Telegram, a *Herald-Tribune*, or a *Sun*, but he disdained the
tabloids and the sensational Hearst broadsheets, the *Journal* and
the *American*. He made up bedtime stories about Mr. Jiggs, the
henpecked hero of the *American*'s "Bringing up Father," and
claimed personal acquaintance with him. On Sundays I visited
my great-aunt Minna, whose bachelor boarder bought the *World*
and the *American*, and I devoured both Pulitzer's "Katzenjam-
mer Kids" and Hearst's rival "Captain and the Kids." (These featured identical characters drawn by the strip's original creator,
whom Hearst had wooed away.)

My interest in journalism was fired when my father some-
how acquired a typewriter. In the sixth grade I was producing a
class newspaper, complete with illustrations, in as many copies
as carbon paper would permit. A penchant for cartooning
yielded a series of comic strips named after their protagonist,
"The Professor." I decided that these deserved professional pub-

lication and visited the office of a newly established weekly, *The Naborhood News*, housed over a delicatessen on Avenue J, the area's principal shopping street. The cigar-chewing publisher and editor bore the impressive name of Charles Socrates Weiss; he was stout and slovenly, and had been lamed by polio. This must have made for uncomfortable trips up and down the rickety staircase to his office, which was impregnated with the odors of pickling spices that wafted from the establishment below.

Weiss wanted to know how many members and friends of my family were likely to become subscribers if he printed my cartoons. His interest subsided visibly when I assured him honestly that no one I knew could afford such an extravagance. But he kept my sheaf of submissions and promised to take them under advisement. The advisement took forever. Repeated return trips to his office were fruitless, and he finally acknowledged that my precious comics, products of so many hours of dedicated efforts, were nowhere to be found. This disappointment should have inculcated in me a permanent distrust of newspaper publishers, but instead it seems to have prompted a heightened awe of their life-and-death powers. Perhaps unwisely, I relinquished my ambition to make a career in comic strips, and instead went on to draw sardonic political cartoons for my college newspaper.

The uninspired readership survey that Zorbaugh commissioned me to analyze suggested to me that the comics might well be a topic of serious interest. I was fascinated and repelled by popular culture, of which the comics were then an important component. At that time a handful of strips, distributed by the major syndicates, accounted for a huge share of the comics' total circulation. Understanding the reasons why particular strips and their characters were attractive to some readers and not to others seemed like an opening to a much more important inquiry into the origins of cultural taste.

Since taste was evidently linked to social characteristics, I wanted to narrow my inquiry to a group of people within the income and educational bracket where newspaper comics readership was most habitual. Gender would certainly affect preferences for individual strips and characters, and I decided to concentrate on men. I had obtained a full-time job and would have to do my interviewing in the evening and on weekends, so it would have to be done in Manhattan. New York then had seven general-circulation daily newspapers, all of which, except for the *Times*, carried comic strips. Since reading preferences had to be matched to an analysis of the content of individual strips, I settled on readers of the two rival morning and Sunday tabloids, the *News* and the *Mirror*, both of which had millions of readers.

The area I picked for my interviews was near my residence in Lenox Hill on the now-fashionable Upper East Side. At that time the Third Avenue elevated demarcated the grand town houses and apartment buildings to the west from the solidly working-class brownstones and tenements to the east. The population was predominantly second generation of Irish, Italian, and Central European origins, and economically homogeneous. It was prime tabloid-reading territory.

I interviewed 121 white men (of whom only 1 in 7 was a high school graduate), recording answers in shorthand to questions that covered (1) exposure to the mass media, especially newspapers; (2) the comic strip reading experience; (3) attitudes and evaluation of the medium; (4) preferences (positive and negative) for individual strips; (5) conceptions and imagery of particular strips and their characters; (6) social characteristics; and (7) personality traits. At this time, especially at the University of Chicago, there was a vogue for projective tests, in which people were asked to free-associate to open-ended or ambiguous stimuli, revealing thoughts they might not wish to express directly. In this case I showed respondents single panels from a number of popular strips. The balloons emanating from the characters' mouths were empty, and I asked what they were saying.

I went door to door, with no formal sampling plan, just as I had done in the Jewish neighborhoods of Chicago in my earlier study. This kind of unsystematic procedure was (in hindsight, regrettably) in the tradition of the Chicago school of sociology, which tended to regard each interviewed person as an informant and each interview as an individual case history to be analyzed and understood. I was not, after all, trying to replicate what had already been discovered from comics readership surveys of large, presumably representative, national samples; I was trying to penetrate the mystery of their readers' likes and dislikes.

By the beginning of the twenty-first century, personal interviewing has been largely abandoned in favor of surveys conducted by telephone. Door-to-door interviewing encounters resistance and is not always safe for the interviewers. But in the relatively low-crime era of the late 1940s, I could enter almost any building without the intervention of locks, intercoms, and buzzers, climb the stairs, ring a doorbell, explain my purpose, and be welcomed inside to ask my questions.

Today, answering machines and popular resentment at telemarketing have steadily lowered the public's willingness to cooperate with telephone surveys. Samples are weighted and balanced to make the findings accurate. At the same time there is more use of group interviews and "mall intercepts" (in which shopping mall visitors are either interviewed on the spot or enticed into a room where they can watch commercials, examine package designs, or taste experimental foods). Most recently there has been a spate of popularity for on-line surveys on the Internet. With all these methods, the samples are not representative of the total population. Yet marketers and politicians give credence to the results as a substitute for the far more costly techniques required to produce projectable findings. In comparison, the haphazard selection of tabloid readers in my comics study seems almost respectable.

My dissertation was peppered with quotations from the interviews and laced with sixty-seven statistical tables. I used a measure of association called Chi Square to establish the statistical significance of the findings worthy of comment. (Chi Square is actually a reverse indicator of the likelihood that the results could be explained by sheer chance). On the faculty committee before which I had to defend my dissertation, Professor William Fielding Ogburn, an eminent statistician,* ordered me to add another measure of association, which he identified only as "T." Unfortunately I mistook his reference to "Tschuprow's T" to mean "Student's t" (a totally unrelated indicator) and momentarily got into hot water. In today's era of prepackaged computerized statistical programs, my exercises might not pass muster. In any case, my qualitative interpretations of the respondents' verbatim responses were in an analytical tradition that would raise eyebrows in the quantitatively oriented world of contemporary sociology.

The comics, I should note, played a vastly more influential role in American life than they do today. Since newspapers were read as a daily habit, most of the strips maintained a continuous running story, daily and Sunday. (This is no longer true as more and more newspaper readers skip issues.) Today high newsprint prices have forced editors to cut the space devoted to comics, reducing their size, legibility, and attractiveness. But at mid-century, 60 percent of the people in towns of over 2,500 read comic strips regularly, and another 16 percent occasionally. Comic-strip characters were featured in movie cartoons and endorsed consumer products. They adorned military tanks and airplanes. Comics were so vivid in the national psyche that (at least in the case of Popeye the Sailor Man) statues were erected in their honor. "Sadie Hawkins Day," in which women took the courting initiative, was widely celebrated on college campuses. It was named after a character in the strip "Li'l Abner."

---

*In his seminar on Social Change, Ogburn interrupted a lecture on the importance of public opinion by asking a Chinese student, "Mr. Wu, tell us about the role of Main Street in the Chinese village." The baffled Wu replied, "In Chinese village is no Main Street. Is ony trails." Ogburn faced him down. "How can there be a village with no Main Street?"

Earlier research on the comics had been mainly historical. The medium had not been of interest to sociologists, though there was a growing amount of psychological and psychiatric speculation and a small amount of empirical research on the related medium of comic *books*, many of which featured fantasies of violence and sex. Their readership had soared during the war. Unlike comic strips, which were read by people of all ages in a family setting, comic books had a concentrated audience among teenage boys and young men in their twenties.

There was a vast literature on tastes and cultural preferences and a substantial body of studies on newspaper reading and newspaper content. Although comic strips were still colloquially referred to as "the funnies," a growing proportion were not funny at all; still, it was necessary to look into theories of humor and the slender file of empirical psychological research on the subject. Background reading suggested questions worth exploring as my original research got under way. It helped fluff out my dissertation to impress the sociology faculty with my scholarly zeal, but it was not highly pertinent to the ultimate findings.

I mention my diligent investigation of previous writings only to emphasize a crucial distinction between academic and commercial research. Academic scholars set out with the understanding that they are merely trying to add a brick to a large existing pyramid of learning. Their efforts are useless if they cannot be fitted into the context of what those who came before them have discovered or what their contemporaries are in the process of learning. Commercial researchers, working under constraints of time and budget, are apt to pay only perfunctory attention to what has been done before, much of which may remain the private secrets of companies in competition with their own clients. Inevitably this means that in the commercial arena there is often a duplication of effort. It also means that studies are planned and questionnaires are written without the theoretical underpinning that provides insight and understanding rather than mere factual detail of transient interest.

THE COMIC STRIPS AND THEIR ADULT READERS (1949)

To what extent do the comics influence the thoughts, values, and actions of their readers? How are they perceived and interpreted? What accounts for their popularity? What gratifications do they provide? How does their symbolic or thematic imagery correspond to the characteristics of their audience?

The insight that art may serve as a "release"—that it may, like fantasy, provide its audience with an outlet from which to escape the dissatisfactions of real life—is closely akin to the kind of interpretation long made in literary and dramatic criticism. We can distinguish between art imagery that is "escapist" in the sense that the audience's tensions are released by a transcendence of immediate problems, and imagery that is "cathartic" because it releases tensions by permitting the audience to act out in the imagination scenes that would be quite different in reality.

Dramatic catharsis, which depends on ideas and symbols, requires interest. Latent tensions must be mobilized and focused. Interest involves empathy and identification. Identification may take place at the level of fantasy, or because of the direct similarity between the depicted situation and that of the audience. Differences of taste reflect the capacity of different themes to reduce tensions for particular kinds of people. But tensions may also be reduced simply by a relief in monotony, by a break in accustomed activity, by the pure mechanics of variety—all characteristics of play.

The comic strips are one of many features that make the tabloid newspaper primarily a vehicle of entertainment rather than information. Without demanding too much effort or attention, these features relieve monotony.

The comics are read "because they're there," as part of the time-consuming process through which the entire contents of the paper are devoured and digested. This does not mean that they have no significance for their readers. Precisely because they—like the rest of the paper—are an essential part of the daily routine, they may be most noticed when they are missed.

Comics reading is a habit. The characters are old friends whose adventures readers have often followed since childhood. As they mature their early interest in the comics wanes, but in most cases the thread of continuity is not lost. The comics are a link to the intimacies of the past.

Most of the strips (especially the popular ones) pursue a continuing course, with each day's episode left in a state of at least partial irresolution or suspense, carrying interest on to the next episode. The small element of interest and variety that they add to the reader's day helps to dissipate those greater, more deeply felt tensions that arise from boredom.

For this reason, interest in the comic strips is independent of the reader's knowledge of how they are going to turn out. Certain elements of each strip's formula remain fixed and predictable. The reader is impelled by curiosity over the *means* by which the expected equilibrium will be attained.

The comics reduce tension in their readers by offering variety and a recurrent focus of interest. Their name implies that they reduce tension through laughter. Actually, comic-strip humor, mostly simple and stereotyped, seems to produce a grim, unsmiling kind of amusement. Genuine, hearty laughs are few. Laughter is a social affair, and the comics (except in the case of a parent reading to a young child) are read by a lone person.

Truck driver, forty: "When I'm with people I do that, but when I'm by myself I just feel like a dope or something. I do the same thing in a movie. I'd laugh if I'm with somebody, but I wouldn't do it by myself."

Just as the comics are read "to pass the time,"
they are talked about for the same reason. Better-
educated men, who talk more about everything, also
talk more about the comics. But such conversation
is largely superficial banter; in groups where talk
about politics or religion could be sensitive and
unwise, men may idly wonder about the next turn of
events in a popular strip, as they might talk about
the weather.

Construction laborer, thirty-one: "Yeah, with a
bunch of fellows on the corner. I'd say, Dick
Tracy is in another scrape; I wonder how he'll
get out of it. Of course we all laugh at it.
And a guy will say, bet you half a dollar he
gets out of it."

Truck driver, twenty-two: "You'd probably have
some daydream of a character, of something you
might have wanted to have been—a flier or a
detective."

Adult readers know, of course, that the
characters do not exist, yet they cannot help
speaking of them as though they really do. Because
the characters are so "real," the authors remain
anonymous even to the most constant readers.
Awareness of the author would destroy the
characters' identity and reduce them to mere
artifice. When readers think of a strip's author,
they often ascribe to him the traits of the
principal character; the man who draws Dick Tracy
is Dick Tracy. The "fantastic" characteristics of
the strips cannot easily be distinguished from
their "realistic" traits. Different readers derive
different satisfactions from the same strips.
The personality traits of readers are not
related to their reading habits or interests. There
is not even a marked association between a man's
overall interest in the comics and the kind of
strip he likes best. Readers of different kinds of
strips show an equivalent range of interest. The
explanation is that people do not read just one

type of strip, either of the dramatic-adventure or the humorous kind. They read and like both types, for different reasons. The reader's eye wanders from strip to strip, irrespective of style or content. Most important is that a strip arouses some feeling, that it engages the reader. A reader's negative attitude toward a particular strip appears in many cases to be an inversion of its appeal.

The response to the cutouts used in the projective question was sparse, dry, impersonal, and unrevealing. This reflects the low level of imagination and the lack of verbal skills among the group interviewed. It also suggests that the comics are for the most part accepted at face value, not invested with strong personal overtones. The characters remain themselves rather than surrogates of their readers. The people who especially like a strip gave the fullest, most imaginative response to it.

There is little indication that the comic strips stimulate much active fantasy; in fact there was a constant rejection of fantasy throughout the interviews. What is disliked is described as "fantastic"; what is good is "real"; the characters "grow." The comics gain acceptance as long as they seem to maintain some sort of connection with everyday life.

The most important benefit of comics for their readers is to break the daily routine. The variety of their imagery is more significant than their actual content. Their recreational "play" aspect is more important than their ideational "art" aspect.

> Stock room clerk, twenty-one: "I just read them for the enjoyment, that's all. More or less to relieve the monotony of the day. I more or less pick up the paper and pick up the interesting points and read it. It's habitual, because I've been reading them every day and I like to read them, because it was the first thing I used to read every day when I was a little kid and now

I'm a little older I'm interested in the news
but I still look at them."

The comics do offer fantasies of aggression,
sex, and achievement, and their appeal for
particular groups of readers can be partly
understood in these terms. But there is no evidence
that readers are drawn to the strips by a conscious
or unconscious lust for vicarious sensation; they
bring their normal impulses to them as to other
life experiences. Fantasies based on these impulses
are brief and have a low emotional charge. The
fantasy images are highly conventional. They do not
express personal longings and strivings. The
literal character of the whole experience is in
keeping with the descriptions that have long
differentiated popular and high art.

Discussion of the popular arts frequently
assumes the form of a polarized argument. Both
critical and defensive positions begin with a
common assumption: the appeal of the popular arts
stems from the fact that they express the dreams
and suppressed fantasies of people living in a
chaotic world. To lives burdened by frustration and
monotony they bring a momentary release. Their
heroes and heroines do all the things that the
reading, listening, or viewing public would like
to do.

The critical position holds that this
gratification is unwholesome. Catering to the
lowest tastes, it turns the audience away from
life's problems rather than to a realistic
grappling with them; it titillates anti-social
aggressive impulses that might otherwise be
checked.

The defensive position maintains that the
pleasures offered by the popular arts correspond
accurately to the psychic needs of the audience;
they therefore serve a positive function for
personal adjustment and provide a harmless outlet
for impulses that would find expression in any
case.

A third point of view, which does not figure much in the debate, questions the strength of the compensatory gratifications offered by the popular arts, and regards exposure to them as very often the result of chance, or the absence of alternative pastimes. This study supports that proposition. For those who were interviewed, reading comic strips was a rather superficial experience. Those with high interest in the comics had no more reason or desire for escapist fantasy than those whose interest was low.

My study taught me that popular culture had less of a hold on the public than was generally supposed. I continued to rediscover this truth when I began to investigate the persuasive effects of communication in the business world.

527147
693604
411082
354755
102986

BIG BUSINESS

■ My research on the comics demonstrates that, while researchers in a university setting may seem free to select their
own subjects, in practice the choices are often influenced by the
scholarly preoccupations of their professors and advisers and by
the availability of grants and stipends for work on designated
themes.

Researchers who work for commercial or nonprofit institutions would seem to be limited to the assignments that others
give them. In fact they may be moved to suggest projects that
arise from their own intellectual pursuits, or to perform analyses
that go beyond the immediate practical purposes that prompted
someone to pay for their work.

Motivation is not the crucial distinction. Scholars at universities are expected to begin with one or more hypotheses to be
tested. Their research is expected to add to the open store of
knowledge (even though their main intent may simply be to advance an academic career). This requires full disclosure of what
they learned and of how they went about learning it.

By contrast, most research done for commercial purposes
aims to provide its sponsors with information that confers an advantage and must therefore remain secret. Occasionally important nonacademic research studies enter the published literature.

But most proprietary studies (and almost all unsuccessful research proposals) remain buried in corporate or institutional files, eventually to be winnowed out and destroyed as they lose their topical interest or possible usefulness to competitors.

My own transition from academia to commerce came about by sheer necessity. The only teaching job I could find in the New York area was at Hofstra University. When I went out to Long Island for my trial lecture, my wallet was stolen at the train station and I arrived late, with only the return ticket and some miscellaneous change in my pocket. My performance was appropriately disastrous. Rejected and dejected, I scurried around, with no immediate luck, for a possible opening in nonprofit agencies or even (as a last resort) in the business world. The first step was to concoct research proposals. I knew very little of how to go about this.

To find a potential client I looked for topical news subjects that posed questions for business management. Federal fair employment practices legislation had hit at the traditional pattern of segregation, first in war industry and later in the full range of employment. Minority-group members were entering jobs that had been closed to them. Interracial contacts had increased, and the issue of discrimination had been dramatized in films and other media. The newly passed New York State Anti-Discrimination Law was forcing department stores to hire blacks for sales positions from which they had always been excluded.

The department store inherited the ancient tradition of the market as a meeting place for diverse groups of people. It was one of the few urban sites where adults of different ethnic and racial origins engaged in face-to-face relationships. In this era, before the rise of self-service and mass retailing, store employees were in close contact with customers. Retailers, like most business executives, assumed that a bigoted public would react with horror to black salespeople. How were the stores changing their personnel policies and handling problems both with customers and with their white employees? More important, how effective were legislative measures in breaking down existing social atti-

tudes and established patterns of group segregation? I made a
proposal to the personnel director of R. H. Macy and Company,
New York's leading department store.

RACIAL CONTACTS IN A LARGE DEPARTMENT STORE (1948)

The people who work in a department store
constitute a part-time community, spending most of
the work week together but geographically dispersed
the rest of the time. Their social positions at
home reveal themselves at work. Conversely, their
activities as employees are an important
determinant of their status in the localities where
they live. In the department store, the hierarchy
of authority, prestige, and material reward is well
defined and universally recognized. It corresponds
to the ladder of status in the larger society.

The great metropolitan store presents a
spectacle of wealth, power, and glamour. It is
impersonal, austere, efficient, and clean. Its
great windows hide an interior mechanism of awesome
complexity. To the masses of its customers the
store offers not so much the promise of a bargain
as refinement, "culture," and a faint hint of
adventure. The salespeople, whatever their actual
social origins, are selected to embody white-collar
upper-middle-class gentility, but these very
attributes make some potential customers insecure
and uncomfortable, giving the sales situation tense
undertones.

To what extent is the breakdown of
discrimination in employment followed by more
intergroup social contacts? What factors make for a
more or less satisfactory integration of minority-
group members into a work situation from which they
were traditionally excluded? What kinds of negative
reaction (if any) are produced through the
enforcement of the Anti-Discrimination Law?

How do interracial contacts in work situations
of low status (like porters' or stock clerks' jobs)

compare with those on the selling floor or those at a more highly skilled or executive level? What factors make for more or less harmonious contact? What differences exist within the hierarchy of sales personnel? (Do black clerks in the bargain basement get along as well with their fellow employees as those selling jewelry or television sets?) Is there a noticeable difference in employee relations between the sales departments and those in which there is no contact with customers? If there is a difference, to what extent are customer contacts responsible, rather than some other factors? Customers who patronize the bargain basement are different from those who buy at the luxury goods counters; in what departments is acceptance of black personnel most complete and least likely to be marred by friction?

What types of work situations are associated with what degrees of intergroup harmony or tension? What are the roles of supervisory personnel, the labor union, and management-sponsored social or educational programs in modifying intergroup beliefs or behavior? How does management handle cases of interracial friction, and with what effect?

My proposal to Macy's was turned down, though many of the questions I posed surfaced again in the design of the 1951 study of desegregation in the army (Project Clear), which appears later in this chapter.

My next proposal landed me a job as a public opinion specialist in the public relations department of the Standard Oil Company (New Jersey), now the ExxonMobil Corporation.

I had read a newspaper account of a contentious stockholders' meeting at Standard Oil, dominated by some rebellious spirits who (though I didn't know it then) showed up at the annual meetings of many large companies to heckle the executives. This report resonated for me with the thesis advanced by Adolf Berle and Gardiner Means[1] that business management and ownership had become not only distinct but antagonistic. It occurred to me that their proposition should be put to the test. Why not do this through a survey of stockholders' attitudes toward a big company, its leaders, and its policies?

I looked up "Standard Oil" in the telephone directory and was dismayed to find listings for Standard Oil of California, of Kentucky, of Illinois, of Ohio, and of New Jersey. (Standard of New York had some time earlier become Socony-Vacuum, after merging with another former subsidiary of the original trust.)* Standard of New Jersey had the greatest number of sublistings and seemed like the logical place to try first. I asked the switchboard operator who was in charge of stockholder relations. It was, she said, the secretary of the corporation. To my amazement, I was able to make an appointment to see him in his handsome office on a high floor of the RCA building (now the General Electric building) in Rockefeller Center. He didn't buy my proposal, but he sent me to see the manager of the public relations department, George H. Freyermuth.

Freyermuth was large, courtly, thoughtful, and energetic, a petroleum engineer who had been given the public relations assignment as a step up the corporate ladder. The company valued field experience in the oil fields and refineries. It moved its executives around to broaden their backgrounds and hesitated to bring in outsiders with specialized knowledge, except in positions subordinate to its loyal career men. (There were of course no women in the picture, except as secretaries; Freyermuth had two, whom he addressed with the same grave formality that they showed him.)

The timing of my first visit to Freyermuth was perfect. He needed someone at hand to keep track of all the company's sur-

---

*Much later, renamed Mobil Oil, it merged with Standard Oil (New Jersey), renamed Exxon.

vey data and to translate them into a form that could be put into action. He gave me the test assignment of summarizing a recently arrived two-volume report and quizzed me when I brought it back the next day to make sure I had not received outside help. He asked his outside public opinion consultant, Elmo Roper, to interview me, ordered a check of my academic credentials, and in short order hired me.

Freyermuth's enormous desk was always covered with high piles of unread documents and correspondence. I once asked him whether his unanswered mail didn't cause problems. He wisely replied that anyone who needed an answer urgently would follow up with a phone call or telegram, but that most of the problems would have solved themselves by the time he got around to them.

Unlike other corporations, Jersey Standard (as the company was informally called, or even more intimately, just Jersey) had a board of directors made up entirely of men who had risen through its own executive ranks. It had only recently established an internal public relations function, in response to scandalous charges that had enveloped it during the war and its aftermath. It had been accused of making secret patent deals with Germany's I. G. Farben and of overcharging the navy for fuel oil.

The company's chairman, Frank Abrams, had a keen awareness of its worldwide social impact and a sense of its responsibilities. Perhaps through the Rockefeller family connection, he had retained a public relations counsel, Earl Newsom, who also handled public relations for Colonial Williamsburg (a Rockefeller project) and for the Ford Motor Company. Newsom advised on the structure of the company's internal public relations department and placed his top speech writer, Stewart Schackne, as one of two assistant managers. Newsom was the opposite of the common notion of what a public relations wizard should be like. He was gaunt, humorless, and withdrawn. He avoided business entertainment and ate a solitary spartan salad each noon while reading a newspaper. In meetings he spoke sparingly and in an almost inaudible croaking whisper, so that all those present had to lean forward to hear him. This gave his most banal utterances an aura of great consequence.

Newsom's account executive for Standard Oil, W. H. ("Ping") Ferry, was moon-faced, with babylike features, but he spoke in a growl. Ferry dressed jauntily, with loud bow ties, and in summer wore a straw hat with a colorful band. Although his father had been president of the Packard Motor Car Company, he liked to come across as a tough street-fighter who had worked his way up from the gutter. He argued forcefully that Jersey should attract attention by speaking out on public issues, even those that did not affect it directly. This bothered me, both in general, because I didn't think a large corporation could be trusted to use its communications power in the public interest, and specifically, because Ferry boasted of "breaking a strike" for his other major client, Ford. On the latter point I needn't have worried, because Ping was, as it turned out, a radical. Having helped guide the Ford family to create its eponymous foundation, he and Robert Maynard Hutchins had set up its affiliate, The Fund for the Republic, which became a stalwart bastion of liberal policy formation during the 1950s and '60s.

Newsom had brought in the pollster Elmo Roper to conduct a survey of public attitudes toward big business, the oil business, and Standard Oil (New Jersey) in particular. Roper had spent his early career as a jewelry salesman and got into market research as a result of interviewing his customers about their preferences. He acquired renown in the 1930s with the *Fortune* Magazine Poll and rivaled George Gallup (whom he admired) in forecasting several presidential elections. Roper faked solemnity but had a wonderful dry wit. He flourished his inseparable cigars with the dexterity of a juggler.

As might be expected, his findings about the public's opinion of the company were grim. They were no less discouraging in a variety of other omnibus surveys periodically conducted by two other polling organizations, the Psychological Corporation and the Opinion Research Corporation, to track the public's view of corporate America. PsychCorp's opinion research was directed by the dignified and self-important little Henry Link, whose Link Audit provided a semiannual barometer reading of attitudes toward a dozen leading companies. Quite apart from the fact that people loved General Electric more than U.S. Steel, I was intrigued to discover that, regardless of the long-term trends, the public loved all these companies more in the fall than in the spring. My efforts to understand the origins of this optimism (in the human estrous cycle, among other things) were unsuccessful. These polls, spring and fall, were awaited anxiously in the public relations departments of the great companies. Their PR directors were called on the carpet to explain to their bosses why the companies' standing with the public had fallen or risen. This was all nonsense; the seasonal changes reflected either forces beyond anyone's control or cyclical variations in the quality of the field work.

Numbers produced by surveys—of audiences, markets, or political preferences—have a life of their own, quite apart from the reality they are intended to represent. That reality often defies quantification. (Data on the number of people exposed to a news item don't tell us how much news is actually being absorbed.) In the worlds of media, marketing, and politics, research is an instrument of power in a bargaining process. Heads are crowned when the numbers look good and roll when they fall, though the numbers themselves may be meaningless.

Intelligent business executives have always understood this and accept the critique when it is discussed in a neutral setting, but on the job they have to make believe that the numbers really make sense and deserve to be taken seriously. Of course they do make sense if one is comparing one kind of bad number with another one waved around by a competitor.

The Opinion Research Corporation was headed by Claude Robinson, an old associate of George Gallup. Robinson (who like Link flaunted his then still-rare Ph.D.) was a salesman with the charismatic style of an old-time evangelist. He described the inchoate and monosyllabic utterances of respondents commenting on test advertisements as "opening a window into the human soul." His Public Opinion Index for Industry combined survey results (always shown to the decimal point, to convey the illusion of awesome precision) with exhortations to his clients to battle the evil forces that fomented anti-business sentiment. One study purported to demonstrate that the best-informed members of the public were also the most pro-business. I pointed out to Freyermuth that the questions used to measure informedness were actually indications of attitudes, so that the results were a tautology. At a subsequent meeting, the project director, Joe Hochstim, a sweet-tempered psychologist, was forced to defend a procedure for which he was obviously not responsible. Soon afterward he quit to become a university professor.

Corporate public relations was still a relatively new endeavor in the late forties. The field had emerged from several distinct traditions. Press agentry—the cultivation of favorable free publicity to advance a commercial purpose—had a venerable ancestry. It was used as an adjunct to advertising to promote entertainers and entertainments, political candidates and causes, and consumer products. John D. Rockefeller, assailed as a wicked monopolist in the century's early years, employed a suave journalist, Ivy Lee, to contrive events (like the indiscriminate distribution of freshly coined dimes) and generate news tidbits that placed him in a new and favorable light. Other imaginative practitioners, like Ben Sonnenberg and Edward Bernays, cultivated their reputations by flamboyant dress or pretentious announcements. They lunched with their clients in the most exclusive clubs and restaurants. Jersey's Washington representatives, the Newmyer organization, disdained to be called lobbyists. Their function, they explained, was to bring industry executives and government officials together to increase their mutual understanding.

The new world in which I suddenly found myself was one that mingled the excitement and glamour of a vast global enterprise with the stultifying ennui of a coddled workforce that cherished routine and fulfilled its chores at a languid pace. I learned quickly to jettison sociological jargon and to be careful of my language in presenting research findings. Once, when a small survey did not warrant intricate analysis, I separated the respondents into two age groups—under and over thirty-five. I could not understand why my audience broke up when I kept referring to them as the "young" and the "old." (I was, after all, twenty-seven, which was virtually middle age.)

Jersey's Public Relations Department was staffed with a large group of specialists who covered a number of different areas. A full-time consultant worked to establish the company as a patron of the visual arts, sponsoring contests and exhibits around the world. A press relations section cultivated what today would be called media relations and extruded a steady procession of press releases. It was headed by Jim Crayhon, a crusty but good-humored character out of *The Front Page*, who kept his shirt collar open and his feet on his desk in defiance of the prevailing decorum. Crayhon's ear and lips adhered continually to the telephone. Although company news was generally desultory and dull, Crayhon maintained an illusion of feverish excitement, as though he were still the city editor of an afternoon paper marshaling his legions to meet repeated deadlines.

The company's slick magazine, *The Lamp*, was distributed to employees, stockholders, and a large number of "opinion leaders." A publications department produced an annual report and innumerable booklets and leaflets on special subjects. An education specialist developed school programs. A genteel community affairs specialist, who might have stepped from the ranks of the original suffragette movement, worked with a slew of civic organizations. Foreign area coordinators trained and supervised the activities of similar departments that had been set up in affiliate companies around the world. Another coordinator worked with industry groups like the Oil Industry Information Committee and its parent, the American Petroleum Institute.

G. Edward Pendray, a genius who coined the terms "laundromat" and "time capsule," was the Oil Industry Information

Committee's public relations counselor. In retrospect he bore a close resemblance to Kentucky Fried Chicken's Colonel Sanders, though his expression was reserved rather than benevolent. The OIIC thought big. At one of its meetings, to plan a radio campaign, we were urged to "hire the world's greatest writers, men like Ernest Hemingway, Maxwell Anderson, Winston Churchill,"— after a moment's search for someone of equivalent stellar literary reputation—"Thomas B. Costain!"

Jersey's liaison man with the Oil Industry Information Committee, Edward Esmay, temporarily took over the direction of the organization. (Freyermuth described this task as "the white man's burden.") This happened when the OIIC's director, Admiral H. B. ("Min") Miller, became the first head of Radio Free Europe after its establishment in 1951. (Miller's exalted military rank was achieved during World War II as a public relations officer; he was not an old salt, nor was he salty by nature, for that matter.)

Esmay was a man of marvelously mild disposition, a quirky sense of humor, a penchant for everlasting telephone conversations frequently interrupted by chuckles, and a strong addiction to pre-luncheon screwdrivers. He consumed these at Toots Shor's, a thriving, bustling, show-business hangout whose Radio City location is still identified by a modest plaque. Shor was a huge, ham-handed, jowly fellow with an insincerely intimate greeting for all comers. At the time the three-martini lunch was still an acceptable standard in the advertising and public relations businesses, but the bar at Shor's drew from a wider clientele of locals and visitors. (The *New Yorker* cartoonist Charles Addams was a buddy of Esmay's at the clubby bar.)

If Shor's was Esmay's midday hangout, his after-work recovery took place at The Little Cottage, a more modest and intimate establishment on West Fifty-first Street, when this was still a block of brownstone residences. Reinvigorated by an hour or so of libation and gossip, he could embark on his extended trip to Grandview, a then still undiscovered village in Rockland County, on the west bank of the Hudson. There, in a Victorian house overlooking the river, his patient wife, Alma, after teaching school all day, superintended the Esmays' tumultuous flock of offspring. (One Esmay daughter married Maté Mestrovic, a historian at Fairleigh Dickinson University, and son of the great Croatian sculptor. On a visit to their modest East Side apartment I expressed interest in his father's works. He took me into a bedroom and opened a closet. It was stuffed from top to bottom with plaster casts of magnificent creations that had never been cast in metal.*)

When Esmay died, at a rather early age, three of his former associates drove up to pay their respects to the deceased, whose remains were on view at a funeral home in nearby Nyack. This was housed in another one of the area's vintage nineteenth-century mansions, with a creaking floor that was far from level. One of the mourners, John Wiggins, who had appropriately fortified himself for the journey, was overcome by emotion at the sight of his departed colleague and fell reverentially to his knees. As he knelt in prayer his head touched the wheel-mounted coffin, which slid away down the canted floor. The sainted Esmay had played a final trick. (Wiggins, another old newspaper reporter, had been a member of Crayhon's press section, and like a number of others, a victim of Demon Drink. He concluded his public relations career as a doorman greeting visitors at a luxurious East Side apartment building, where we suffered mutual embarrassment when I came to visit a resident.)

Executives who commuted long distances from distant suburbs led compartmentalized lives. An office romance with a secretary led one of my colleagues to leave his job, wife, and three children, whom he vowed never to see again. (He didn't.) At the age of forty-two he registered with the Forty-Plus Club, an employment agency serving the superannuated. After prolonged unemployment, he got a doctorate in psychology, a new career, and another child, and died of a heart attack while working in

---

*He returned to Croatia after Yugoslavia's breakup and became ambassador to Bulgaria.

the garden against doctor's orders. His widow then discovered that she had been number three, not number two.

The jewel of the public relations department's operations was the photographic section, headed by Roy Stryker, who had established and run the famed photographic unit of the Farm Security Administration during the New Deal era. Stryker had assembled a team of the country's best photographers (including such luminaries as Arnold Newman, Esther Bubley, and Gordon Parks) to document the role and impact of the oil business on all aspects of life, in the United States and elsewhere. The resulting photo library covered every conceivable subject of human, social, and aesthetic interest. Shortly before my arrival, Stryker had retained the great filmmaker Robert Flaherty to make a movie. The idea was to present the oil business as one that was run by sympathetic people, cared for the environment, and was essential to the nation's economy. Flaherty disappeared into the bayous of the Mississippi delta and was heard from only with appeals for more money as he ran far over budget. The outcome was the memorable documentary film *Louisiana Story*.

One of Stryker's unfulfilled pet projects was to provide Brownie box cameras to platoons of small children and to send them out to photograph their worlds. He wore rimless glasses and a broad-brimmed Western hat. His lips were pursed but his eyes twinkled. Shortly after I arrived he sat me down in his office, told me that I was the first Jew ever hired by Standard Oil, and advised me to refrain from speaking up at staff meetings until I knew what I was talking about. It was wonderful advice.

To counteract the impression that the contemporary oil business was unchanged since Ida Tarbell's 1909 description of its monopolistic practices,[2] Freyermuth had funded a team of Harvard Business School historians to write a company history.[3] This pioneering effort was given unrestricted access to the archives, which were being sifted by a field team quartered in a section of the office where my desk was initially located. Its leader was a Minnesota economic historian named J. Sterling Popple, who would periodically arise, guffawing, from immersion in the ancient files to share a morsel from some outrageous memorandum. "The mighty Popple," as we called him, had taken the Twentieth Century Limited to Chicago one evening, settled down in the rear observation car with a book and a drink, and found himself seated behind two Jersey executives in frank and ardent discussion of the very subject he was researching. They hardly expected the stranger next to them to understand what they were talking about.

The desk closest to the window in this suite was occupied by a Texas belle, Ruth Sands Bentley, whose principal work responsibility, it appeared, was to gossip on the telephone. Most of her one-sided conversation consisted of deep sighs and complaints about her husband John, a writer and devotee of racing cars who kept her up all night with the clacking of his typewriter and spent his weekends spinning around the Bridgehampton track.

The semiprivate office to which I was subsequently promoted was shared with Richard Wilcox, a Yalie whose ample waves of blond hair and double-vented tailored suits emulated the style of an English country gentleman. Dick had worked as a foreign correspondent for *Life*, but his most fascinating life experience had come during the war as an officer in the Coast Guard. He had been assigned as the minder for the former heavyweight champion Jack Dempsey, who had been awarded a commission and sent around the world on the premise that his presence would boost troop morale. Dempsey was also a "goodwill emissary" to foreign dignitaries, like the viceroy of India, of whose wife he asked, at dinner, why her husband was known as "noncombattan' Mountbatten." At an appropriate moment he also asked Lady Mountbatten, "Where does a man get his ashes hauled around here?"

The studies I had conducted up to this point were individual endeavors from start to finish. I decided what questions to ask, went out and asked them myself, tabulated and analyzed the responses, and wrote up what I had found. Now I was engaged in research that involved many other people—the bosses and associates who defined my agenda, and the professionals at research organizations who carried out the field work of surveys on a national scale. I thus became aware of the politics of research, both in its internal execution as the product of specialists with different skills and perspectives, and also as a negotiating tool within the corporation and in its relationship to other institutions. The company was engaged in a variety of expensive projects aimed to modify public opinion about it and the oil industry. Were these efforts successful? Again and again throughout my professional career I faced the same question: What are the effects of mass communication?

Our most ambitious project was sponsorship of the Sunday afternoon concerts of the New York Philharmonic Symphony Orchestra, broadcast over the CBS Radio Network during the 1948–1949 season. In this last phase of radio's golden age, the networks reigned supreme, and their managements still felt impelled to defer to the public interest by dedicating a certain amount of air time to programming of quality, like weekly symphony and opera broadcasts. NBC maintained its own symphony orchestra under the direction of Arturo Toscanini. High culture was accessible to the mass audience.

For Jersey Standard, the questions about this project were simple: To what extent did listeners connect the Philharmonic broadcasts with their sponsor, and did this influence their sentiments about the company?

The first problem was to locate listeners. Devotees of classical music were a small elite. What seemed appropriate was a series of surveys to compare knowledge and attitudes before the broadcasts began, in the middle of the season, and after the season's close. Instead of trying this on a national scale, we concentrated on two cities, Boston, where Esso was a well-established brand name, and St. Louis, where the company had no marketing operation. The research was to be carried out by Roper's firm; the project director was Julian Woodward, a former sociology professor whom Roper had employed despite his ostentatious wariness of academicians. Woody was dour and took himself very seriously. He was intrigued by the notion of "opinion leadership," which had been advanced in a much discussed study of the 1940 presidential election.[4] The idea was that in every stratum of society there were individuals who expressed themselves more freely than their peers and whose ideas were more influential. Our surveys incorporated a series of self-rating questions intended to identify these people; an implicit assumption was that they were endowed with superior aesthetic sensibilities and therefore more likely to be admirers of classical music.

The idea that one season's broadcasts could show detectable aftereffects in large-scale surveys was considered ridiculous by CBS's vice president for sales promotion, Victor Ratner, a bald, grinning, gap-toothed man of strong convictions, enormous copywriting talent, unfailing optimism, a colossal sense of humor, and somewhat coarse personal habits. Regrettably, our surveys more or less proved him right. Because the number of listeners was small, it was hard to find any statistically significant evidence that the broadcasts were having a powerful effect on public awareness or attitudes toward the company. The sponsorship was not renewed.

Ratner left CBS a few years later to take over the sales promotion department at Macy's, at the then unheard-of annual salary of $100,000. When I asked him whether the salary difference after taxes really warranted the move he replied, "No matter how much they take, they always take a little less than you make." Over the remainder of his lifetime, Ratner and I often debated the subject of popular culture, which I scorned and which he strongly defended, differentiating art from entertainment. His view was that "Art takes us deeper into [the endless] mysteries [of life]; entertainment takes us away from them—into fictions of artificial gaiety or artificial tragedy or artificial love—all enjoyed precisely because they are not like life, and are not seeking to improve it or understand it better."[5] This dichotomy was never one I could accept.

Ratner confided some of the difficulties of working for his boss at CBS, Frank Stanton, for whom he had great and deserved admiration. Stanton personally reviewed every typewritten document that went to a client and refused to accept a page to which a correction had been made, however minor. Another account of Stanton's perfectionism came from Gerhard Wiebe, his former colleague in Ohio State University's psychology department and later his executive assistant. Wiebe was both awed and dismayed because Stanton never left his office unless every message, letter, and document on his desk had been answered or disposed of.

Gus Wiebe had the appearance—but decidedly not the temperament—of a kewpie doll. He started at CBS as a member of its outstanding research department. Its director was Oscar Katz, lean, bald, and animated, an alumnus of the Office of War Information. Katz's solemnity hid a zany streak. (He had a fanciful idea for a televised game show to be called "Mr. Fuck.") Oscar used his insights into popular entertainment tastes to become a successful investor in Broadway shows. When CBS split its broadcast operations in the early 1950s, he had the foresight to go with the fledgling television network, even though the audiences, money, and power still resided with radio. Eventually he became head of programming, moved to a mansion in Beverly Hills, and acquired a choice table up front at the Brown Derby, then Hollywood's prime rendezvous point. There he held court as patrons trouped by and greeted him with purposeful heartiness. His meals were interrupted constantly by importuning calls that he took on a telephone plugged into an outlet beside his seat.

The pride of CBS's research department was the program analyzer, an invention of its former director, Frank Stanton, and of Columbia sociologist Paul Lazarsfeld. (It was known at CBS as the Stanton-Lazarsfeld Program Analyzer and at Columbia as the

Lazarsfeld-Stanton Program Analyzer.) The device permitted the elements of a radio program to be tested. Variants of it have since become a staple feature of audience research on broadcast and film entertainment. They are also used to evaluate commercials, including the political variety. Thus they have found their way into the testing of reactions to candidates' speeches, allowing both the style and substance of what they say to conform to the liking of the voters.

The program analyzer tallied moment-by-moment responses to what listeners heard, registered by push buttons held in each hand, the right one pressed to show approval, the left one for disapproval. In 1948 CBS used two versions: Big Annie, which was used with large groups assembled in a theater, and Little Annie, in which a dozen or so participants gathered around a table, seminar style. The researcher in charge, seated in a control booth, took notes on each individual's reactions to the various episodes or sequences. Returning to the testing room, he could then confront each in turn: "Number Seven, why didn't you like the part where . . . ?" The ensuing discussion, recorded by an aide and tagged to the elements of the program, provided valuable insights into the shifts in audience interest.

Tore Hollonquist, who ran these sessions, was a heavily built Swede who set aside his normally glum demeanor to effect an air of hearty conviviality with the out-of-town visitors recruited from studio audiences for the tests. His wife was a small, cheerful Italian with whom he communicated in English; they seemed as compatibly paired as an owl and a chickadee. The area around CBS headquarters was blessed with a number of Swedish restaurants providing ample noonday smorgasbords, of which Tore generously partook, with appropriate accompaniment of aquavit and beer. He spoke dejectedly of Stockholm's long winter nights and of the restrictive Swedish laws on the purchase of alcohol.

The program analyzer could detect the strengths and weaknesses of a communication, but not its effects. To gauge the impact of Jersey's public relations ventures, I looked beyond the large-scale surveys of which Ratner had been correctly skeptical. In two other studies I tried more intimate techniques of gauging the impact of the Philharmonic broadcasts and of their intermission feature. The first was a systematic analysis of letters and cards the program had generated from listeners—229 that came unsolicited and 515 received in response to a direct appeal made on the last broadcast.

FAN MAIL FOR THE PHILHARMONIC (1948)[6]

In the past, a performer or political speaker was in intimate contact with the audience, could shift style to meet the murmurs and gestures of the crowd, and could usually sense the effect. In modern mass media, the speaker talks into a void. The radio artist may be surrounded with a studio audience to preserve the illusion of intimacy, but the response of the invisible hearers remains a mystery at the moment of contact. Seated in their individual homes, the listeners can react only by continuing to listen, or by tuning out.

For the producers of radio programs, fan letters can never be an index to the reactions of the audience as a whole. The people who write in are not representative—if only because they take the subject seriously enough to write—and it is a naive producer who regards the number of letters as a measure of the program's appeal.

The proportion of listeners who actually write depends on (1) the type of program—the degree to which it mobilizes the full attention of the listening public (dramatic programs do this more than musical ones), (2) the degree of controversy that the program excites (its novelty or "shock" effect), and (3) the incentive offered.

The writers of fan mail usually sign their names, and the postmarks reveal their addresses, but there is no really reliable way of knowing whether they are rich or poor, old or young. In the absence of interview data, the social and

personality traits of the writers and also their
motivations for writing must remain a matter of
inference from nuances of style and handwriting.

The New York Philharmonic Symphony Orchestra
broadcast had four major elements: (1) the music;
(2) the commentator, Deems Taylor—composer, music
critic, and an established radio personality
[Taylor was bald, had horn-rimmed glasses, a jaunty
bow tie, and an elfin manner. He was a serious
musician with a common touch]; (3) the intermission
feature ("Weekend with Music"), with three high
school students brought to New York each week from
different parts of the country; and (4) the
company's "institutional" messages, delivered by
Taylor in a low-pressure, anecdotal fashion.

Listeners who wrote in during the season's
course were to a considerable extent interested in
things extraneous or peripheral to the program
itself. Many asked for advice, autographs, copies
of the script, or gifts. They complained of the
commentator's pronunciation or of coughs from the
audience in the concert hall. They were usually
concerned with some particular aspect of the
program.

The comments in the solicited postseason mail
were more widely diffused among the elements of the
program and were also far more approving in tone.
Taylor was identified both as the commentator and
master of ceremonies and as the man who "ran" the
show. He received comments not only on those
aspects of the program in which he played a part
but on anything else connected with it.

"I want to congratulate you for having
enlightened a soulless corporation in making
such a handsome gift to the young musicians of
America."

Taylor humanized a "high-brow" program. He
sounded like a pleasant, easy person to know, and
he bridged the gap between home and Carnegie Hall.
In this role, Taylor received musical and literary
compositions to be criticized, warnings of the

approaching millennium, old photographs and
reminiscences, and a request from two young nurses
that he map out an itinerary for their New York
visit. Listeners felt they "knew" him and addressed
him as a personal friend. Even when they were
critical, they often preferred to think that Taylor
secretly shared their views. One demanded, "Quit
this degrading job which is beneath you!" Another
wrote,

> "Aren't you ashamed to deliver that drivel
> handed to you by your sponsor but, please, oh
> please tell me you do not believe a word of
> it."

A large part of all the criticism came from
people whose animus seemed to be directed at the
American system of sponsored broadcasting rather
than at this particular program.

The people who addressed their comments to such
impersonal agencies as the broadcasting system, the
orchestra, the sponsor, or the local radio stations
were somewhat more critical than those who wrote to
Taylor. Those who ventured at least one unfavorable
comment covered more territory in their letters and
evidently had a more intense interest in the
program.

Among the listeners who wrote in were crackpots
and naifs who seemed to reason that prominent
persons were rich and powerful; it was therefore
proper to appeal to them for help or advice on
personal problems, or to offer them counsel:

> "I suppose this sounds fantastic, but you see I
> would so much like to have a colection of
> clasics that I could play at my leasure."

While radio fan mail does not provide a true
cross section of the listening public, it expresses
almost all the nuances of individual reaction that
could have been found through more elaborate
audience research. Writers of fan letters are
impelled by the notion that they are serving some

useful or important end. What they hear or see has
to generate sufficient feeling to make the effort
worthwhile. Much depends on the importance they
assign to the program on which they comment, and on
what they expect the letter to accomplish.

It is easy for listeners who dislike what they
hear to switch to another station. If they take the
trouble to write in to express dislike, there is
evidently something about the program that strongly
attracts them. Letter writers start with high
expectations and considerable involvement in what
they were about to hear. They might write in either
if these expectations were fulfilled or if they
were in some way disappointed. Almost every letter
addressed to a radio program is, in a sense, a mark
of approval for that program.

The fan-mail analysis, like the large-scale surveys, was national
in scope. A secondary aspect of the Philharmonic sponsorship
was at the level of the local communities from which teenagers
were selected to appear at intermission. How and to what degree
did people become aware of such an event? This raised the
broader and more interesting question of how news travels. For a
case history I picked Rapid City, South Dakota, the jumping-off
spot for the scenery of the Black Hills. The highways entering the
town were lined with guest houses and tourist cabins. In the
business district, old-fashioned small-town storefronts alternated with the trim façades of new department stores. Rapid City
had grown phenomenally, from 14,000 in the 1940 census to
25,000. Chiefly responsible for this boom was the nearby air
force bomber base.

Together with a hastily recruited Greg Stone, who had
moved on to teach sociology at the University of Illinois, I arrived in Rapid City two weeks after the broadcast on which a
local teenager had been a "Weekend" guest. We made two hundred telephone interviews during evening hours and did personal interviews in sixty-three homes, half in a comfortable
upper-middle-class district and half along the unpaved streets of

a working-class neighborhood. The personal interviews were completely informal, with no fixed questionnaire. We never raised the subject of the "Weekend" directly but gave our respondents every opportunity to bring it up voluntarily.

A WEEKEND WITH MUSIC (1949)[7]

The *Rapid City Daily Journal*, which placed heavy emphasis on local news, could not ignore the honor won by a local girl, but at first its editors were reluctant to provide publicity. A long-standing feud between them and Radio Station KOTA kept even the daily radio log out of the paper.

The local director of the Girl Scouts: "The impact was terrific. We all just went hog wild. . . . I think definitely that everyone was listening that Sunday."

Others had the same impression of universal interest and excitement:

Plumber, forty-five: "Of course, all the men mentioned it in the shop the next day to see if we'd heard it."

Wealthy widow, sixty-eight: "I think everyone turned the radio on that Sunday."

Was "everyone" in town actually aware of the event? Half of those interviewed by telephone indicated some knowledge of it. In the personal interviews, people who at first exhibited no knowledge of the "Weekend" often showed that they really knew something about it when someone else in the room brought up the subject.

Among the "informed," three-fifths said they learned the news from the paper. Half heard it on the radio and a fifth from conversation. Conversation, gossip, and casual chitchat were not the primary source of news. But through such talk, stimulated by the mass media, people expressed

their interest and reinforced their recollections.
Nearly two-thirds of the "informed" said they had
talked about the "Weekend" with someone—if only with
a spouse at the breakfast table. They were sometimes
left with a garbled version of what took place:

> Wife of a real estate operator, forty-two: "The
> Chamber of Commerce paid her way east. . . . Just
> to give the child an opportunity."

How is it that some people knew about "Weekend"
while others knew nothing or were so uninterested
that they failed to mention it to the interviewer?
When general questions of broad political interest
are raised in surveys, one normally expects to find
the people of better means and education to be more
informed than those lower on the social ladder.
"Weekend" seemed more at the level of gossip. It
was the kind of local news that might have been
expected to hold interest for all layers of the
community, being simple, easily grasped, and set in
a familiar scene. Yet the news about "Weekend" was
known to three-fourths of the people with some
college education, and to only one-fourth of the
least educated. The better-educated also discussed
the event much more.

At the upper and middle social levels, men knew
about "Weekend" as often as women. Women in the
low-income brackets are generally less informed
than men on public issues; this was reversed in the
present instance of local "gossip."

Did Rapid City's "Weekend with Music" make new
friends for Jersey Standard? It was hard for people
to think of advertising in any terms but sales
promotion.

> High school principal: "Not that I'd buy any
> more Standard Oil products. It must be of
> advertising value or the company wouldn't do it."

He evidently associated the "Standard Oil" of
the program with the Standard of Indiana service
stations in town. He was asked about that.

"As far as I know, that's Standard Oil of New
Jersey and that's the parent company of all of
them. We around here are something else. I
would think they're all connected."

Few people seemed to question why a big company
would be interested in sponsoring this activity.
Big companies were just expected to do things of
this sort, perhaps without any special selfish
reasons.

Wife of a shoe repairman, twenty-four: "They do
it for the same reason as any other company.
Look at what the soap companies do. They give
away them prizes all the time."

What was the place of the Philharmonic radio
program in the life of Rapid City?

Wife of a Sioux Indian linoleum fitter, thirty-
eight (indescribable squalor, five young
children clambering over her, the youngest
nursing): "I listen to it every Sunday. I can't
say I understand it, but I listen to it. I
don't really know why. I just sort of got in
the habit. I don't have any musical education
of any kind."

In the isolated community of Rapid City, CBS,
Jersey Standard, and its advertising agency
descended like *dei ex machina*, changing lives and
causing a stir. To some small degree, their
intrusion affected the way residents saw themselves
and their relationship to the wider world.

This little study demonstrated the role of the mass media as a
stimulus to conversation.[8] The research found that discussion of
"Weekend"—a strictly local news event—increased with social
status, just like discussion of larger national and world issues.
Was this because of the particular nature of the subject? If a
young person had been selected because of accomplishment in
baseball rather than in music, would the pattern of discussion
have been different?

Briefly the powers-that-be considered a more modest inter-mission feature, and raised the possibility of finding a host to substitute for Deems Taylor. David Anderson, the public relations department's point man on radio, narrated messages and introductions for a specially prepared tape of short musical selections, identifying himself as "John Donne." I then conducted tests on a series of studio audiences, asking them to select a host among several alternatives. I included "John Donne" along with the names of the two best-known radio hosts of classical music, Milton Cross and Ben Grauer. John Donne came out far and away in the lead, thereby teaching me a valuable lesson about the public's inevitable preference for what was already in place.

Anderson was far from being a professional radio announcer. Once a United Press reporter, he had been hired by Crayhon from the NBC newsroom to handle Jersey's publicity releases and contacts with radio stations, which still broadcast news in those days. Pursuing the romance of travel and the satisfaction of uplifting the impoverished and downtrodden, he sought out tropical assignments, first sailing off to Venezuela in a majestic stateroom on the SS *Brazil*. After Castro's triumph in Cuba, he developed a program to train the new government of guerrilla warriors in the arts of management and administration, hoping to win them over to the cause of what was still called "free private enterprise." Driven out of Cuba, he became enthusiastic over an effort to distribute kerosene burners to Haitian peasants so that they would stop burning down their forests for charcoal. In Libya he tried to propagate Western ideas and was expelled again, this time by Qaddafi. In his postretirement job at the American Institute of Certified Public Accountants, he struggled to upgrade that craft into a profession by developing a code of ethics. Low-keyed and self-effacing, Anderson embodied both the vicissitudes and rewards of a career in public relations.

An important part of Jersey Standard's effort to sway "thought leaders" or "influentials" (in then-current public relations jargon) was by reaching out to educators. Each year the company invited a small, select group of college professors, mainly economists and other social scientists, to a two-day "Round Table" to discuss topical issues with leading Jersey executives. This highly limited but intensive interaction with a tiny academic elite succeeded (in my observation) in changing perceptions on both sides and was presumed to have a ripple effect.

Company publications were also mailed to public officials, journalists, and college faculty. As with every other costly element in the company's ambitious public relations effort, this program had to be justified to management with proof of its effectiveness. In 1950 the flood of unsolicited promotional material that now fills America's mailboxes was still a mere trickle. Then, as now, a conventional approach to determining whether the mailings were worthwhile could involve large-scale surveys or the mailing of questionnaires to recipients (perhaps matched against comparable nonrecipients), asking about their knowledge of and attitudes toward the company. But my instinct was to go out and talk directly and at length to the targets of this program.

College professors were generally regarded as important and prestigious. Their numbers had grown with the enormous postwar increase in college enrollment. Teaching as a profession encouraged a critical and analytical view of things; it was also financially unrewarding. Surveys showed that college teachers, reconciling high status and a middle-class style of life with a low income, were more hostile to business than the public at large. What was the effectiveness of mailing them the company's annual report and annual meeting transcript? To find out, I conducted intensive personal interviews with sixty-six professors at a wide range of colleges and universities.

Their comments showed the difficulty of swaying opinion through impersonal mass communications and illustrated the kinds of ideas and insights that come from listening to informants individually and in depth rather than recording replies to a structured questionnaire.

JERSEY'S PUBLICATIONS AND COLLEGE TEACHERS (1951)

Three main elements account for the great variety of mailing pieces that flow across educators' desks:

(1) *The academic field.* Teachers of engineering and of business are high on the list for outside mailings, because their work often brings them into close contact with industry, while teachers of the humanities, pure science, and theoretical social science are low on the list.

(2) *The personality of the individual teacher.* Instructors teaching identical courses differ widely in the degree to which they use outside materials and solicit instructional aids. This is dramatically exhibited by two professors of chemistry teaching identical courses in two adjacent institutions. One cites the great amount of material he requests from private companies. The other bemoans the fact that his course is so tight and crowded that he has no use for anything more.

(3) *Special research or teaching interests.* The amount of outside literature a teacher gets depends on the courses taught. Certain economics professors are heavy consumers of materials from business, unions, or government agencies; others whose courses are more theoretical have little use for such materials. A professor may receive no material at all, or up to twenty or thirty pieces a week.

Why do some mailing pieces receive more attention than others? Everyone at least glances at the material. Some keep only what is of special interest; others spend a good deal of time. Prompt special attention for unsolicited literature seems to depend on the following considerations: (1) Its relevance to the professor's actual teaching or research interests. (One may be interested in a company official's speech because it spells out an argument in which he is interested, while others may use it as an example of business English, of a public relations device, of corporate propaganda,

or of logical argumentation.) (2) Its human
interest or curiosity appeal. (3) Its technical
quality: the degree to which the material is
typographically and visually appealing, the quality
of paper, the style, and the format. An elaborate,
expensive, impressive-looking mailing piece is not
readily discarded.

> Professor of Political Science, Eastern College:
> "The thing that impresses the students about
> Standard Oil is the magnificent paper that they
> can afford to use."

None of the professors expresses resentment
over receiving Jersey's annual report. However,
those in fields rather remotely connected with
industry are puzzled as to why it was sent to them.
"I don't know whether it's propaganda or
educational."

The comments spontaneously offered on the
annual report are, almost uniformly, very
favorable. It is singled out as an outstanding
example of presentation—typography, graphs, even
the paper stock. Still, some teachers simply glance
at it and discard it:

> Professor of Law, Southern University: "A lot
> of money is wasted on that stuff. I'm not
> interested in investments, so that a thing
> that's encouraging me to invest I wouldn't
> spend any time on."

In an economics, business, or accounting class
the annual report can be taken simply to illustrate
a balance sheet or a profit-and-loss statement. In
a graphics or English course, it might be used as
an example of report construction or presentation.
It may be selected to exemplify a public relations
technique, or presented quite differently as a
picture of the social organization and structure of
a large modern corporation. It is used to bolster
an ideological argument—to destroy anti-business
prejudices or (more rarely) to instill them.

In the judgment of their professors, students appreciate anything that smacks of real life and the practical world of business as a contrast to mere "theory." Many instructors distribute the transcript of the stockholders meeting to illustrate how democratically a large corporation is run, or simply of how it is run (without pros or cons). Others, however, think the transcript documents their own convictions that management controls a corporation like Jersey with little or no regard for stockholder wishes or interest:

> Instructor in Economics, Eastern University: "It gives some of the students an impression, as it does me, that it's a big stage show and that the real power is still in the hands of the people having control."

> Professor of Chemistry, Southern University: "Very many of the students have the idea that a large corporation is some sort of crooked outfit, that it became large because it is dishonest. I think they get to realize that these large companies usually are large because of the way they operate."

> Professor of Geography, Midwest University: "I don't know how that could be of overall value to the company, from a financial value point of view. Unless it's to justify the high price of oil, I don't know what you accomplish other than goodwill."

Some instructors assert that the chief benefit is to keep the company's name before a section of the public, and regard this as a rather dubious benefit.

> Professor of Geology, Midwest College: "From the standpoint of sales they're gaining nothing. Whether they do it for income tax purposes or not I don't know. I presume they can write these things off, can't they?"

What motives do professors ascribe to the companies that send literature to them? A considerable range of sophistication appears in the opinions on this point.

Instructor of Geography, Midwest University: "Maybe to show—in this time of labor strife—to show their employees with happy smiles on their faces."

Professor of Economics, Southern University: "I'm no different from everyone else. I like to return a favor. I wouldn't drive down three or four blocks to buy a gallon of Standard Oil products, but I think of these as indirectly building goodwill."

Other educators argue that sending literature to the colleges serves the same function as any other type of advertising—sales promotion.

Professor of Chemistry, Southern University: "The motive of any company is to make money. A great many students are likely to use the product later on."

A variation on the sales theme is the argument that the company's motive is to recruit new employees among college graduates, or to gain new stockholders.

Another group of professors think in terms of the usefulness that the materials had for them and regard the company's motive as altruistic. Large companies are interested in education, they say; they just want to help out the teaching profession, and they have lots of money to give away.

The most positive responses come from the very people who least need to be convinced—instructors of business, accounting, and engineering who tend to be politically more conservative than teachers in the social sciences and humanities.

I concluded that it might be far more important for the company to contact English or psychology teachers than teachers of advertising or business. To reach those who were critical or suspicious might mean broadening the circulation of some existing publications or creating new ones. More effort should be given to dramatize and personalize the material. Speeches by company officials might, for instance, attain a wider readership and command more attention if they contained a photograph of the speaker, with a brief biographical sketch. A casebook, or series of casebooks, adapted to different academic fields could illustrate situations depicting the life of a large corporation.

The detailed conclusions of this report exemplified a crucial element, and also a crucial problem, in applied research. In presenting recommendations the researcher must abandon the stance of objectivity, necessary for the integrity of the investigation, and apply imagination to solving a problem facing the organization. The researcher thus oversteps the permissible limits of scientific inquiry but is likely to be judged by the utility of the recommendations rather than by the technical quality of the research.

At the time I joined Jersey Standard, the company was still reassembling the pieces of its far-flung empire, which had been badly battered during the war. In Eastern Europe the newly reacquired subsidiaries were being nationalized by the Soviet satellite regimes. In Western Europe the oil industry was converting itself to a peacetime economy. (In Nazi-occupied France, Esso had become a distributor of the charcoal that fueled vehicles as a substitute for gasoline, and the public relations directors of the French and German subsidiaries had conferred at congenial lunches on the Champs Élysées.) At Jersey's first international public relations conference in 1948, opinion surveys were promoted as a valuable tool for affiliates who were just learning how to set up programs in this domain.

Standard Oil of Brazil had just engaged a newly formed company to conduct what may have been the first properly conducted opinion poll in that country. International Public Opinion Research had been formed as a partnership of Elmo Roper and Joshua B. Powers, a former journalist who ran an advertising sales representative firm for Latin American newspapers. They had hired Elmo C. ("Budd") Wilson, the former research director of CBS, to run the company.* Wilson, once a journalism instructor at the University of Minnesota, had spent the war working for the Office of War Information in London. He had a pleasant round ruddy face, red hair and a bristling red mustache, a merry air, and a taste for good food and wine. Wilson's maxim for his company was, "1. Do a good job. 2. Have fun. 3. Make money." He was successful only on the first two points.

In late October 1948, Budd and I flew separately to Rio de Janeiro to sell local management on the value of their impending poll and to supervise the design of the questionnaire and the organization of the field work. Frank Surface, a homely, silent, elderly chemist in the company's marketing department, was another member of the team, bringing his wife along on what may have been a preretirement boondoggle.

The oil industry was in a hot spot at that moment in Brazil's passionate political life. The military dictator, Getulio Vargas, was under strong pressure to nationalize it; ubiquitous graffiti proclaimed, *"O petroleo e nosso!"* (The oil is ours!).

Wilson and I found ourselves in the office of Esso Brazil's president on Rio's downtown waterfront the morning following the presidential election in the United States, a day on which large headlines in the local press announced, "Dewey to Be

---

* Later renamed International Research Associates, this company's subsequent history is a cautionary tale about the hazards of private entrepreneurship in the research business. After Wilson's death in 1968, ownership passed to his former associate, Helen Dinerman, who had worked with Paul Lazarsfeld at Columbia's Bureau of Applied Social Research. It was then folded into a new entity, Starch/INRA/Hooper, which merged several specialized research companies. That company was acquired as an investment and taken public by a group headed by Oscar Lubow, an advertising executive with no research background. Their get-rich-quick scheme didn't work. Lubow was ousted and Wilson's son Jay took it over. He bought the Roper Organization from Elmo's son Burns and renamed the company Roper Starch Worldwide. A later acquisition was the Response Analysis Corporation, founded by two former employees of the Opinion Research Corporation. The enterprise was eventually sold to United Business Media, a British holding company, which also acquired Audits and Surveys. (That firm's president, Sol Dutka, once Roper's statistician, had earlier taken it public, with no success in the stock market.) In 2002 the company's name was Roper ASW. Mediamark Research became part of this empire.

Elected Today." As we discussed plans for our poll, the short-wave radio kept bringing us the surprising election returns. We explained to the assembled executives that Truman's lead merely reflected the fact that the Democratic big cities were the first to complete their count. As the day wore on and it became apparent that the infallible pollsters—Elmo Roper, George Gallup, and Archibald Crossley—had things all wrong, our tack changed to assurances: Our survey for Esso Brazil was intended to investigate broad issues rather than engage in the hazardous prediction of who would turn out to vote. The company's managers were more sophisticated than I might have expected; the survey proceeded on schedule. My next international project fared less well.

Creole Petroleum was another important and profitable Jersey Standard subsidiary, the dominant oil producer in Venezuela. That country had survived a lengthy dictatorship and a long series of unstable governments, generally established by coups d'état. Henry Pelke, Creole's public relations manager, was short, tough, and earthy, a veteran of Texas politics. He wore a broad grin, metal-rimmed glasses, and thinning hair slicked back in a comb-over. Pelke explained cheerily that one of his tasks was to call on local and provincial officials, distributing envelopes of cash to assure their "goodwill."

Much of the crude oil produced in western Venezuela was exported by tanker to the nearby Dutch West Indian colony of Aruba, site of a refinery operated by another Jersey subsidiary, the Lago Oil and Transport Company, Ltd. (The now-popular vacation resort was then a remote and sleepy tropical island.)

The material needs of Lago's expatriate American employees were supplied by a commissary supported by Jersey's purchasing department in Radio City. Purchase orders from Lago listed all the necessities of life: five hundred bottles of aspirin, six cases of toothpaste, one hundred gross of condoms, etc. This last item brought blushes to the cheeks of the modest ladies who filled the orders in New York. The word went back that condoms should henceforth be ordered under the code name "Aruba specials." The next purchase order dutifully came through as: "six cases of toothpaste and one hundred gross of Aruba specials (condoms)."

This anecdote, which circulated gleefully through the executive ranks at Jersey, whetted my curiosity about Aruba. Here was an extraordinary case history of a backward, isolated, traditional society whose people had been suddenly thrust into the industrial age.

The oil companies were the first true multi-national corporations. The managers of their overseas subsidiaries, men selected for their technical knowledge and executive ability, were abruptly required to cope with the personalities, values, institutions, and politics of alien societies. They came armed with the style, procedures, and precedents that had evolved in the company's domestic activities. Among these was the philosophy of "human relations in industry," with its attendant apparatus of incentive programs, profit sharing, retirement benefits, and "employee communication." Lago's managers were solidly rooted in the traditions of the parent company. Charlie Smith, who directed employee and public relations, told me, "You have to have been with this company through a depression and a war to appreciate what it gives you."

In 1950, after attending a short executive training course at the Harvard Business School, Lago's two leading executives decided that they needed an "employee attitude survey," and I was summoned to fly down for preliminary reconnoitering—a feasibility study. In a briefing before the trip I was told, "Americans down there act like God Almighty. They get a 25 percent pay increase and a cost-of-living allowance plus perquisites. It's a lazy, comfortable life."

I spent about ten days on the island talking to executives, employees, and other residents. I took an overnight trip on a tanker to Venezuela's Lake Maracaibo, an almost enclosed arm of the Caribbean whose surface was punctuated by a forest of oil derricks. (The ship's officers were multi-national but all white. They ate in total silence at their mess. The crew were all either black or what would today be called Hispanic.)

The trip to Aruba brought me face-to-face with what has become one of the principal social challenges of the twenty-first century: accelerated migration from poor countries to rich ones. The broad outlines are familiar: Western medicine and sanitation have spurred high population growth in poor countries. At the same time, low birthrates and rising living standards have increased the Western demand for inexpensive labor, attracting immigrants. As a result, the host countries face changes in the composition and age structure of their population, growing income disparities, and in many cases a heightening of ethnic tensions. In these conditions the seeds of terrorism have sprouted.

The field notes that follow represent snapshots of a small isolated society in the process of transformation. They touch upon a number of issues that remain highly topical: the movement across borders of people in search of a better life; the subsequent clash of cultures; the managerial dilemmas faced by global corporations operating within an alien political system and a multinational workforce.

Ordinarily the first step in preparing a questionnaire for a survey is to talk informally with people of the kind to be interviewed later, and to cover the assigned subject in the broadest possible way to see what ideas turn up. In the case of Aruba, the specific issues of employee morale and loyalty could not be disengaged from the dynamics of a complex little world in a ferment of social change. Although the object of the exercise was to design a survey, I had to approach the scene in the same way as I had the Peace Mission movement nine years earlier, more as an ethnologist than as a researcher of opinion.

ARUBA: THE TRANSFORMATION OF A TRADITIONAL SOCIETY (1950)*

Aruba was first colonized by Spain in 1528 and acquired by the Dutch in 1634. Because the island, about the size of Washington, D.C., is arid and

---

*The statements in quotation marks are from the shorthand transcripts of my dozens of interviews.

infertile, it never supported the typical West
Indian plantation economy, based on the importation
of African slaves. Few of Aruba's inhabitants are
dark-skinned, as they are on most West Indian
islands. The Arubans are a mix of the original
Arawak Indian stock, "less warlike and less
advanced than the Caribs," and of the Spaniards,
Dutch, and assorted buccaneers who moved in and out
over the centuries. The native inhabitants speak
Papiamento, a linguistic cocktail that includes
elements of all their languages, with Spanish at
the root. With their inbred population, Arubans
share a small number of family names. Individual
isolated communities are distinctive in their
subcultures.

Before World War I, the island's men used to
migrate seasonally by schooner to Cuba, Colombia,
and Venezuela to work as agricultural laborers.

"Arubans used to help each other, like in
building a house. If a man slaughtered a sheep
one week, he'd distribute the meat to his
neighbors. They'd give him meat the next week."

Although three-fourths of the islanders are
Catholics, folk traditions persist. Old women
called *curiosas* give advice and dispense herbs.
Sick people consult the Broea-man (in Spanish,
Bruja) or witch doctor. *Curados* (quacks) are
consulted more than doctors. TB and syphilis are
regarded as the workings of witchcraft. There are
always evil spirits around, especially at dusk.
Arubans "fear blades and scissors" as well as black
cats and owls.

How has the oil business affected this static
traditional society? Lago started a storage
operation in 1924 and finished building its
refinery in 1930. The island's population soared.
In 1947 it was 47,800.* Lago accounts for about
two-thirds of the island's total workforce.

---

*It was 66,000 in 1995, after the island had become a popular winter resort. The
refinery's production diminished in the 1960s. It was closed in 1985 and reactivated
in 1993.

An oil refinery operates around the clock, with
three work shifts. It requires a labor force that
encompasses both skilled technicians and menial
laborers. From the start, Lago relied on
experienced Americans to handle the technical and
administrative jobs. The native Arubans (27 percent
of Lago's eight thousand employees) are ill-
equipped to meet the rigorous demands of a modern
industry, so recruits from throughout the Caribbean
basin have been admitted on temporary work permits,
renewed only as long as their employment continues.
Arubans are in the lowliest unskilled jobs; many
are illiterate and speak no English. In higher-type
jobs, there are mainly lighter skinned BGs (natives
of British Guiana, mostly of Indian descent),
Surinamers, and Arubans.

The presence of so many foreigners places a
severe strain on the island's facilities. In rural
Aruba, housing is primitive. "Often there are no
outhouses." In the absence of public
transportation, the towns can be reached only on
foot and are inaccessible to rural people. Boys of
fourteen or fifteen in the village of Noord have
never been in Oranjestad (the principal town), two
or three miles away.

The stresses of industrialization have brought
changes in the Aruban personality. A gentle,
"backward" people have developed "egoism,"
"aggressiveness and suspicion," prejudices, and an
"emphasis on prestige symbols."

"People are different now. Everybody drinks,
there's more crime. You used to have family
feuds before, but at the end of the year people
would make up to each other. Now there are more
killings, which you never had in the old days.
People run around. They have more money,
movies, radio, frigidaires. They don't take
care of the old folks. They spend their money
drinking and don't care about their parents."

"The Arubans drink themselves into inanity on
payday." Bay rum is "Aruban champagne."

With its total domination of the island's
economy, Lago is at the same time a force for
radical change and one that maintains the status
quo by reinforcing existing institutions and codes
of conduct. Lago management recognizes the
importance of expanding opportunities for the
native Arubans. They get first choice in hiring,
and as a result, "A lot of dead wood has been
hired."

The managers, industrial technicians concerned
with the processing of petroleum products, find
themselves entangled with an incredible array of
human problems. They have to pacify a variety of
incompatible constituencies—the Dutch authorities,
established economic interests, unpredictable
populist demagogues in Aruba's provincial society,
and the multiplicity of occupational and ethnic
groups among employees. Real inequities, imagined
inequities, pride, and self-interest create
tensions that cannot always be resolved
reasonably.

For want of alternative suppliers, Lago
provides educational programs and electrical power
and subsidizes the staples of life. As the company
has taken on responsibility for social services, it
faces new problems. "The hospital is a sore point.
Twenty percent of the expense goes to deliver
babies." The company discontinued selling bedsheets
in its commissary for locals because of pressure
from the town merchants. The battle over this
seemingly petty matter has severely damaged the
company's efforts to establish a dialogue with its
non-American workforce.

For centuries, Arubans maintained their stable
cohesive society with a minimal Dutch colonial
presence. Like other West Indians, they traveled
freely from island to island and to the Venezuelan
mainland in search of employment. Race and
ethnicity became a central preoccupation after the
arrival of the oil companies and their massive
importation of foreign workers.

"The situation here is the world in miniature,
with the white man owning and controlling
everything."

The (solidly white) American expatriates who
run the refinery live with their families in a
well-policed enclave known as "The Colony," whose
neat houses and well-tended lawns resemble those of
any suburb in the United States. Their off-duty
social lives are largely confined to this
settlement and its central institution, the Esso
Club. The uniformity of housing reduces
distinctions of occupational rank and salary. The
fence around the Colony is to keep out the goats,
say the Americans. To keep out the Arubans, say the
Arubans. The servants in the Colony are all West
Indian Negroes. (Arubans do not do domestic
service.) A number of Lago's top executives are
from the South; they speak of "niggers" without
self-consciousness.*

There are two parallel status systems, that of
the workplace and that of the societies from which
employees have come. A police corporal with low
status in the refinery is head of the Negro Masonic
order (The Mechanics) for the whole territory of
Curaçao.

Dutch law forbids racial discrimination. All
Dutch, Aruban, and Negro children go to the same
schools. There are no color barriers in the lively
Flamingo Room bar; the manager cannot exclude
Negroes, but he seats them (including his
daughter's tutor) in the back.

The company's racial and national hiring
practices are set deliberately.

"Top management decided in 1940 not to employ
any more [Chinese-origin] BGs and Surinamers
although many had been hired prior to that.

---

*In 1950 racial segregation was enforced by law in parts of the United States,
including Texas and Louisiana, oil states from which many of Lago's American personnel were recruited.

They were very intelligent and good workers but they were radicals and troublemakers."

Management also makes distinctions among the black natives of the various West Indian islands. No Jamaicans are hired. "They're of very low-grade intelligence; very bad political background; troublemakers. Very poor physical specimens."

A dense network of voluntary associations reinforces the social bonds within the various ethnic groups and thus inhibits rather than encourages contacts. A party for government employees had to be held at the Golf Club, not at the company-sponsored Esso Club, which has never been used by nonwhites. "Management said the Colony would object."

In spite of the intense club activity, the absence of after-work recreation (particularly acute because of the three daily work shifts) is most upsetting to the thousands of displaced and unattached men.

"You've got to work hard here because there's nothing else to do."

Management is aware of the employees' boredom but feels there are limits to what it can do. "We've encouraged sports. If you don't watch out you'll take care not only of their work life but of their home life as well."

For a population of men away from home, company-sponsored sports are not a substitute for female company.

A Grenadan: "If you want a girl here you don't have money for a shirt for your back."

One in five local employees suffers from venereal disease. A boisterous establishment, the Hotel del Día, just outside the entrance to the refinery, provides round-the-clock recreation for Lago's bachelor workforce. There are other, less formal brothels in the village. Prostitutes are flown in from South America under government supervision.

"The government makes you go on the beach like an animal; you can't take her to the house."

Ambivalent feelings are expressed toward an employer who is both benevolent and demanding:

"The company is the only popular thing on the island. They're good; they discipline you with their thrift plans and their vacation plans. Everyone would like to work for the company."

Lago's refinery has no unions, and management wants to keep things this way. The company's creation of elected employee representative groups inevitably has brought new personalities to the fore. A native of British Guiana, B. K. Chand, a butcher in the plant commissary, was elected to the Employees Advisory Committee, against the opposition of "blood sucking semipolitical parasitical political jobbers." When he left this post he was honored with a farewell poem by colleagues who hailed "Chand of happy memory, fearless Chand." "Brave son of India born in heat / Could well execute the sale of meat / But to work in that icy cold / Was not a job you'd like to hold." (Chand wrote a book about himself: *B. K. Chand: The Man.*)

Lago built its refinery in Aruba (rather than in Venezuela itself) because of the colony's political stability.* A number of political parties contest for power: The AVP (Aruban Volkpartei) appeals to the poor and arouses anti-Dutch feeling with the slogan "Aruba for the Arubans." Its leader, Henny Eman, is called "the Führer" and

*Worldwide in 1950 colonialism was beginning to fade, and the Dutch East Indies had become the independent republic of Indonesia. The Netherlands was in the process of turning its West Indian colonies into a commonwealth.

accused of strong-arm tactics and much else. At the
AVP election victory celebration, according to the
opposition press, "Nuns were hooted and
intimidated. Men were dragged home like beasts,
dead drunk. Children of ten and eleven were carried
out of the Flamingo Room in a state of
intoxication."*

What do Lago's managers want to learn from
research? ("We don't know what they're thinking,
what goes on in their heads.") Some of their
questions appear to be raised in the expectation
that the results would confirm what they already
surmise:

"There's always been the psychology that the
oil industry won't stay here. What does the public
think of the stability of Lago?"

"Just what do they think of us as an economic
contributing factor?"

"Does the public think that Lago controls the
government?"

"There's this emotional feeling of nationals
vs. non-nationals. How much of that shows up?"

"What do they think of the foreign staff group,
off the job?"

"What are their attitudes toward local
supervisors?"

"What is the alien's viewpoint toward his
longtime outlook in Aruba? Would he take Dutch
citizenship and stay here if he could?"

"What do people think of the future of the next
generation?"

"What's the state of home ownership, especially
among the alien groups?"

"Clubs range from the swanky down. Is that the
recreation pattern?"

"How influential are the BGs with the rest of
the British groups?"

---

*In 1990, fearing a loss of Dutch subsidies, Aruba canceled its proposed inde-
pendence agreement, which was to have taken effect in 1996. In 2002, Henny Eman,
Jr., was Aruba's prime minister.

"How would workers react to a shift in work shift hours?"

"What do they like best about Lago? What do they like least?"

The purpose of research, I told Lago management, is not to solve problems but to provide a base for action and settle questions with the help of facts. I outlined a survey proposal to cover a number of topics:

1. Race relations. How much intergroup contact is there? When racial tension arises, where does it start and how? How does it affect the work efficiency of and attitudes toward the company?

2. Productivity. Is the company getting the best labor force it can? How do social changes and problems affect aspirations and productive capacities? How do workers' values change on the job?

3. Social and political realities. What is the state of family life, housing, education, recreation? What indicators are there of social pathology: drink, crime, prostitution? Who is considered to bear political responsibility, the company or the government? Who is thought to control what?

4. Labor grievances. How is the Employee Council regarded? What are workers' attitudes toward supervisors and management?

5. Communication. What are the sources of news and information, both in general and about the company? How much social isolation is there among the various nationality groups? What is their importance?

I proposed two questionnaires, one for an employee survey, another for a general population survey to be conducted later. In the end, Lago's management decided that a survey would stir up too many sentiments that were best left dormant and unexplored. A survey would certainly have provided hard data to resolve questions on which informed people within the company

disagreed. It might have made managers more sensitive to grievances of which they were already well aware. It is doubtful
whether it would have led to important changes in the way the
company recruited, hired, compensated, or motivated its workforce. In retrospect, the statistics that might have come out of a
survey would probably have lent authority to my short series of
observations, but not changed the story.

My employment at the heart of the big business establishment
kept me ideologically stretched. (I could not share with my associates the information that my new wife, Agnes, was an organizer
for the Textile Workers Union of America, CIO.) But I soon discovered that Standard Oil was full of unexpected incongruities.
One day Freyermuth presented some of my survey findings to
the company's directors, and I was suddenly summoned upstairs
to be on call, in case there were questions. The board's anteroom
was adorned by the presence of John D. Rockefeller's own magnificent rolltop desk. Although the staff at company headquarters was otherwise exclusively white, the attendants in the
sanctum sanctorum were all elderly black gentlemen dressed in
black. Like funeral directors, they padded about silently, their
demeanor grave and their voices hushed. I had rushed up from
my office without reading matter, and as time passed, one took
pity and asked, "Would you like a newspaper, sir?" He reached
into the bottom drawer of Rockefeller's desk and asked, "Which
would you like, sir, the *Times* or the *Compass*?" (The *Daily Compass* was a short-lived radical tabloid that sought to replace Marshall Field's defunct *P.M.*)

Standard Oil was ahead of its time in the field of employee
relations, with a well-qualified full-time executive to counsel actual or impending retirees, and a series of "management semi-
nars" that reached down to include even those at my peon level.
I masked my skepticism as we were indoctrinated in the rudi-
ments of the free-enterprise system, and foolishly neglected to
invest in the company's stock through its corporate contribution

plan. Nonetheless I basked in the glory that accrued to me through my place of employment. In commercial research circles my lowly position was invested with the awesome aura of the company itself. But in academia, where the idea of employment in commerce represented a sellout, I encountered disdain and suspicion. "Tell me," I was asked by an instructor at a small Midwestern college who had received a master's degree with me at Chicago but had never gone on for a doctorate, "do you ever find that your graduate work in sociology is of any use to you now?" I said yes but failed to ask, "Is yours?"

The glory days of Frank Abrams's public relations department had faded long before Jersey Standard changed its name to Exxon and moved its headquarters to Houston. Whatever money was saved by slashing the public relations budget to the almost-vanishing point was a pittance compared to what was lost by the company's blundering response to the disaster of the Exxon Valdez's Alaskan oil spill—something that could never have occurred on Freyermuth's watch.

In the spring of 1951 I took leave from Jersey to direct a series of surveys on "The Utilization of Negro Troops" for the Department of Defense. Budd Wilson's company had been retained to do this work by the Operations Research Office, a cover operation set up through Johns Hopkins University to tap civilian expertise for the army.

Project Clear began in Korea and continued at military bases throughout the United States. Although President Truman had proclaimed the principle of equal treatment for blacks in the armed forces, the policy had not been implemented, and a series of high-level commissions had prepared conflicting reports and recommendations.

Opposition to racial integration came partly from the inertia of the military's huge bureaucracy and partly from simple prejudice. Truman had federalized a number of National Guard divisions, including several from Southern states, where the

all-white Guard was rooted in small-town, "good ol' boy" culture. Paradoxically the war's manpower demands brought these
units into active service and thus became a source of resistance
to desegregation, yet those same manpower demands led to the
emergency use of urgently needed black replacements for casual-
ties in combat units.

The research team was assembled hastily, partly by me and
partly by Wilson. Data processing was to be handled by American University's Bureau of Social Science Research, which
Robert Bower, a former student of Lazarsfeld's, had established
on the model of his mentor's Bureau of Applied Social Research
at Columbia. In New York, I recruited another Lazarsfeld-trained
sociologist, John Morsell, whose work as an interviewer and as
an analyst was so good that he quickly became my principal associate on the project. Morsell had earned his doctorate at Columbia while working at a dead-end municipal civil service job.
With his pipe at an upward angle, John managed to look thor-
oughly civilian in his baggy army uniform. He had grown up in
Pittsburgh, and the indignities of Southern segregation were
quite new to him. He regarded the workings of Jim Crow through
his horn-rimmed glasses with the bemused detachment of a Ma-
linowski examining the habits of the Trobriand Islanders. (John
stayed on with Wilson's company when our project ended, and
spent the remainder of his career as Roy Wilkins's associate director at the NAACP.)

Social scientists are not always disinterested observers of
the phenomena they study. In Project Clear our assignment was
to investigate how the army could best use its black troops. If I or
my colleagues on the research team had been segregationists, or
perhaps simply unimaginative, we might have defined the task
as one of measuring the degree to which white soldiers accepted
racial integration. In that case a straightforward survey of attitudes would have revealed the prevailing prejudices and acquiescence in existing practice; the findings would have put a brake
on changes to the status quo. Instead, circumstances allowed us
to contrast the opinions of men serving in segregated units with

those in units that had already been desegregated under battle conditions. The results demonstrated that integration imposed from above led to acceptance. But these results reflected the prior conviction of the researchers that attitudes were malleable.

I left for the Korean War from Seattle, the sole civilian on a military aircraft loaded with reservists who had been summoned back to active duty, given uniforms, and shipped off in short order, without any freshening-up training to prepare them for combat. The plane chased the sun; we were served an endless succession of breakfasts, both on board and at our two stops, in Anchorage and on the dreary island of Shemya in the Aleutians, where the wreckage of Japanese fighter planes lay scattered beside the runway.

In Tokyo, Americans still played the part of all-powerful occupiers. I was horrified to see four huge soldiers picking up a small (unoccupied) Japanese car and slamming it down, just for fun, while passersby giggled politely. In our civilian clothes, Bob Bower and I did not feel bound by the "Off Limits" signs that the army had placed on certain establishments in the Ginza. We ventured upstairs into an enormous, festively lit nightclub where the hostesses and many of the patrons were dressed in gaudy carnival costumes as medieval European knights and ladies, Renaissance princes, and Victorian horse guards. Loud American popular music played in the background, beer was consumed from two-liter bottles; the mood was one of unconfined hilarity. Six years after Hiroshima, this felt weird.

Taegu and Pusan were the only two Korean cities that had not been captured by the Communists in their initial advance and that remained intact. In the port city of Taegu, a large part of the population appeared to be engaged in laundry services for the American troops. Laundries were identified by crude signs reading "Clean and Kind." On a cloudy day, after a long exploratory walk through the city's winding back alleys, I found myself hopelessly lost. A small crowd of bemused civilians gathered around as I tried to ask for directions to the city center. This was the first time in my life when linguistic skills were totally useless. (This has happened to me twice since: once at night in the suburbs of Helsinki, and once, disastrously, when I tried to find a toilet in Hangzhou.) How does one communicate with gestures that one has to find one's way home? I must have eventually done so.

The humble hovels of Korea's rural inhabitants (the GIs called them "hooches") were made of reeds and wattle. Many had been burned or abandoned and vandalized. The brick houses of the towns were damaged by machine-gun and artillery fire. The city of Seoul was a wasteland through which army trucks raced in a steady procession. In the countryside the unpaved roads exhaled clouds of dust in good weather as vehicles passed; they were rivers of deep mud when it rained, which it seemed to do interminably. Long lines of military traffic barely moved along. At intervals along the roads, signs warned of mines; some were adorned with a skull and crossbones, others were signed, "Signed, The Thing." (*The Thing*, a recently released horror movie, had captured the fancy of the troops.)

The tide of the Korean War had turned with the entry of Chinese "volunteers" who had driven American forces back from the border after General MacArthur unwisely pushed to the Yalu River. The Chinese prisoners I talked to were tiny and wizened, poorly uniformed and dispirited, as any prisoners must be. A group of them sat on the ground, cross-legged with their hands tied behind them, and sullenly submitted to interrogation. The interrogator, to my surprise, was a Mandarin-speaking Japanese civilian (wearing an American uniform), evidently a former intelligence officer, who essayed a translation of their grunted words for the American captain who posed questions. I found it rather surprising that our army did not have Chinese-speaking specialists of its own.

At this point the war had settled into a stalemate, much along the present line of demarcation between North and South Korea. As we approached the front lines, barely camouflaged artillery batteries fired methodically and with brutal sound. The sweet stench of death permeated the woods. Unburied corpses of men and horses remained by the side of the road. We passed files of ROK (Republic of Korea) troops, returning from battle positions to rest. In utter silence, filthy, bowed down by their heavy rifles and equipment, they trudged wearily away from danger. The front line was also surprisingly silent, though any movement visible to the enemy was apt to be met with an explosion of heavy gunfire. The work of our team was not done on the line but back at division headquarters, generally about half a mile to the rear. We slept luxuriously on canvas cots under tents, upon which a steady rain was usually falling.

Altogether twelve thousand soldiers completed our questionnaires in the Korean study and in the second stage of research at military bases in the United States. We also conducted open-ended personal and group interviews with about two thousand officers and enlisted men. In the group interviews we talked to members of a squad who had fought or served together and shared common experiences that they could discuss or argue about in the interviewer's presence. This was quite different from the current practice of running group interviews with people recruited individually and brought together for the first time to talk about what they often consider to be a trivial or irrelevant subject.

In Korea the questionnaires and pencils were given to men who had been rotated from the front lines to the rear for "rest and recreation." Their morale was boosted by hot food, volleyball games, and an occasional concert by a division's band. Except under emergency conditions, each of the three battalions in any regiment was periodically rotated out of the lines. One evening, when the rain was not falling, there was an open-air screening of a film. It was *The Battle of the Bulge,* about World War II, starring Van Johnson—just the sort of escapist fantasy to take soldiers' minds from the horrors of war!

An urchin named Rhee had been adopted as a mascot by one division headquarters company. A member of our team, Ira Cisin, a pudgy and good-humored professor at George Washington University, instructed him to engage in a minstrel-show dialogue. Cisin: "Rhee, why does a chicken cross the road?" Rhee: "I dunno. Mus' be for some foul reason." "That's a mighty poor pun for a man of your ilk!" "Ilk? I'm a Mason!" "I didn't know you were a lodge man." "Oh, no. Ony a hunded ten poun."

The questionnaires we gathered were sent back to Tokyo for processing. (Because of the intense time pressure, the transfer of the information to IBM punch cards could not wait until the research team's return to the United States.) At one point there was a snag in the data-processing operations, and I was summoned back to Japan to deal with it. This involved a helicopter ride from the front to an air base, a bumpy trip in a small plane to Pusan, and then a chilly flight to Tokyo in the hold of a C-47 cargo plane.

In a sardonic German documentary film about World War I,[9] sequences showing soldiers under shellfire in the muddy trenches are juxtaposed with scenes of Hindenburg, Ludendorff, and other extravagantly beribboned officers of the high command playing court to fashionable ladies at a Berlin garden party, where snappily attired military orderlies serve Sekt and canapés. This bitter incongruity came to mind when I returned to my room at the Dai Ichi Hotel in Tokyo and found an officers' dance in progress, with men in dress uniform and ladies in long ball gowns. (The families of officers in the American occupation force in Japan had remained in their quarters when the Korean War began. Enlisted men's wives had not been brought over.) I felt the same indignation I had experienced in New York when I returned from devastated Europe in 1945 and found crowds battering one another to get into the subway at the rush hour. But this was normality.

To my surprise, as a former enlisted man, I found the generals whom I interviewed to be impressive in their intelligence and temperament as well as in their concern for their troops.* I asked one of them why he thought the North Koreans had fought so much better than their southern counterparts. Was it the Com-

---

*One exception was Lt. Gen. Edward Almond, whose surly manner conveyed suspicion of any project that might alter the established racial order.

munist ideology that motivated them? He argued that the difference was only one of training and organization. In the Vietnam
War the same question became even more compelling and was
never satisfactorily answered.

Somewhere behind the battle lines I had a disquieting conversation with an army psychologist who was enthusiastic about
the opportunity to test soldiers' reactions to the stresses of battle.
He described the war as a wonderful "laboratory" for his research. While I was offended by his callousness, the term "laboratory" does accurately describe the variety of experimental
conditions that shaped our own study. We were able to compare
the responses of both white and black soldiers in combat and
noncombat units to situations in which troops remained racially
segregated or integrated in differing proportions. Our reports
were based on these comparisons, which showed that contact increased acceptance and that integration improved the performance of blacks without diminishing that of whites.

The reports quoted directly from our personal interviews,
including all the crude expressions. I overrode Wilson's suggestion that these should be excised, both because I felt that the language was authentic and because the term "motherfucker,"
widely used by black troops, was an obstacle to their successful
integration. In spite of Wilson's concerns, a couple of hardened
middle-aged female typists turned out the text without fainting.
The language was, however, used by the Pentagon as a pretext to
keep the reports classified "Secret." It took a twenty-year struggle on my part to get them declassified and published, but by
that time the fully integrated army was again embattled in
Vietnam.

In today's wars, most men go into battle because they have to
rather than because of compelling fervor for their cause. But it is
generally assumed that their motivation to do well depends on
their acceptance of the righteousness of their side. For this
reason our study included questions that dealt with soldiers'
feelings about the war as well as assessments of their own well-
being, their officers, and their units.

During the Vietnam War, troop morale became a burning

issue in news coverage and in domestic politics. For that reason I decided to exclude from my book on Project Clear[10] certain information, not directly related to the subject of integration, that raised sensitive questions about the attitudes of American soldiers toward their military duties in wartime. These findings can now go on the record.

TROOP MORALE IN THE KOREAN WAR (1951)

A military unit can perform its functions only if it remains cohesive. Cohesion requires acceptance of the military code of obedience. It also entails the interdependence of individual soldiers and their mutual loyalty and trust. (The intimacy of military life was invariably cited as the main justification for racial segregation.) In units engaged in active combat, death and injury reduce the number of comrades to whom an individual soldier relates. It is difficult to form new close relationships with men who may soon be gone, and newcomers are treated impersonally, even callously.

Soldiers' enthusiasm, and presumably their performance, were very much determined by the conditions they faced. Most soldiers rated their own units highly, though some were in outfits that were disasters in the making. Of fifteen integrated units in Korea and Japan, seven were described as performing "very well" by 80 percent or more of their members, and another six were rated this highly by two-thirds or more; three received lower scores. (Only a fourth of the enlisted men in one company said it was performing "very well.")

Among white combat infantrymen in Korea, both in all-white and in integrated units, half said the morale of the men in their outfit was "very high" or "high." Among soldiers in two companies of a California National Guard division on (noncombat) duty in Japan, the white Guardsmen, both in segregated and integrated units, gave a higher assessment of morale than did other soldiers (draftees and enlisted reservists); these men,

though incorporated into their ranks, were
apparently perceived, and perceived themselves, as
outsiders. Morale in one of these companies was
assessed as highly as it was by the infantrymen in
Korea; in the other it was much lower. Apparently
morale was produced by the military unit rather
than by the predispositions of its individual
members.

Not surprisingly, the stress of battle affected
men's feelings. A third of the combat infantrymen
replied "Yes, often," to the question, "Are you
ever bothered by nervousness?" but only a sixth of
the garrison soldiers in Japan gave that answer.
Most notably, a majority of the combat soldiers did
not report such symptoms, though they revealed
their stress on another question. Only one-fifth of
the combat troops said they were "hardly ever
worried and upset," compared with two-fifths of
those in Japan.

Less than half the infantrymen said they could
do most for their country by "being in the army"
rather than in a civilian job or by going to school
or college. Among the noncombatant soldiers, the
proportion was about one in four. Having a military
job that was relatively safe led to the illusion
that one's services were not really needed.

High school graduates were more likely than
those with less education to think they could do
more for their country as civilians than as
soldiers. Enlisted men were more likely to give
this answer than were the better-educated officers
and the senior noncommissioned officers, many of
whom were career military men. Men who enlisted in
the regular army were more positive than draftees
or reservists. However, even among these
volunteers, two of five had apparently had second
thoughts and said they could serve the country
better as civilians.

In spite of the miseries of the war in Korea's
uninviting terrain, a fourth of the combat troops
preferred "my present job in my present outfit" to
the alternatives ("the same kind of job in some

other outfit," "a different kind of job in my
present outfit," or in "some other outfit").

Similar answers were given by the non-Guardsmen
in Japan, but the Guardsmen were substantially more
positive. They were in a unit for which they had
volunteered in the first place and with hometown
(or at least home-state) buddies untouched by
battle. Two-thirds of the Guardsmen, but only two-
fifths of the other men in their units, said their
work was as important as any other job they might
be doing in the army. These non-Guardsmen appeared
to feel somewhat alienated; fewer than half of them
(compared with solid majorities in every other kind
of unit) said their officers "can count on the
willing and wholehearted cooperation of the
soldiers."

The men whose lives were on the line were most
skeptical about their mission. Half the combat
infantrymen said they "very often" "get the feeling
that this war in Korea is not worth fighting." Only
a third of the troops who were safe in Japan gave
this answer. Similarly, a fourth of the combat
troops, but two-fifths of the troops in Japan, said
"it was wise for the United States to help the
South Koreans." In both cases, it should be noted,
a majority thought otherwise.

The infantrymen were also much more willing to
stop the war "if the Communists were to offer to
stop fighting now on condition that we let them
keep control of Northern Korea." Only one-tenth
wanted to "keep on fighting until they give up
completely." Among the soldiers in Japan, who had
not faced the realities of the war, one in six
wanted to hold out for total victory. In the
absence of a clear-cut win, the more protracted the
war, the greater the disenchantment among those who
carried the burden.

The findings on troop morale were only a footnote to our surveys, which had been commissioned, after all, to study "The Uti-

lization of Negro Troops." The process of racial desegregation was inevitable, and in the next dozen years it quickly extended from the military to all aspects of American life. The successful integration of the army was often cited as evidence, as the props of institutionalized racism were demolished by the courts and by the pressures generated by the civil rights movement.

Ellis Johnson, who headed the Operations Research Office, told Wilson that he considered Project Clear to be its most important accomplishment. A few days after our last report was submitted, I sailed for Europe for a postponed start to an academic year as a Fulbright research fellow. Shortly afterward, Bob Bower crossed the Potomac to summarize the findings for the top brass at the Pentagon. When he finished, the presiding general turned to the others and said, "This is *it*!"

527147
693604
411082
354755
102986

THE PROFESSION

■ A profession is distinguished from a trade in several ways: it has generally accepted qualifications for entry into its ranks; it practices according to agreed-upon ethical rules; and it proclaims its social responsibility, at least in principle. In all these respects, the field of work in which I had become a dedicated practitioner has always revealed ambiguities.

Immediately after World War II, commercial research was a small world in which my own path kept intersecting those of a relatively limited number of others. Even in the twenty-first century, although commercial research is a substantial business in the United States, it employs only some fifty thousand full-time people, of whom at most a few hundred constitute a mutually acquainted elite. As in any occupation, the personal connections among those at the top are fostered through a network of associations, business and social contacts, referrals, and job recommendations.

The American Association for Public Opinion Research played a crucial role in providing a sense of professional identity to members of the fledgling craft.* I joined AAPOR in May 1948 at

---

*It had been founded in 1947, a year after opinion researchers were first convened at Central City, Colorado, by Harry Field, who had started the nonprofit National Opinion Research Center in Denver to work on surveys in the public interest.

its second conclave in Eagle's Mere, a small resort in the Pocono Mountains of eastern Pennsylvania.

Election forecasting was a major topic of discussion that spring, before the political party conventions. No one questioned the ability of the national polling organizations to predict the outcome. Some critics felt queasy about their use of the "quota" method of sampling, which had come into general use over the course of the preceding quarter-century. It allowed interviewers to select respondents according to certain designated categories of gender, race, and social class. There was much talk of the more complicated procedure of probability sampling, pioneered by government statisticians in their wartime surveys. This method selected the location and identity of households and individual respondents impersonally and by chance.

Nonsurvey methods were also up for discussion. Louis Bean, a former government statistician with a distinguished-looking thatch of white hair, analyzed historical voting records district by district, related them to economic data, and came forth with a set of predictions. Samuel Lubell, a journalist, claimed excellent results from the informal interviews he personally conducted with hundreds of voters in areas where the outcome was uncertain. Sam did not like to climb stairs, and it delighted him that people sitting on their front porches were so readily accessible. His system was described as "possibility sampling" by the California Poll's canny Mervin Field.

The early AAPOR conferences had occasional dramatic moments. At one, the frenetic founder of psychodrama, J. L. Moreno, demonstrated his therapeutic role-playing technique. He summoned from the audience a reluctant participant from the newly established state of Israel and proceeded to interrogate her about her personal interactions with Arabs. (The notion of "Palestinians" had not yet been invented.) To her mind such people were nonexistent, except for a gardener called in to do occasional jobs. Another audience member was recruited to play the role of the Arab, but the Israeli really had nothing to say, except that the roses needed watering. As Moreno badgered her to give vent to her innermost feelings, she turned heatedly on him. Moreno was delighted. "Ah, ze psychodramatic shock!" he proclaimed proudly.

Elmo Roper agreed to chair the plenary session at the 1956 conference, at which Lazarsfeld and the political scientist Harold Gosnell were to speak. One of Roper's rising young project directors, Louis Harris, had promised to sign up a third speaker—his friend, the newspaper columnist Joseph Alsop. Weeks and months passed without confirmation from Harris, who was bright, intense, and dark in manner, spoke deliberately, and smiled too readily. The program went to the printer, but there was still no word about Alsop. Harris never showed up at the conference itself. The reason became clear when Elmo returned to his office on Monday. Lou had used the occasion of everyone's absence to clean out his files and set himself up in his own business, taking with him the clients he had worked for at Roper's. He was not the first to conduct private polls for political candidates, but he was the first to demonstrate that success in political polling had commercial rewards. He stepped beyond the research function to manage the unsuccessful gubernatorial campaign of Franklin D. Roosevelt, Jr., in 1962 before making his name in public (or published) polling in presidential elections. Others followed, establishing their names by guiding successful candidates and using their fame to capture market research clients.*

AAPOR's membership was extraordinarily varied. The presidency of the organization alternated between commercial and noncommercial members, who were about equally represented. (Academics have since gradually become a majority.) From the academic side came sociologists, psychologists, political scientists, statisticians, professors of journalism and communication, plus an occasional economist. Other noncommercial types included demographers and specialists in public health. Most of

---

*Among these were Pat Caddell, President Carter's boy pollster; President Reagan's pollster, Richard Wirthlin; and Robert Teeter, the first President Bush's pollster.

those on the commercial side were self-taught practitioners. They included newspaper reporters who had drifted into political polling, women who ran interviewing services (the interviewers themselves were almost all women), and assorted executives and employees of research firms, advertising agencies, corporations, and trade associations (like the Life Insurance Agency Management Association, a fount of surprisingly good studies of American life). The diverse mix of backgrounds and interests was a stimulant to discussion. This was especially true in the organization's early days, when there were few concurrent sessions of the kind that subdivided the meetings of larger professional associations.

The favorite of all AAPOR meeting places was the Sagamore, a large rambling structure on the shore of Lake George in the Adirondacks. There the assembled pollsters dined on bounteous meals and midnight snacks. The highlight came at the end of the Saturday evening banquet, when the lights were dimmed and the entire kitchen staff paraded ceremonially around the dining hall, bearing platters of flaming baked Alaska.

The organization's membership was still small enough to be intimate. Lively and sometimes angry debates enriched the working sessions. There were late-night drinking parties, songfests, and poker games (sponsored by a Society for the Study of High and Low Statistics). The camaraderie of these meetings bonded individuals from all parts of the nation with wildly disparate work interests.

AAPOR had adopted a code of standards and ethics at its inception, but it was framed in vague generalities. By 1958, when I was chairman of the standards committee, clamor was mounting to make the code more specific and binding on the membership. The two principal opponents of this pressure were, curiously enough, two rigorous statistical methodologists. Shirley Star (formerly my fellow graduate student at the University of Chicago) had been a collaborator of Samuel Stouffer's in his landmark World War II study, *The American Soldier*. Passionate in nature, neglectful of her appearance, and incisive in her arguments, she

resisted the idea that the rules of good research could be codi-
fied.

My Project Clear colleague, Ira Cisin, took an even stronger
position than Star. He argued that AAPOR was not a professional
organization since it had no requirements for membership other
than an interest in the field and a pledged intent to adhere to
whatever code existed. "It's nothing but a chowder and marching
society!" No research report that cited the public's answers to a
single question met his own standards, which required the use of
statistical scales developed from a battery of questions that
probed at the nuances of a given topic. (We scaled many of the
questions we asked in Project Clear, but the resulting computa-
tions never added to the knowledge we got from the answers to
individual questions.)

There was also the matter of enforcement. This came to a
head several years after the new code was adopted, when the
standards committee received a tip from a researcher at the Ford
Motor company. He had discovered that a well-known firm,
Gilbert Youth Research, was obtaining sales leads for the company's dealers in the guise of conducting consumer surveys. The
culprit, not a member of AAPOR, was Eugene Gilbert, once a boy
wonder, now middle-aged. When the AAPOR council asked him to
cease and desist, he stormed into my office, threatening legal action. At considerable expense, the association incorporated to
spare its membership from legal liability.

The AAPOR code has since been revised to become even more
specific and demanding, but there has been ever greater abuse of
survey research by companies and individuals who, like Gilbert,
are outside the organization. The increased dependence on telephone interviewing has coincided with the growth of telemarketing, leading to fakery and confusion, and contributing to the
public's growing reluctance to cooperate. In politics a disturbing
development has been the use of "push polls," in which respondents are fed derogatory charges about a candidate to influence
their voting preferences rather than to sound them out. And political polls based on bad questions, poor samples, and shoddy
interviewing are routinely reported in the press, which has

shown remarkably little aptitude for distinguishing meretricious "surveys" from the genuine article.

Like any profession, research has continued to have its share of phonies, with derelictions both small and larger in consequence. There was William Yoell, whose speeches at research conferences reverberated with the authority added by a nonexistent NYU doctorate in psychology that he had awarded himself. There was Allan Jay, the fast-talking president of Videodex, a television ratings service. Golden-haired and sun-bronzed the year round, Jay looked like a movie star. I repeatedly asked him if I could visit his research operations, and he finally invited me to his enormous Art Deco penthouse office, which had previously been used by Eddie Rickenbacker when he was president of Eastern Airlines. There were, however, no other rooms in the suite. As a congressional investigation later discovered, there were no research operations elsewhere either, only booklets that printed Jay's "ratings." Although Videodex closed down soon after these revelations, Jay continued to attend professional meetings, where he was treated with respect by peers and former clients.

Then there was Norton Garfinkel, who satisfied the advertising business's inane appetite for a "single source" of data on media and markets with his Brand Rating Index. The Index quickly rode to stellar success, and Garfinkel sold his company to the Arcata Corporation, a West Coast forest products company with dreams of becoming a giant conglomerate. BRI foundered after a presentation to the 1970 Advertising Research Foundation conference by Willard Simmons, whose company measured magazine readership as well as product consumption. Simmons's presentation demonstrated an uncanny resemblance between BRI's magazine figures and his own, as well as between BRI's television data and Nielsen's. In this case, too, the service went under, but Garfinkel remained on the party circuit.

Even before I joined Jersey Standard, several large corporations had begun to open up to social research. Robert Ford, an industrial psychologist, had instituted a far-reaching program of re-

search on employee attitudes at AT&T (still known as "Ma
Bell").[1] In the early 1960s, General Electric hired the sociologist
Nelson Foote to initiate studies that dealt with a wide range of
subjects, from the broad social trends that would ultimately affect consumer and industrial buying patterns to the minutiae of
audience responses to individual television commercials. Foote's
eyes twinkled, conveying a perpetual sense of amusement at corporate foibles. He operated with great autonomy, pursuing his interest in Caribbean music on trips to Jamaica, where he departed
from his disengaged professorial demeanor by selling a hugely
expensive GE generator to the newly independent government.
Two alumni of Columbia's Bureau of Applied Social Research,
Lee M. Wiggins, Jr., and Joseph T. Klapper, and the sociologist
Richard Maisel, joined Foote in this research.

Wiggins was fascinated by the problems of analyzing data
from panels of people who were interviewed repeatedly—a preoccupation of his teacher, Paul Lazarsfeld. Lee was a South Car-
olinian in rebellion against his father, who had risen from a
laborer's job to the presidency of the Atlantic Coast Line Railroad. The son was irreverent, sharp-witted, and irrepressible. As
a youthful activist at the University of North Carolina, he had
been national president of the American Student Union and was
fast disillusioned with the Communists who tried to control it. In
1944, as a captain in the air force, he was ferrying a bomber
across the South Pacific, far from the usual traffic lanes, when
the plane developed engine trouble and had to be ditched. In the
confusion of evacuation onto the inflatable rubber lifeboat, an
airman broke his leg and most of the emergency rations were
lost. From the debris floating on the water, Lee fished out the
book he had brought with him, Arthur Koestler's *Darkness at
Noon*. He read and reread it repeatedly, tried to comfort his de-
spairing crew, and after several days was miraculously spotted
and rescued.

Klapper was also the son of an eminent father, the first president of Queens College, part of New York's City University.
Easygoing and fun-loving, Joe had a strong sense of the ridicu-

lous and was an unfailing source of bizarre anecdotes. He was studying mass media's effects; he looked for a convergence of theory derived from large-scale before-and-after surveys sponsored by the media themselves and the small-scale laboratory-type experiments of academic social psychologists, usually carried out on captive undergraduate students.

Klapper left GE to head a new Office of Social Research at CBS that supported an impressive variety of university-based studies. The most famous of these were Stanley Milgram's experiments on obedience to authority, which showed how easily people abandoned their judgment and their usual ethical code if they trusted the person who gave them orders. Klapper's office also turned out research on such important subjects as television's influence on election outcomes (he did not believe they were affected by TV's early vote projections) and on children's behavior ("Where is all this violence I keep hearing about?" he asked.)*

Another distinguished recruit to General Electric was Herbert Krugman, who directed the company's opinion and institutional advertising research from 1967 through the 1980s. Krugman maintained a somber mien but flashed a wide smile and uttered yelps of enthusiasm as he engaged in the process of intellectual discovery. He had worked as an industrial psychologist and in product design before entering the field of advertising at the McCann-Erickson agency (after I left). The prevailing corporate culture of GE was infused with the powerful heritage of innovative engineering research that dated back to the era of Charles Proteus Steinmetz. For the company's in-house social scientists, this made for an atmosphere of great permissiveness, which Krugman compared to that of a research university. He drew on GE's technical resources to study perception and communication. In the 1980s, Krugman's research was to become

---

*Klapper's principal extracurricular project was as chairman of AAPOR's site selection committee. (His wife Hope was the other member.) They enjoyed sampling the hospitality of the modest resorts whose pricing was in an acceptable range.

highly pertinent to my investigations of the newspaper reading process, especially after he introduced me to an eye camera invented by Norman Mackworth, a Stanford psychologist. It was as cumbersome as a diver's helmet, but it proved useful in demonstrating that readers took in and screened vast amounts of reading matter that they never consciously remembered.

As academic and commercial research intersected, career lines branched off from one domain to the other.* David Wallace, who had started out writing promotional copy for *Time*, became its research director. He took this new skill to the Ford Motor Company, where he aroused suspicion by choosing to live among the weirdos in Ann Arbor rather than in manicured and nearby Bloomfield Hills. Wallace tooled back and forth from work in a sporty red convertible. He was craggy-faced, droll, and unpredictable. (He wrote the words to the association's unofficial anthem, "*Je vous aime,* AAPOR.") At Ford his most notable project was the selection of a name for the ill-fated Edsel car, which had been invented by market research to fill a middling gap in the company's product line and make it more competitive with General Motors. Various possibilities were churned out by the Foote, Cone & Belding advertising agency, but the imaginative Wallace decided that a poet might be a more adventurous source of ideas; he enlisted Marianne Moore. An elaborate program of consumer research followed. Finally, Wallace wrote Moore: "We have chosen a name out of more than 6,000 candidates that we gathered. It has a certain ring to it. An air of gaiety and zest. At least

---

*John W. Riley, Jr., a sociologist who worked in opinion surveys for the military during the war, briefly combined teaching with work for the Market Research Corporation of America, a firm founded by his father-in-law, Percival White. He went back to his professorial career at Rutgers University, then returned to what was sometimes called "the real world" to become a senior vice president of the Equitable Life Assurance Society. He arrived there through the suggestion of Robert K. Merton, Lazarsfeld's colleague at Columbia's Bureau of Applied Social Research. Jack Riley and his wife Matilda were a handsome couple, high-spirited and enthusiastic athletes. She was a longtime associate director of the National Institute on Aging.

that's what we keep saying. Our name, dear Miss Moore, is—Edsel."

After the failure of the Edsel, Wallace returned to New York. He became disenchanted with commercial research when he found that his next employer, Arch Crossley, checked his election polling results with Gallup and Roper before releasing them, to make sure they were not too far apart. Wallace earned a doctorate in sociology at Columbia and became a college professor. Dressed like a beachcomber, he hailed me one hot day in the produce market at Taormina in Sicily. Two days later, when I returned from my trip, I read his one-inch obituary in the newspaper.

If frustrated business researchers were tempted by the tranquil life of academe, college professors were even more likely to move into industry when the incentives were right. A later research director at Ford was George Hay Brown, a former professor at the University of Chicago business school and later a director of the United States Census. Brown scoffed at my innocent inquiry as to why the automobile industry was not promoting mass transportation systems, to stem the depopulation of city centers if for no other reason. (They were already in the bus and people-mover business.) He insisted, correctly, that Americans' addiction to personal transportation was not amenable to change.*

The 1948 Eagle's Mere conference was also the occasion for the organizational meeting of the World Association for Public Opinion Research (WAPOR). The development of polling in Europe, ar-

---

*Another researcher at Ford in the 1960s was the psychologist Valentine Appel, later a specialist in print audience measurement. While at Ford, someone in the executive ranks learned that he was a friend of the historian August Gilbert, who had written a book about the Nuremberg trials. Appel was asked to see if Gilbert would consult with Ford, so that they might tap the secrets of Nazi propaganda on behalf of their advertising and promotion. (Apparently the spirit of the founder's *Dearborn Independent* still hovered over the company.)

rested by the war, was in a new and exciting phase. The meeting was marred by the denial of a U.S. visa to a scholar (Laszlo Radvanyi, married to the German novelist Anna Seghers—both Communists, as it later turned out) from Hungary, which was already firmly under Soviet control. I introduced a resolution that passed without dissent at an AAPOR business meeting, condemning any impediment to the free movement of people or ideas. This was later reported as suspicious behavior to my new employer at Standard Oil by a colleague from the company's marketing side.

WAPOR meetings in the following years reflected the growing sophistication of European researchers. As president (in 1965–1967) I followed Karl-Georg von Stackelberg of the Emnid Institut in Bielefeld, Germany. Karl-Georg wore a monocle. He brandished the obsolete title of *Graf* ("count"). His face was impressively bitten by dueling scars. Before his discovery of polling he had been the author of a number of books extolling the heroic exploits of the Luftwaffe and the Condor Legion (Hitler's expeditionary force to Spain, most notorious for the bombing of Guernica, which was practice for the mass destruction of cities in World War II). The books turned out, on examination, to be run-of-the-mill military propaganda, without detectable ideological overtones.

This was not true, however, of a book written by another German pollster, Elisabeth Noelle, which paid homage to Joseph Goebbels, expounded upon the cult of the Leader, and included anti-Semitic diatribes. In an article I published in 1966, I quoted from the book's disparagement of democracy.[2] This drew no attention.

Noelle was plain-featured, dressed in tweeds, and wore no makeup. She had a hard gaze and great self-confidence, telling a *Life* magazine researcher, Clark Schiller, "There's no problem I cannot solve."

Noelle's activism in the Nazi youth movement had been rewarded in 1937 with a fellowship at the University of Missouri. This came after a year's special political training. According to her ex-boyfriend Karl J. Eskellund (later a famous Danish travel writer), she was "very proud that she was invited to a tea party all alone with Hitler before she went over to perform her patriotic task in America." Her "patriotic task" was to learn American polling methods, but she also helped with letters to the *Daily Missourian* extolling the Nazi cause.

During the war she served in Goebbels's propaganda machine, writing anti-Semitic and anti-American articles in his organ, *Das Reich*. Her husband, an SS-man named Erich Peter Neumann, directed propaganda for the Nazi Gauleiter of Dresden. Immediately after the war's end, they founded the Institut für Demoskopie with the backing of French military intelligence, which had no squeamish ideological scruples. The Institut became Germany's leading polling firm, and Noelle became an ever more visible figure at professional meetings.

Noelle's second book, *The Spiral of Silence*, elaborated on the commonly expressed thesis that people keep their mouths shut if their opinions are different from what they perceive to be the majority views of those around them. This tendency toward conformity, she felt, was deeply rooted. (She quoted an animal psychologist, Erik Zimen: "To a wolf, the howling of another wolf is a powerful stimulant to follow suit." To me this was reminiscent of the Polish Communist dictator Wladyslaw Gomulka's explanation of his political philosophy—"When one runs with wolves, one must howl.") In Nazi Germany, dissenters were silent, but in democracies they spoke out, especially on most of the topics of survey research, which carried no particular political charge.

In the 1990s, Noelle's influence became ever greater. She was a prominent political advisor to Chancellor Helmut Kohl. Her book was constantly praised and commented upon in the UNESCO-funded *International Journal of Public Opinion Research*, which she co-edited. When revelations of Noelle's Nazi past continued to accumulate, she stonewalled all the charges, citing as a witness to her non-Nazi credentials her mentor Emil Dovifat, au-

thor of the Nazis' official textbook for journalists.* Noelle tried to
stymie the granting of tenure to a young American political scientist who had published a devastating critique of her theory.
The resulting scandal received prominent play in the *Chronicle
of Higher Education* and then in Germany's leading news magazine, *Der Spiegel*. To all of this the worldwide opinion research
fraternity continued to turn a blind eye.

WAPOR's annual conferences alternated with those of AAPOR and of
Esomar (the European Society for Market and Opinion Research).
Esomar's meetings were huge, impersonal conventions in which,
during the social hour, the delegates clustered together in tight
little groups of their countrymen. In 1965 I lunched in Dublin
with the officers of Esomar and the prime minister of Eire, an engaging and unpretentious politician who came accompanied by a
military aide. The conversation turned to the recently ended
New York World's Fair. The prime minister, Sean Lemass, be-
moaned the modesty of the Irish pavilion, whose most notewor-
thy exhibit was the Book of Kells. Italy, by contrast, had sent over
Michelangelo's *Pietà*, which was a major tourist attraction.
Lemass had been particularly taken by the talking statue of Lincoln at the Illinois pavilion, which accompanied a recorded
speech with suitably animated gestures. Esomar's head was an
Englishman who had evidently studied elocution with Colonel
Blimp. In a fruity aristocratic accent, he cunningly suggested that
a talking statue of Cromwell might have drawn more crowds to
the neglected Irish pavilion. The prime minister withdrew the
pipe from his mouth. "That would have been all right, as long as
we could have written the script."

*A sample quotation: "Out of a ripe understanding of the people and of human
beings, and unique success in leading the people and the masses, Adolf Hitler has
given practical form to fundamental principles, the principles of propaganda. . . . The
political concept that Adolf Hitler has presented is very enlightening for the mission
of newspapers."

At that time empirical social research was practiced somewhat furtively within the Soviet sphere, where public opinion was to be manipulated, not investigated, and where the probing of human irrationality and complexity might erode confidence in the implacable tenets of Marxist-Leninist ideology. Yet here and there were pockets of officially sanctioned inquiry: sociologists studying juvenile delinquency, demographers examining human longevity, investigators of broadcast programming preferences, economists measuring consumption trends as an aid to government planners. In Poland and Hungary, universities harbored a new intellectual generation that closely followed the academic literature of the West.

The Yugoslavs, after Tito's break with Stalin, maintained a high level of autonomy within the confines of their Communist dictatorship, with its own quaint doctrine of "workers' self-government." A Yugoslav market researcher with the characteristically Dalmatian name of Fedor Rocco organized WAPOR's first regional meeting, held in 1965 in Dubrovnik. This was a watershed event, marking the first official recognition of survey research within the Communist world, and bringing together for the first time researchers from almost all the countries in the Soviet bloc and a respectable number of curious Western European counterparts. The delegates from East and West Germany circled and sniffed at each other warily at the opening reception and soon became engaged in intense conversation. The meeting itself was opened by a government minister, a hefty and imposing lady reputed to be Tito's mistress.

On the last evening the participants were taken in a procession of buses up a winding road that led to the crest of the brooding mountains that overlook the jewel-like medieval city. In what had been a wartime Partisan lair, crude wooden tables were set with a torchlit feast of green salad, bread, and barbecued lamb. As bottles of red wine were emptied and quickly replaced, the murmur of conversation gave way to melody. The Yugoslavs had launched into the fierce and melancholy songs of the Partisans.

Earlier in the meeting I had fallen into conversation with the head of one of Italy's leading polling firms. I remarked that his last name was Croatian and asked whether he understood the language. He confided to me that he was a Croatian, had fought with the fascist Ustashi during the war, and had escaped to Italy and created a new life. This was his first trip back to Yugoslavia, and he was clearly nervous about it (with good reason, I thought). As the Partisan songs resounded, I looked over at him. He had joined in!

527147
6936 04
411082
354755
102986

IMMIGRATION, AS IMMIGRANTS SEE IT

■ My first encounters with the Arab world came after I left Standard Oil. They came about accidentally, like many of my other research adventures.

In 2002 some four million residents of France are of North African descent, including several hundred thousand who are native-born French citizens. The great majority come from Algeria, which in 1962 won a bloody guerrilla war for independence that had started in 1954. Most of France's immigrant population now live in the drab suburbs of large cities, many in public housing. Their presence evokes resentment, expressed in the xenophobia of Jean-Marie Le Pen's National Front. A *cause célèbre* was created by the insistence of Islamist schoolgirls on wearing traditional head coverings in defiance of France's long-standing ban on religious symbolism in its schools. Such resistance to cultural integration contrasts with the painless assimilation of Poles, Portuguese, and Italians in France. As I write this, the recruitment of French-born Algerians for the Al Qaeda terrorist network has brought the subject greater visibility.

In 1951 the postwar immigration from North Africa was already attracting attention. The newcomers shuttled across the

Mediterranean by steamer or crammed into what can only be described as the steerage class of DC-3 airplanes operated by Air Algérie, an Air France subsidiary. The Algerians were in fact French citizens. Their country had been colonized by France in 1830, long before the protectorates of Tunisia and Morocco were established. It had been divided into three *départements* under de Gaulle's Fourth Republic.

I was steered in the direction of the Algerians by Jean Stoetzel, whom I knew from meetings of the World Association of Public Opinion Research. Stoetzel, a professor of sociology at the Sorbonne, was also the director of the French Gallup Poll.* His easygoing and jovial persona masked his erudition and analytical virtuosity. Stoetzel was a scholar-entrepreneur of indefatigable energy and curiosity whose books spanned the subject matter of the social sciences. He had great charm and the French intellectual habit of making brilliant, sweeping, and sometimes controversial statements. (At the height of the cold war he told me that the real struggle of the twentieth century would not be between capitalism and communism, but between Christianity and Islam. I took this to be a metaphor for the industrialized and poverty-stricken worlds. In retrospect I should have taken him literally.)

In conversation with Stoetzel, I drew an analogy between the situation of the North Africans I had seen on the streets of Paris and that of the Puerto Ricans who had begun to flood into New York. Stoetzel told me that the North Africans were a hot subject and sent me to see Alfred Sauvy, the director of the Institut National d'Études Démographiques (National Institute of Demographic Studies). Sauvy offered to harbor me during the academic year, and Stoetzel wangled a small grant from UNESCO to cover my interviewing costs. Sauvy was a savant, a prolific essayist for *Le Monde* on a wide range of subjects. His institute was

---

*He had reestablished polling in France with a survey for the U.S. Office of War Information a week after the Germans left Paris.

staffed by a mixture of scholars with academic affiliations (like the great historian of Paris, Louis Chevalier) and civil servants who greeted one another formally every morning, making the rounds and shaking hands with all their co-workers.

One resident scholar was engaged in a fascinating study of France's *fausse noblesse*, which outnumbered the fast-dwindling but authentic hereditary aristocracy. He provided instructions on how to acquire a title. The first step was to buy a house in a country village, say a place called Nemours. If your name was Jacques Dupont, you could begin adding this village name to your return address on letters. Soon the bank statements and electric bills you received in Paris would arrive addressed to Jacques Dupont de Nemours. If the postman began to call you Monsieur le Comte, there was no reason to object, and soon you could add the title to your visiting card. (Visiting cards were of course a big thing. It took strong restraint to keep from ordering one identifying myself as *ancien élève de P.S. 99.*)

The Demographic Institute was conducting a series of studies on immigration to France (mostly by Poles and Portuguese), and my project fit right in.

In Algeria the steady population increase had outstripped the rate of economic development. The rise in living standards had not kept pace with felt needs and appetites, stimulated by the presence of a large European colony and growing familiarity with European culture, technology, and amenities. The migration prompted by population pressures in the impoverished rural areas had fostered the growth of the large cities of North Africa and had also been directed toward France. French language and culture were in greater or lesser degree part of the heritage and daily life pattern of every Muslim North African. Colonies of North Africans existed in France even before World War I. During World War II large numbers served in the French military, and many remained or returned after the war's end.

When Algeria became part of France in 1917, movements of Algerians to France were as free as those of any Frenchman who went from Dijon to Paris. The number of North Africans in France rose from 22,000 in 1946 to about 300,000 in 1951. This last figure did not tell the full story, for the Muslim minority was the residue of a far greater number who came and went each year.

The migration was made possible and necessary by a kinship system that imposed heavy economic responsibilities on male members of a family but also enabled them to leave their families for years in the care of a relative. It was not merely a migration from an Islamic to a European milieu but from small towns and villages to great cities and industrial centers. The North African who left his native society—strongly traditional, patriarchal, and closely knit—was suddenly plunged into the urban mass as an isolated individual without female companionship and normal family ties.

The psychic strains imposed by this condition were aggravated by material problems. Most of the immigrants lacked the experience and skills that might qualify them for industrial jobs; they became floaters at the lowest level of the employment pyramid. Being visibly different from the average Frenchman in their speech, clothing habits, and, very often, physical appearance, they were subject to discrimination by employers who shared a widely held impression of their instability, intractability, and incapacity.

Half the North Africans in France were without regular employment. They eked out a miserable existence through occasional odd jobs, public charity, or the generosity of friends and relatives. The employed were concentrated in the lowest-paid and most insecure jobs.

I described the Algerian immigrants as follows:

France, traditional haven of the oppressed and defender of man's individuality, is today faced within her own borders with a full-scale minority problem. The minority are the North Africans who have arrived in a continuous stream of migration since the end of World War II. Their presence has aroused increasing alarm and alarum from the press, a certain uneasiness from the public, and a kind of gingerly indecision and inaction from the authorities.

The American tourist or casual visitor might not notice their existence. Perhaps, sitting at a sidewalk café in Montmartre, he may be accosted by the rug peddler, a tall Berber whose fierce upturned brown mustaches suggest his military past. On his head is the small, tight-fitting blue beret—both a concession to the European mode and an expression of obedience to the Koranic edict that man's head shall remain covered in the presence of God and the world, with no brim or visor to interfere when he bows his head to the ground in prayer. The rug peddler shuffles from table to table, offering his wares in silence, his dour mien unchanging. He wears slippers, a grey smock, and shapeless trousers. His woolly rugs are crudely emblazoned with purple camels and scarlet pyramids.

The rugs slung over his shoulders, he holds forth in his one free hand a cluster of rawhide wallets stained brown or red. Among the bearded artists and derby-hatted *lycée* professors of café society, he may appear to be only another eccentric resident of the Left Bank.

Then there is the peanut vendor, a youthful, sallow-faced Arab with thick lips, high cheekbones, and an eye half-closed by inflammation. He is bareheaded, his thick curly black hair flowing over the back of his neck. His basket of peanuts rests in the crook of his arm. Regardless of season he wears the same flimsy summer suit, patched at the seat, frayed at the sleeves, and worn through at the elbows.

As a result of the war, France's birthrate was declining, and some of its social policymakers were convinced that the solution was the full integration of Algeria into France. They liked to refer to Algerians as Frenchmen of Muslim faith, and proudly pointed out that some of them could pass as *Français du Midi* (Frenchmen of Southern France).

My initial impression was that real assimilation was a hopeless objective. This judgment was affirmed when I visited Algeria, which had more than a million and a half residents of European descent—French, Spanish, and Italian. Their comfortable lives, in gleaming commercial centers and elegant residential quarters, offered a sharp contrast to the medieval squalor of the Casbah. On a hillside overlooking the splendid harbor of Algiers, French children played nursery games in a small park that had a fountain adorned with a large mosaic image of Mickey Mouse.*

During the 120 years of their occupation, the French authorities had politically exploited the rift between the Arab-speaking urban population and the Berbers of the hardscrabble mountain villages, the source of many of the emigrants who had gone to France to improve their fortunes.†

The emigration at this point was more than 90 percent masculine, yet a few men brought along their wives and children to Europe. As in the pattern of immigration in the United States, men came first and sent for their families when they had earned enough to pay their passage and provide them with housing. But the first indications were that many of the Algerians had no intention of resettling when they crossed the sea. They couldn't make a living at home, but home was where they wanted to be. Why, however, did some of them want to make a new life for themselves in what was, after all, a strange country? This was the focus of my research.

To conduct a study I had to have access to Algerians in France. I needed interviewers with whom I could speak French, but who could themselves speak either Arabic or Berber, de-

---

*I did not visit Algeria again until some thirty-five years later. In the city center of Annaba (formerly Bône) stood the Municipal theater, a handsome *beaux-arts* building carrying the names of Molière, Racine, Corneille, and Hugo atop its façade. Pigeons flew in and out of its broken windows.

†In one of those villages, an elderly turbanned gentleman who had served in the trenches during World War I recited for me, in somewhat fractured French, a lengthy hymn of hate against the kaiser.

pending on the origins of the respondents.* I went to a municipal agency that had been set up in Paris to serve the immigrants'
social needs. This brought me to the attention of the Sureté, the
secret police unit that monitored possibly subversive foreign activities. They apparently decided that my investigation must
have been initiated by the U.S. government as part of a plan to
wrest control of North Africa. Fortunately, Stoetzel was able to
stave them off.

My next obstacle was the haughty director of the agency
where I had requested space for the interviews. He was a jowly
old North African hand, bristling with suspicion and thinly disguised contempt for the Algerians whose interests he was supposed to be serving. He invited himself and his mistress to be my
guests at an elegant and costly lunch, and as he tossed down his
repeated postprandial liqueurs he kept repeating, *"L'Unesco est
riche!"* (My Fulbright stipend was $100 a week.) The investment
paid off. The next day, totally no-nonsense and businesslike, he
gave me the access I needed. To give him credit, he paid back
with a much more modest lunch at the Cercle Nord-Africain, a
private club of retired colonial officials, some of whom appeared
to be veterans of the original 1830 conquest.

The interviews each ran between two and a half and five
hours, and sometimes required several sessions with a given
respondent. They were conducted in either Arabic or Kabyle,
but the responses were written down for me in French. One hundred interviews with Arabic-speakers and forty with Berber-
speakers were conducted in March and April 1952 in Paris and
its industrial suburbs. (The line between Arabs and Kabyles is
cutural rather than ethnic, and small differences in their re-

---

*I recruited the interviewers with the help of Father Jacques Ghys, a bearded,
sandal-wearing anthropologist-priest who published a learned journal of North
African studies. With his cowl and soiled white robe flapping behind him, Ghys re-
sembled a giant seagull as he loped rapidly through slum streets. He belonged to the
Pères Blancs (White Fathers), missionaries dedicated to the salvation of the heathens.

sponses reflected the preponderantly urban origins of the Arabic-speakers.)*

Ould Ferhat was the most conscientious of the four inter-viewers on the project. Married to a provincial Frenchwoman, he had three or four young children who had joined him in a climb to the top of the Eiffel Tower, which he considered good exercise. When they ailed he took them not to a physician or clinic but to a *guérisseur* (a healer). Earnest and mournful in manner, he was a diligent and productive worker—a prototype of one of the three kinds of immigrants I identified in my research.

THE ALGERIANS IN FRANCE (1952)[1]

Like members of any immigrant group, most Algerians tend to cluster together in the shelter of existing associations and familiar folkways.

> "I usually go to a café where most of the people are from my home village. The customers are Kabyles; so is the owner. We do what the Kabyles generally do: discuss the latest news from home, play some games of cards or dominoes, take a cup of tea or coffee. Sometimes we take a meal there or just relax and listen to some music or songs from home."

Creating miniature ghettos, they are noticeable to the French as a strange ethnic minority in their midst. Thus they attract to themselves a collective stereotype fashioned from their least attractive elements.

> "They consider us work beasts; we always get the dirtiest and toughest work."

> "They hold us in contempt and consider us as inferior, in order to exploit us."

---

*Religion was never mentioned by any respondent, though it could have been brought up spontaneously at many points in the interviews. (I had been advised not to question directly about the regularity of religious observance, which seemed to have little significance in the immigrants' daily lives.) In 1952, Islamic fundamental-ism had not emerged as a political force.

"They always imagine us holding a knife."

"A lot of us don't have jobs; they think it's because we don't want to work. They think we're fakers, liars, and thieves, because the press puts anything an Algerian does in big headlines."

"They take us for people without dignity, but they don't know that if we take the worst jobs at the lowest pay, it's because we're pressed by need."

"They think we're people from another planet, without a past or a culture. For them, 'Algerian' means savage, brute, thief, whatever you want. They don't understand our language and don't want to know us better."

"They consider us savages who can live on bread and water."

Is external accommodation to the demands of the new environment accompanied by internal accommodation, by the acceptance of values from the dominant culture, and a shift in personal loyalties, identification, and self-imagery? To what extent does accommodation reflect the individual's previous experiences? How much does it depend on the accidental or idiosyncratic circumstances governing experiences in his new habitat? Since North Africans range in physical types from Nordic to Negroid, does their appearance determine French acceptance of them as individuals?

The fact that the great majority ultimately (sooner rather than later) return to their homes indicates that they more closely resemble migratory workers than immigrants, uprooted to reestablish life in a new land. Mere luck may decide whether a man ends up in a situation sufficiently attractive to bind him to France for life or floats from job to job, or from job to no job, and ultimately returns discouraged to his former home.

What is the typical life course? Swaddled into immobility as an infant, a three-year-old is

rapidly weaned, toilet-trained, and turned out into
the narrow, muddy streets of the village to play.

"I was very young when I started to go out into
the fields to guard the flocks, sheep, goats,
and cattle. At first I was accompanied, then
after two weeks I was sent out alone."

From helping his father in the fields it is a
short step to helping an artisan in his shop or a
neighboring French colonist on his farm, or even to
becoming an errand boy in a nearby town. But these
are unenviable and poorly paid occupations,
especially for a younger son (as are over half the
respondents) with no hopes of inheriting the family
property. His native village seems a place without
a future.

Now arrived in France, his *chéchia* (turban)
packed away in his cardboard suitcase, he sets out
to follow the trail of rumor or chance to a town
or neighborhood where some relative or fellow
villager was last reported to have lived. Here his
problems begin.

He has come to a world that is alien without
being altogether new. Even at home he experienced
the conflict between what is right and proper by
Muslim standards and what is acceptable in France.
Even in the most isolated mountain village, the
forbidden delights of Europeans—wine and motion
pictures—are known about, at least secondhand. In
substituting a beret for his *chéchia*, fez, or
burnoose, he has already taken the first step of
compromise. To get along in his new environment,
certain outer conformities are expected of him.

"In the Metro, people stared at us with a
shameful curiosity and with smiles. There was
nothing about us to make them laugh; simply our
skin color and our language were different from
theirs."

The first adaptations are in the outer details
of dress and language. But there are wide
variations in the degree of change in the

individual's behavior and thinking, in the rules he
lives by.

A critical distinction can be made between
those who have definitely left their original
homes, in spirit as well as in fact (I call them
émigrés, and they represent over a third of the
sample), and those (whom I call *migrants*) who look
forward to the day of their return to Algeria.

How do the well adapted, the émigrés, differ
socially and psychologically from the others? The
less familiar the immigrant is with France and its
way of life, the less likely that he will become a
permanent settler. For the illiterate, the problem
of communication is preeminent. The individual's
education reflects his social origins and the size
of the place he comes from. The émigrés are from a
milieu in Algeria with greater access to the good
things in life. The migrants appear to have been
driven by economic pressures; the émigrés more
often say that they would have come to France
anyway.

Émigrés and migrants do not differ in age, and
the same proportion have left wives behind in
Algeria. Their family responsibilities are similar;
there is no difference in the proportion of oldest
sons. But the émigrés come from more stable family
situations, with paternal authority functioning
firmly. Their parents are more likely to be living;
they have moved less often in Algeria. They have
fewer sisters, and thus fewer dependents.

Émigrés' early experiences appear to have made
them happier, better adjusted, and more able to
cope. More relate specific pleasant episodes, and
they have happier recollections of their parents,
especially their fathers.

For the migrants, life in the formative years
and on through to the present is more apt to have
been dreary, painful, and filled with worries. The
émigrés tend to have less rigid and stereotyped
reactions; they hold fewer people in low esteem and
describe them by attributes or characteristics
rather than by categories like "French colonists"

or "politicians." The émigrés are less isolated.
Even the bachelors are more apt to be sharing a
room or apartment and therefore less likely to be
lonely and maladjusted.

There is no significant difference in the
proportion of émigrés and migrants among those of
European appearance and those with distinctively
North African features, but there are fewer émigrés
among those whose looks fell into the intermediate
category, and who may feel most marginal.

Immigrants who had been in France longest have
more often found stable employment, but compared to
newcomers their jobs are no better and they are no
more likely to want to remain in France
permanently. The proportion of émigrés is the same
among the employed and the unemployed. But émigrés
more often have a stable job history, a skilled
occupation, and (on their present or last jobs) are
employed in a large enterprise where North Africans
are a small minority and regarded as individuals
rather than as members of a distinctive "out-
group."

Émigrés are likely to be satisfied with their
jobs and to have made greater advancements in grade
and salary. With better, more stable jobs, the
émigrés earn more than the migrants. They can
afford to buy newspapers and go to the movies, and
command of the language gives them greater access
to the media that speed cultural adaptation.
Although their housing accommodations are slightly
better, the émigrés are actually less satisfied
with them, probably because their aspirations are
higher. Émigrés do not have more opportunities for
daily contact with French neighbors, but they
cultivate contacts that the migrants shun.

While the émigrés' ties to France have been
forged by their more frequent and more pleasant
contacts with French society, their old connections
do not vanish. Equal proportions of émigrés and
migrants send money home to their families, in
about the same percentage of their incomes. Émigrés
are only slightly less apt to say that they have

Algerian friends, and are no less likely to
frequent Algerian cafés. Even the most acculturated
immigrants express loyalty to Algeria and its ways.
Yet émigrés have fewer romantic illusions about the
country they left. Hardly any of them fail to
mention aspects of North African life from which
they are glad to be away; hardly any mention North
African customs as things they most miss.

A critical distinction is that half the
émigrés, but only a tenth of migrants, live with a
Frenchwoman or are married to one (as a fifth of
them are). The émigrés are more likely to say that
their opinion of France and its people has become
more favorable since they arrived. In almost every
case they assume that the French generally accept
them personally as Frenchmen. This is the first and
necessary condition for them to feel French
themselves.

The immigrants receive their greatest setbacks
in the material conditions of life rather than in
social acceptance. For the most part unprepared to
handle the skills of the machine age, they are
employed at the simplest level or not at all.
Impoverished newcomers in a country with scarce
housing, they are forced into the worst lodgings.
Discouragement over life's material problems
reinforces their disillusionment. Many who start
out with a strong desire to adapt or assimilate
feel rebuffed.

In these discouraging circumstances, it is
remarkable that there are any North African émigrés
at all. But they do exist—men who are French not
only in their outer conformity to standards of
dress, language, and behavior, in their decision to
remain and raise families in France, but in their
own sense of identity, in their transformation into
individuals who think as Frenchmen rather than as
North Africans when the two value systems are in
conflict.

The internalization of European values is not
confined to the émigrés. It occurs to a lesser
degree among many who do not like France or the

French and are anxious to return to Algeria. The
traditionally minded Algerian who adopts French
customs or habits of thought does not necessarily
believe he is becoming more like a Frenchman; if he
is aware of the process, he thinks of it as
becoming more modern, more advanced (*évolué*). The
émigré, however, thinks of himself as becoming
French.

The émigré's higher state of psychological
security enables him to adjust to the shocks of new
experience. His emotional resiliency lets him make
the best of present reality while the migrant takes
refuge in past associations and in fantasies of the
future.

The length of time spent in France is not a
crucial factor in determining whether an individual
is an émigré or a migrant. Adaptation does not
occur gradually as an immigrant matures and comes
to fit in; it starts during the formative years
before emigration. The very factors of social
background and personality that make some men adapt
successfully to France are those that make them
more likely to succeed if they stay at home.

527147
693604
411082
354755
102986

On the Edge of the Cold War

■ Our sojourn in grimy Paris began in a fifth-story walk-up apartment above a fur establishment on the rue Bergère, a street frequented by sadly overweight and dilapidated streetwalkers. The nearby Grands Boulevards provided round-the-clock entertainment. (Edith Piaf sang a block away.) Our apartment had its limitations (the refrigerator was the windowsill), and we found a new one near the École Militaire. It was sublet from a countess (most likely a member of the *fausse noblesse*) who became infuriated by our daily use of hot water and demanded payment of a supplement to our rent. She declared imperiously, *"Je ne paierai pas pour les bains des Américains!"** An extra couch in her apartment was equipped with a throw made of a lion's skin. Mary Jane ("Emjay") Mairs, who was the date of our friend Richard Appleton Walsh, came over for a postdinner drink, had one too many, passed out, and was put to rest on the couch. When she awoke the next morning, her ultra-chic little black velvet cocktail dress was covered with lion hair.

Dick Walsh was one of a heterogeneous crowd of American expatriates who had descended on the Left Bank after the war. Dick hinted darkly of his days with the CIA but patriotically re-

---

*"I shan't pay for the baths of the Americans!"

fused to divulge the precise nature of his strenuous undercover duties. He lived on a stipend from a father who had sired him in his old age and with whom he had only distant relations. Walsh was prematurely bald (he had been known as "Knobby Walsh" at Harvard and detested the name), chain-smoked, and had a hyenalike laugh which he employed frequently, because he found life extremely amusing. His French was of minimal utility, but he knew all of the hidden secrets of Paris.

Carol and Abby Mathiessen, two sisters from Minnesota, hosted bring-your-own-bottle revelries in their room high up in a disreputable medieval residence on the rue du Bac. At one of these I met Ivan Kats, a half-Jewish Dutchman whose family had fled the Nazis and relocated to New York. He had served in the U.S. Army and was attending the Sorbonne on the GI Bill. Mischievously humorous but deadly passionate about ideas, Ivan went to work for the (secretly CIA-backed) Congress for Cultural Freedom, which sought to provide support for Europe's non-Communist intellectual left. His subsequent career was a kind of one-man Marshall Plan of the mind.*

The real Marshall Plan worked through the Mutual Security Administration, which employed a number of veterans of the American labor movement, among them the United Auto Workers' Victor Reuther. On a rainy winter's night, his wife Sophie entertained a small group of kindred spirits at their suburban villa. One of the guests had come in a government car, whose French driver was sitting in it, waiting to take him back to the city. When someone suggested that he be invited in to warm himself, Sophie objected. "Where should he go, down in the cellar with the dog?"

At the American embassy in Paris, the mother hen for the

---

*He entered into correspondence with Mokhtar Lubis, an Indonesian writer and editor who had been imprisoned both by Dutch colonialists and the Japanese occupiers and was subsequently jailed by the dictator Sukarno. They set up a foundation called Obor (The Torch) to publish Indonesian translations of significant Western books for a country that had been insulated from contemporary thought. Ivan made Obor his life's work, expanding the foundation's activities to Thailand, Pakistan, Bangladesh, the Philippines, Vietnam, and Morocco.

Fulbright brood was Beatrice ("Bibi") Braude—plump, bubbly, and justly proud of her impeccable French.* With our car fueled with the help of her official discount gasoline coupons, she accompanied Agnes and me on a trip to Spain the following spring. I had cried at the death of the Spanish republic and embarked on the journey with mixed feelings of excitement and apprehension.

We entered the country on a stormy late afternoon along the crumbling remnants of the sea-battered highway that followed the Basque coast. In places it had been reduced to a single lane on the edge of a cliff trailing down to the churning waters. We finally found shelter in San Sebastián, in a large, noisy café filled with young men wearing identical grey raincoats. Even under Franco, life seemed to go on. The Spanish roads had not been maintained since the outbreak of the civil war in 1936, so the trip was enlivened by frequent blowouts. There were no replacement tires for a Chevrolet available anywhere, so the garage mechanics stuffed miscellaneous strips of old rubber between the worn spots and the inner tubes.

My relief driver was Hal Brav, a writer who had been driving a taxi in Detroit since his discharge from the army. He was now struggling to survive in a Left Bank garret, with a precarious income derived from dubbing American voices in French films. Nightly we sought accommodations suitable for our three widely disparate levels of income, explaining to bewildered innkeepers that Bibi and Hal were *not* sharing a room.

In Madrid, Bibi lost the wallet from her purse. The young Spaniard who found it methodically traipsed to all the major hotels to find where she was registered and was waiting for her in the lobby of the Ritz when we got there. He refused a reward but agreed to have dinner with us. He avoided serious conversation

*Bibi Braude lost her State Department job the following year—an early victim of McCarthyism. The damning evidence against her was revealed when she was exonerated of "disloyalty" charges forty-three years later, and eight years after her death: she had once talked to a Communist and had been seen entering a Communist bookstore in Washington, and her name was found in the address book of a Soviet spy whom she detested. Meanwhile she became a professor of French literature at the University of Massachusetts.

during the meal, then suddenly loosened up after two men at an adjacent table left the room. They were members of the secret police. I asked why they should be interested in us. No ordinary Spaniard, he told me, had dinner with foreigners in the dining room of the Ritz. It was my first encounter with the realities of dictatorship.

Another Fulbright researcher in Paris at this time was the sociologist Arnold Rose, Gunnar Myrdal's collaborator in his landmark study of race, *An American Dilemma*.[1] Though a renowned scholar, Rose was unpretentious and meek. While other Fulbrights sought inspiration by inspecting passersby from the tables in front of Les Deux Magots, Arnold remained diligently attached to his typewriter. He and his formidable and vivacious wife, Caroline, and their three small children, shared a tiny room in a sleazy hotel in Montparnasse, from which he reluctantly emerged only for frugal dinners and conversation. (In 1969, Arnold left life in grand style; as he lay dying in his upstairs bedroom in Minneapolis, he said good-bye one by one to colleagues and friends while the boisterous revelry of his premature wake took place below.*)

My year in France, 1951–1952, occurred at a time when the Soviet Union was mobilizing its political allies in Western Europe in bitter opposition to American influence and to the continuing American military presence. The hot war that Stalin had helped initiate in Korea was being fought in Europe with angry words.

The operating principle that "Truth Is Our Weapon"[2] placed stringent limits on American propaganda. The Soviets faced no such constraints. How does one account for gullibility, whether to Father Divine's proclamation of his own divinity, or to the assertion of Egypt's leading cleric that the Jews destroyed New York's World Trade Center on September 11, 2001? Joseph Goebbels, Hitler's minister for propaganda and public enlighten-

---

*He was president of the American Sociological Association when he died.

ment, enunciated and practiced the principle of the Big Lie, so outrageously bold that no one could imagine it to be wholly fictional. At the same time in the United States the Young Communist League counseled its argumentative activists, "If you don't have the facts, make them up!" This principle was well illustrated in *Beautés Américaines*, a rotogravure picture magazine that could have been found on any Paris news kiosk in 1952. On casual glance it belonged to the genre of *Paris-Nues, Nuit et Jour*, and other publications with cover photographs of scantily dressed young women. Actually this was a special issue of *Regards*, a French Communist magazine. The pinup girl on the cover was the official "dream girl" of the 182nd U.S. Infantry Regiment. Not by chance, she was shown against a background of stacked rifles.

AMERICAN BEAUTIES (1952)

American Beauties is a concentrated capsular version of all the things the Communists try to tell the world about America. The magazine exemplifies the rules of Communist propaganda.

1. *Use pictures* (sexy ones are good) *to attract attention*. The skeptical reader may question the wording of a quotation or the accuracy of a statistic, but a photograph seems like a literal and true representation of what exists. A photograph can be retouched or faked, given a false or misleading caption, or used to illustrate a generality when it really shows a particular.

2. *Use pictures to gain believability.*

3. *Use opposition sources to damn the opposition; this too heightens believability.*

4. *Flatter the reader by creating the illusion that he is being allowed to make up his own mind.*

5. *Disarm the reader by denying that you are about to distort the truth; this gives you full opportunity to lie as brazenly as you wish.*

The editors portray the United States with photographs taken almost wholly from American

sources, and with quotations from American
publications or from French periodicals friendly to
the United States. Nothing, says the introduction,
is tricked, altered, or falsified.

"We have allowed ourselves some indispensable
interpretations and commentaries, but we have
guarded against any exaggeration or any
generalization from isolated facts. We leave
the reader to draw his own conclusions."

To the foregoing rules another can be added,
also as a device to achieve credibility:

6. *Don't paint the adversary as being utterly
without merit, particularly if the audience is
already aware of his positive side. Acknowledge
that he has qualities, but couple this with a
vigorous denunciation of his faults.*

The Communist editors wisely admit America's
technological accomplishments, if only in passing,
and if only to brush them aside. America is
essentially weak but at the same time has dangerous
and menacing power.

7. *Don't hesitate to contradict yourself; just
be sure you're saying different things at different
times.*

8. *Deny the truth of America's claim to enjoy a
high living standard. This serves two purposes: It
shows Americans as weak and unworthy of emulation,
and it shows them as braggarts and liars.*

"If there is really one car for every three
persons, why are the subways, the buses, and the
trolley cars always crowded?"

9. *Use the deviant case to represent the whole;
if it can be illustrated it may be accepted as a
valid generalization.*

The unfortunate Americans have no place to
sleep or eat. Beneath a scenic snapshot of the
Manhattan skyline, a homeless veteran sleeps in a
Los Angeles park.

Three men munch sandwiches at a stand-up
luncheon counter. Here the caption reads, "Few or
no eating places; the workers lunch at their place

of work or in the yard, and drink ice water or Coca-Cola, which is found everywhere." (Soft drinks, incidentally, are reportedly advertised in the United States with such slogans as: "Christ on the Cross wouldn't have suffered if he could have drunk a Coca-Cola.")

10. *If there is no suitable quotation to prove your point, invent one. Don't be concerned over how preposterous it is; if there are quotation marks around it, the reader will assume it's correct.*

The littered backyard of a Washington, D.C., slum is juxtaposed with a photograph of an unharvested Idaho potato crop. "Policemen and private guards of the landed capitalists are assigned to the task of keeping people from taking any of this precious rotting stuff."

11. *Find the germs of truth, the points of vulnerability; then distort the importance of the faults you uncover.*

Naturally, the ingenious capitalists profit immensely from the misery of the masses. A crowd of grinning young men are identified as unemployed standing in line in front of an employment office. (Actually they are grinning because hiring is in progress.)

12. *The wrong caption on the right picture can do just as effective a job as a doctored photograph. Assume that the audience won't know the difference.*

"Unemployment is the great menace from which the worker is never sheltered; the monopolies have an interest in it." This analysis is bolstered by a "quotation" from the *Wall Street Journal*: "A worker who sees a line of unemployed outside his shop will lay twice as many bricks in the same amount of time, without asking for a raise in salary."

13. *Confuse the past with the present, if there are unfavorable images* (like those of the depression) *that can be summoned out of the past.*

"This year a considerable number of American children will join the army of twenty million

illiterates that exists today in the United
States."

(This "quotation" from *U.S. News and World
Report* is a fiction, but a chart in the article
cited shows that there are twenty million children
attending school in the United States.)

14. *Portray the adversary as morally corrupt by
claiming the universality of whatever elements of
corruption actually exist, and by interpreting as
corrupt activities that are actually quite
harmless.*

The national sport of the U.S. is wrestling,
either in a mud-covered ring ("a sport especially
destined to elevate the human person") or between
male and female participants. American wrestlers
generally perform in rings covered with mud, peas,
feathers, or rotten fish; football matches are
conducted on fields carefully soaked with water, to
produce the filthiest and thus the most titillating
spectacle.

> "These are the heroes whom America proposes for
> us: alcoholics, madmen, murderers, gangsters,
> naturally, informers, dope dealers, drug
> addicts, maniacs."

15. *Juxtapose unrelated items to suggest that
they are actually connected.*
16. *Identify opposition to yourself as
criminal.*
17. *Bring out the old Marxist clichés. They're
still meaningful to a lot of people. Show that the
U.S. is run by a small conspiratorial clique of
criminal capitalists.*

To Al Capone ("the noted American gangster") is
attributed a statement making it quite clear who is
behind anti-Communist sentiment in America:

> "Bolshevism is knocking at our door; we mustn't
> let it through. We must organize against it,
> tighten our ranks and hold fast. America must
> remain a healthy and untainted union."

Lest the reader conclude that Al Capone and his heirs are the only major force in American politics, *American Beauties* presents a portrait gallery of "the real bosses." "The policy of the Department of State is elaborated in the offices of 'Standard Oil.'"

Number One on the list of America's real rulers is, perhaps not surprisingly, the long-dead "John P. Morgan." Political life in America is merely a façade, characterized by "infantilism and corruption." Item: in return for a free ride on a model train at the Chicago Railroad Fair, senators vote enormous sums for the benefit of the railroad financiers.

Civil liberties are a mockery and a myth in the United States.

"Attached to each government office there is an 'organism for the political control of thoughts,' that is to say, an office for informers, which keeps track of all denunciations and which hunts all those suspected of having manifested the slightest intellectual liberty."

18. *Seize on any violation of civil rights in the United States to document the proposition that America lacks freedom.*

The headline on a two-page spread of photographs of interracial violence is a quotation from the grand dragon of the Ku Klux Klan ("considered by the official press as a patriotic organization"): "If Negroes are accorded equal rights, blood will flow." The biggest and most impressive photograph in this section, depicting a lynching in Georgia, is, to judge from the clothing styles, about twenty-five years old.

19. *Show America as a nation inspired by the Nazi ideology of racial arrogance and designs for world conquest.*

A full page pictures a football lineman crouched for action with his features set in mock ferocity. The title is "God has chosen us," probably derived from a statement by Senator Albert Beveridge, who died in 1827.

"God has not prepared the English-speaking
peoples for a millennium only to engage in a
vain and lazy self-contemplation. No! . . . He has
made us fit to govern, so that we might rule
the barbarian and senile peoples. And among all
the races, he has chosen the American people to
lead the world finally to its regeneration."

20. *Portray Americans as war criminals.*
A heavily retouched photograph shows prisoners
being tied to the stake prior to execution. The
heading is, "Hundreds of Korean patriot hostages
were thus executed by the American interventionist
forces in Korea." The faces of the soldiers in the
picture are obscured; they are wearing World War II
Japanese helmets.

21. *Bring the argument down to earth by showing
that America is a menace to the reader in his own
country.*

The Communist propagandists are not so much
trying to create new images of the United States as
to strengthen existing impressions. Falsehoods are
especially convincing if they bolster what already
seems plausible. Lies can be contradicted, but the
element of truth in the Communist attack exposes
the areas in which America is most vulnerable and
where words alone are not sufficient to prove its
case.

Content analysis of the sort I have just recorded is a necessary
tool in the study of mass communication. At Jersey Standard I
had used it in my study of the Philharmonic's fan mail. I had
used it also to evaluate one of the nonprofit organizations to
which the company contributed funds—an independent international shortwave broadcasting operation, WRUL, which transmitted English-language programs from its Boston headquarters. Its
unique virtue, in the eyes of its managers, was that, unlike the
Voice of America, it was nongovernmental. What was its audience? What effects did it have? The only evidence was in letters
from listeners in response to continuing appeals. I discovered

that most of this mail came from expatriate Americans in far-off places rather than from the foreign nationals who were the real target. The company withdrew its support, and the operation eventually foundered.

Another assignment in the area of international broadcasting came at the end of my Fulbright year in France. The CIA had just established Radio Free Europe to broadcast to the Eastern European countries under Soviet occupation, and the Oil Industry Information Committee's Min Miller had been selected to run it. He asked me to go to RFE headquarters in Munich to examine the operation and suggest how its effects could be assessed. Munich was just emerging from the rubble that had filled its downtown at the end of World War II, when I first passed through it. Temporary one-story structures lined the main shopping streets. Hitler's Haus der Kunst housed an American officers' club in which a melancholy string band played *"O mein Papa!"* a popular song lamenting Germany's bleak postwar condition.

Unlike the State Department's Voice of America, which openly represented American interests, RFE was intended to act as a "surrogate" for the free media now absent behind the newly dropped Iron Curtain. A group of passionate exiles, with mixed—and sometimes highly unappetizing—political views, prepared the programs. A prodigiously well- informed historian, William Griffiths, supplied policy guidance and nudged his unruly charges into a semblance of conformity at the morning staff meeting.

In the highly charged atmosphere of that time, after the armed struggle with communism in Korea, there was a sense that the situation in Eastern Europe was still fluid. The selection of programming and content had not yet been reduced to a routine; it was a genuinely creative process. In Germany the postwar Displaced Persons camps were still functioning, and refugees from the east kept trickling in with new horror stories. These fugitives were, in fact, principal sources of intelligence about what was happening, but they were not being systematically interrogated. There was, moreover, no procedure in place to estimate the size

of the audiences for RFE broadcasts or the reactions of the listeners. The operation badly needed a research department that
would collect information about audiences and obtain listener
reactions to different kinds of programming content. I proposed a
detailed plan for its organization but resisted Miller's urging that
I stay on in Munich to set it up.

Shortly after I embarked on my study of the Algerians, Budd Wilson had arrived in Paris to organize a series of surveys through
his firm's network of affiliated research companies. Wilson's
biggest client continued to be the federal government. Opinion
research had shown its usefulness during the war, with surveys
of American troops and of German prisoners. With the invasion
of Germany came the Bombing Survey, an extensive series of
studies that investigated how and why the enemy's civilian
morale had remained impervious to the destruction of its cities.
The onset of the cold war brought a heightened interest in the attitudes of the public in Europe, Japan, and the Middle East.

As Wilson's pan-European polling expanded, he needed a
full-time European representative. This was Eunice Cooper, one
of several alumnae of the Columbia Bureau distinguished by
their extraordinary analytical skills. Eunice was tiny, hunch-
backed, and possessed of a deadly and often malicious sense of
humor. Her months in Paris were largely occupied with the intricacies of getting permission to conduct business in France. She
held prolonged discussions with an exalted notary, a hand-
wringing lawyer, whom she addressed as *"Maître,"* and innumerable petty bureaucrats in a variety of government offices.

This was the heyday of the effort to apply social science
knowledge to the ideological conversion of Germany and to assure the success of the Marshall Plan by building support for
U.S. policies. Research was sponsored by the State Department
and by a number of other agencies, including a mysterious arm
of the newly spun-off air force, the Human Relations Research
Institute (HRRI), headquartered at Maxwell Field, Alabama. This

organization had commissioned Wilson's IPOR to study the attitudes of Europeans toward the United States and its policies.

HRRI's civilian research director, and an occasional visitor to Paris, was Frederick W. Williams, who had earlier run surveys of the German population on behalf of the Psychological Warfare division of SHAEF (General Eisenhower's headquarters). Williams was tall, slightly stooped, and as gaunt as a Giacometti figure. He wore rimless glasses, flashed a wry, wistful grin, and chuckled gaily as he pronounced his political opinions, which were ultra-conservative. At one point his office at the CIA was close to that of his friend Howard Hunt, later immortalized by Watergate. Williams saw the signs of Soviet conspiracy everywhere. His wife, Rosika, a Jewish refugee from Romania, was a pretty, self-indulgent woman who was herself most opinionated. She humored Fred's views but did not share them.

HRRI's European research director was Max Ralis, whose eventful life was a distillation of the terrible twentieth century. Born Max Israel in revolutionary Russia, he was taken to Berlin by Social Democratic parents fleeing the terrors of civil war, then to Paris to escape the Nazis. With the outbreak of World War II he was drafted into the French army, and when the front collapsed in 1940 he managed to make his way through the unoccupied zone, over the Pyrenees, and miraculously to New York. When he was, inevitably, drafted into the U.S. Army, his multi-lingual skills were put to use in intelligence operations, where he served as a chauffeur to the sociologist John W. Riley, Jr., and thus, by a kind of osmosis, apprenticed as a student of public opinion. When the war ended, he joined Lazarsfeld's Bureau of Applied Social Research.

Ralis exuded an illusion of unflappability. He puffed on a pipe, flashed a Cheshire-cat smile, and spoke in leisurely fashion in all four of his equally accented tongues. In Paris he ran a one-man show with the help of a French secretary. But he was not alone. To support his efforts the air force had assigned a DC-3 aircraft, an assortment of military vehicles, a chicken colonel, and a staff of half a dozen officers and men whose main duties consisted of monitoring one another's travel orders; there were also a number of French civilian secretaries and drivers. Ralis's research activities, which involved continual perambulation around Europe, were punctuated by the necessity of composing long memoranda replying to longer memoranda laboriously composed by the "commanding officer" in the adjacent office. (When Max tried to get me permission to use the military post exchange, the colonel spent a full day writing a four-page single-spaced memorandum explaining why he had denied the request.)

Ralis returned to the United States to get a Ph.D. from Cornell University with a thesis based on a study of Indian village life. Two years later he was back in Paris as the director of audience research and program evaluation for Radio Liberation (later renamed Radio Liberty). This had been set up under CIA auspices as a counterpart to RFE, which dealt with the Soviet satellite nations. Radio Liberty beamed accurate news and dissident views past the broadcast-jamming barriers that surrounded the Soviet Union itself. RL's director, Howland Sargeant, an even-tempered and seasoned diplomat, had assembled a lively and politically diverse collection of American Sovietologists and Soviet refugees who squabbled among themselves but were united in their dedication to restoring freedom to the USSR. In the ensuing quarter-century, Ralis's research unit devised ingenious ways of capturing information about radio listening habits and interests as well as about the broader currents of thought and social concerns. (It amassed an extraordinary collection of popular anti-regime jokes.)

Max Ralis provided crucial guidance for an organization that conveyed truth and offered hope to the peoples of the Soviet Union and helped inspire the political forces that killed it off. How could one penetrate the Iron Curtain and obtain a true sampling of public attitudes and behavior? Ralis's unit contacted travelers, Soviet and foreign, in a variety of European locations, engaged them in carefully planned but inoffensive conversations, and extracted data that were vital to the tasks of planning broadcast program schedules. Specialist consultants* were employed to help solve the methodological challenge of producing projectable estimates of audience size. A sign of Ralis's effectiveness was the frequency with which he was denounced by name in *Pravda*. He never ceased being bewildered and indignant about the horror stories he heard daily, or being amused by the ridiculous follies of the Socialist Paradise. He met and was befriended by virtually every significant Russian intellectual and artist who made his way to the West. And when the Soviet empire imploded, he knew that this had not happened altogether on its own.

In 1976, Radio Free Europe and Radio Liberty were combined into a single organization; lately they have been given expanded responsibility for broadcasts to such places as Iraq and Afghanistan. For years these surrogate radios assumed that their listeners sought them out, sometimes at considerable personal risk, and listened with enormous interest to news and political messages from abroad, messages that were otherwise inaccessible. Shortwave broadcasts later became less important than the rebroadcasting of RFE/RL's programs on locally owned medium-wave stations. Today, when people can freely tune in to anything they want, they listen more casually. Thus in the 1990s, radio in Eastern Europe and the former Soviet Union underwent a difficult and fascinating transition. Its function as a disseminator of official propaganda was reduced, if not eliminated, and it became more than ever a vehicle for the diffusion of popular music, as it has long been in the West.[†]

---

*Among them were the political scientist Ithiel de Sola Pool and Alex Inkeles, a sociologist and scholar of the Soviet system.

†When I addressed the managers of RFE/RL's affiliated stations in 2000, I reminded them that they now faced some tough questions. How could they maximize their profits by producing advertising revenues that reflected their ability to attract audiences? And was there any criterion, other than the size of profits, by which their success could or should be measured?

THE AD BUSINESS

■ When I returned from Paris in the fall of 1952, my old job at
Jersey Standard was being held open for me, but I passed it up to
take a better-paying position at the company's principal advertising agency, McCann-Erickson. The history of the two organizations was closely linked. The youthful Harrison K. McCann had
been the Standard Oil trust's advertising manager before the
1911 court decision that split up the company. The agency he
founded (and ultimately merged with one started by his contemporary, Alfred W. Erickson) was immediately awarded the accounts of the various successor Standard Oil companies,
including the surviving Jersey Standard, and the Standard Oils
of Indiana, California, and Ohio as well as Standard Oil (New
Jersey)'s numerous overseas affiliates. They were served by a network of offices that led the transformation of the advertising
business in Europe, Latin America, and Asia.

Harry McCann was still a stately presence treading the
agency's executive thirteenth (his lucky number) floor when
I joined McCann-Erickson. Marion Harper, Jr., who cross-
examined me before I was hired, was a prodigy who had become
the agency's president at age thirty-one after a whirlwind success
as research director. Tall, bald, with tiny facial features, he ex-

uded charm when this was necessary (but only then) and radiated devotion in the pursuit of his ambitions. Harper anticipated the rising tide of corporate mergers and created Interpublic, the first umbrella organization that permitted service to competing clients through an aggregation of autonomous agency units. He amplified the company's cash flow and ruptured the profit ceiling imposed by the traditional 15 percent agency commission by creating subsidiaries to handle ancillary activities. He foresaw the globalization of business and expanded McCann's international scope, bringing a coolheaded Brazilian, Armando Sarmento, to New York as the agency's president—a dazzling move in its time.

I was hired over lunch by Sidney W. Dean, Jr., McCann's senior vice president of marketing. Marketing now seems like a commonplace function, but it was new at the time. The term "marketing" was slung about rather loosely, and still is. In some companies it was a grander word for the sales department. In others it was a euphemism for sales promotion. In still others it encompassed a slew of departments—sales, advertising, promotion, merchandising, public relations, and market research. Research was intended to be the underpinning. The premise was that, unlike the nineteenth-century manufacturers who figured out how to make goods better and then hired people to sell them, modern companies had to start by understanding the public's "needs and wants" and then design products to suit. There were, however, different ways of learning what consumers needed and wanted, and great pressure to get answers on the cheap.

Dean made it immediately clear that he was not a Republican. His career had covered a series of remarkable revolutions. When he first joined the J. Walter Thompson agency, the advertising business was not far from the scene described by Theodore Dreiser in *The Genius*—a world in which even creative directors were soft-spoken Ivy League gentlemen in Harris tweed vested suits, and the word "damn" was considered an unseemly oath. This was the dawn of the radio age, which transformed not only

advertising but American culture. The advertising world underwent another great revolution after World War II, with the birth
of the consumer society and the age of television.

Dean presided over an unusual mix of prima donnas, some
of them talented, others not so, but all exceptionally assertive,
opinionated, and ambitious. One of the agency's clients was
Westinghouse, then second to General Electric in the appliance
market and a major manufacturer of television sets. At that time
about 25 percent of the homes in the country had television, and
the client needed an authoritative and scientific estimate of how
quickly the market would grow. The task was assigned to two
very bright economist-statisticians who went on to become important figures in advertising—Stanley Canter and Alvin Achen-
baum. They did a careful analysis of the evidence and produced
a forecast that extrapolated the existing slow growth, which had
been caused largely by a freeze on new station licenses in much
of the country. By 1960, they forecast, television would penetrate
half of U.S. households. Dean looked at their chart, listened to
their explanations, and then took a pencil and drew a steeply ascending curve that got the level up to 80 percent. The economists
tried to reason with him. "There's never been a growth curve like
that in the history of new products!" they said. "There is now,"
said Dean, and of course he was right.*

Dean was a man who could exude righteous indignation—
not always an endearing quality, but in his case tempered with
charm, tact, and strong good humor. Although his work career
was dedicated to serving corporate clients, venture capitalism,
and financial institutions, he maintained a marvelous ability to
stand apart from the conventional perspective. He pursued his
ideas with passion. He knew that any role for government in the
realm of mass media was to be regarded with mistrust. Yet he
also knew that the electronic spectrum represented an asset of

---

*I should have taken this lesson to heart when, after a talk I gave about the fu-
ture of mass media at Boston University in 1989, a student asked why I hadn't mentioned the Internet. "Look," I said, "The Internet has 100,000 users and newspapers
are read every day by over a hundred million people. How can you compare them?"

society as a whole, that its allocation and use necessarily required government regulation, and that such regulation demanded primacy for the public interest. When cable emerged to widen the array of viewing choices, he was among the first to note that it could not be allowed to operate by the same rules as over-the-air broadcasting. He saw the danger of having the system operators who disseminated the signals also produce the programming content.

The heart of Harper's McCann-Erickson was the new business operation. A full-time researcher studied corporate balance sheets and trade publications in search of leads to companies that could be pried loose from their present agencies. The single-mindedness with which Harper pursued new business paid off. A strong sense of dynamism pervaded the organization. Employees scanned the ad column of the *Times* each morning to see what new accounts had been won. Some came by sheer brute deal-making, as in the case of the Bulova watch account, which was "owned" by a tough character named Terence Cline, who could apparently make the owners dance through hoops.

McCann's command of the Esso Standard account was consolidated by its purchase of the Marschalk and Pratt agency, which had handled Esso's broadcast billings (and also the parent company's Philharmonic). Other business was wooed slowly and deliberately with the aid of elaborate presentations based on original research. The peripatetic Victor Ratner labored for months on a spectacular show that won the Coca-Cola business. (Ratner had already solved the problem of producing a slogan for a brand of whiskey that was indistinguishable from its competitors. "If you can find a better whiskey, buy it!")

Personalities were crucial to the task of winning new business, as in the case of Emerson Foote, who was instrumental in getting Chesterfield cigarettes as a client. Foote's original agency, Foote, Cone & Belding, had long represented the American Tobacco Company. His relationship with its crude chairman, George Washington Hill, was fictionalized in a best-selling novel about the advertising business.[1] Benign, saturnine, and with a

lofty gaze, Foote deserved to have had his portrait painted by
George Romney. He became chairman of the agency when Harper
moved to head his newly created Interpublic Group. After his retirement, and as evidence of the ill-effects of smoking accumulated, Foote became a militant activist against tobacco.

In December 1957 a McCann-Erickson team flew to a London meeting of Chrysler's European executives to plan a new
marketing campaign. Our plane caught fire on takeoff, delaying
the trip for several hours. The passengers were met at Heathrow
by a fleet of Rolls-Royces. The following day we met in a chilly
office warmed only by a small coal fire. The Chrysler man in
charge stood with his back to the glowing hearth while the rest of
us shivered. Unfortunately he was so carried away by the agenda
he was setting for us that he failed to notice that his trousers had
caught fire. Our carefully prepared project was subsequently
aborted, though not because of this catastrophe.

Harper made advertising history when he resigned the huge
Chrysler account to take on that of General Motors' Buick division. Chrysler was a difficult and demanding client, resistant to
research and sluggish in its marketing posture. In 1958 the automobile business was in deep recession, and Chrysler was hurting
very badly. Along with many other executives of the agency, I
was sent out on a special project to interview automobile dealers
across the country to learn how they felt about the state of the
market and about automobile advertising in general. We thought
we were working on a project for Chrysler, but Harper had something else in mind. He used the results of that crash study to
make a play for the Buick account, which he had courted surrep-
titiously. While it was common for clients to toss out their agencies, the reverse was unheard of. We felt it was unseemly and
improper. Harper established the principle that the agency was a
proud and independent entity in its own right. He had correctly
assessed the incompetence of the Chrysler management and concluded that the company was going nowhere; General Motors,
with its great worldwide presence, represented a great growth
opportunity for McCann-Erickson.

Harper stockpiled talent without taking the time to consider how to use it. Newly hired executives were deposited in offices without being given assignments. Some self-starters developed projects and kept on going; others grew bored and found new jobs; still others were suddenly removed from the payroll. Harper spent money wildly. He acquired a company plane for his personal use. He ordered dozens of silk shirts at a time from the shops of deluxe hotels and charged the cost to his room. With a native Oklahoman's affection for livestock, he bought the Deep Hollow cattle ranch in Montauk, Long Island, and put it on the books as a corporate retreat and conference center to which selected executives were invited for weekends.

Eventually such excesses threatened to plunge the company into bankruptcy, and Harper was fired by a board of directors whose members he had himself handpicked. He welched on personal debts and drank himself into incoherence and disgrace, ending his life as a recluse living in the home of his mother in a small Oklahoma town. He lamented, "I have been captured by what I chased." But he had changed the face of the advertising business.

In the mid-1980s I proposed Harper for the Advertising Hall of Fame and sent a copy of my nominating letter to Neal Gilliatt, who had been Interpublic's vice chairman. I hoped that he would second my nomination, but he wrote back, "This should be a posthumous award!" It was. In 2002, Harper's baby, Interpublic, was (along with its rivals, Omnicom and WPP) one of the world's largest advertising companies.

Harper's orbit intersected surprisingly with that of Paul Lazarsfeld, a towering figure in the history of twentieth-century applied social science. The connecting point was probably the Radio Research Council, founded in 1943, with Lazarsfeld as the first president. The council brought together a small group of network and agency research directors and independent researchers for monthly luncheon discussions of methodology and

listening trends. Lazarsfeld was at this time director of the Office
of Radio Research, which he had established at Princeton and
then transferred to Rutgers University. In his studies of listeners'
response to radio programs, Lazarsfeld collaborated with the
young research director of the Columbia Broadcasting System,
Frank Stanton, who had done his doctorate at Ohio State on the
subject of radio ratings. The Office of Radio Research ultimately
came to Columbia as the Bureau of Applied Social Research.

The profession of public opinion and marketing research in
America bears the indelible imprint of scholars and practitioners
who were exiled by the growth of Nazism. A significant number
of them fled Austria after (or in Lazarsfeld's case, in anticipation
of) the *Anschluss* of 1938. Lazarsfeld's first two wives, Marie Ja-
hoda and Herta Herzog (with whom he maintained warm friend-
ships after their respective divorces), were core members of this
group. Other members were Hans and Ilse Zeisel (brother and
sister). All brought to the examination of social data an extraordinary capacity for analytical insight, whether the subject matter
concerned the impact of the depression on a small Austrian industrial town (Marienthal), the political effects of mass media, or
the peculiarities of consumption habits and brand preferences.
In an era before technology encouraged the routine expectoration
of vast and redundant measures of statistical significance, their
approach to evidence was highly intimate. In those days the
numbers produced by surveys represented counts of real people
rather than computer-adjusted sampling abstractions, and the Vienna school (and those they trained in this country) treated them
respectfully as such. Each person interviewed constituted an individual case history; the data were ransacked to understand the
reasons behind every answer.

In this quest a division between quantitative and qualitative
research was inconceivable. Lazarsfeld and both Zeisels loved
numbers and had strong mathematical training. All were also
steeped in a uniquely Viennese art: the psychoanalytic interpretation of human motivation and behavior. (Lazarsfeld's mother,
Sophie, was a psychoanalyst who resumed her practice in New

York.) The teachings of Freud (himself an active presence on the local scene) brought a keen awareness of the unconscious impulses that found their way into respondents' answers to an interviewer's questions. The analyst's unstructured interaction with the analysand provided a model for the interviewer's technique of discovering attitudes that could not necessarily have been anticipated. The depth interview emerged as the direct offspring of the analyst's "Ah hah, verrry interesting! Tell me more."

Lazarsfeld is a subject of innumerable legends and was a mentor of many outstanding practitioners. Perpetually grinning, clutching or clenching the stump of a cigar, he was witty, warm, and outgoing. He was also sly and caustic in his private comments on colleagues. He was an imaginative theorist, a perspicacious data analyst, a methodological innovator, and a clever organizer and politician. On one occasion I persuaded him to speak before the Public Relations Society of America. He proclaimed that as a hardheaded pragmatic social scientist he was appalled by the soft-minded, romantic, and impractical illusions of businessmen. His English was fluent but unmistakably accented. He asked a student, "How come t-o-m-b is pronounced 'toom' when w-o-m-b is pronounced 'wahm'?"

The Bureau of Applied Social Research was a training ground for graduate students who combined statistical and psychological approaches to the analysis of commercial problems. At McCann-Erickson, Marion Harper hired two of Lazarsfeld's protegés, his former wife, Herta Herzog, and Hans Zeisel.* Originally trained as a lawyer, Zeisel left commercial research to become a professor at the University of Chicago law school, where he conducted important studies of the jury system and of the judicial process. Zeisel was bald, slight, short, dark, and handsome. He was incredibly quick, impatient, brilliant, and

---

*It was Zeisel who recommended me to McCann-Erickson, which he had just left to become research director of the Tea Council. When I told him I might be too young to warrant a good salary, he retorted, "They *pay* for youth!"

acerbic—a devastating critic of pretense and the meretricious. (After listening to a forty-five-minute presentation of a costly and involuted new study by John Howard, a senior professor at Columbia's Business School, Zeisel asked him, "What exactly did you do and what did you find out?")

The Vienna group was suffused with the tradition of Social Democracy, which combined distaste for the existing political and economic power structure with revulsion at the powerful forces of Austrian right-wing jingoism and the emerging totalitarianism of the Nazis and Communists. As much earlier in Great Britain and the United States, social science was seen as a forerunner of social reform. When the Nazis took over Austria, Zeisel's sister Ilse outwitted their search for the membership records of the Social Democratic party by smuggling them into a locker at the Vienna railroad station. Her good looks helped her charm the stormtroopers who controlled exit visas from the Great German Realm. She rejoined Lazarsfeld's team as a staff member at Columbia.

Ilse was what the French call *une force de nature*. She had strong convictions but expressed them gracefully, punctuated with a throaty laugh. She did consumer motivation studies in company with her close friend, Herta Herzog. As with Herta, Ilse's reports were hardly ever published, but they showed superb interpretive skill. She was an indefatigable field worker who enjoyed trawling for the information that respondents didn't even know they had. At the age of eighty-five she married a former colleague, Frederick W. Williams, and announced that he had made her "an honest woman."

Herta Herzog was a handsome woman with an engaging temperament. Her right arm had been crippled by polio, and she scrawled her reports in a left-handwriting that only her secretary could read. As she wrote, she rubbed her greying blonde hair as though looking for inspiration. Her specialty was the interpretation of lengthy "depth interviews" conducted by an elite corps of interviewers whom she had recruited to probe consumer motivations. Her analyses were inspired, and her Viennese accent entranced clients. At the height of Senator Joe McCarthy's sinister influence, she found herself seated next to him on a flight to Chicago and buried herself in her work, trying to ignore his presence. He persisted in an attempt at conversation and was curious about what she was writing. By the end of the trip he had offered her a job on his staff, fighting communism.

Ironically, Herta's second husband, the sociologist Paul Massing, had himself been a Red in his youth in Germany, though his principal current interest, aside from teaching at Rutgers, was operating a tractor at his New Jersey farm. Massing's former wife, Hede, had become a professional anti-Communist, a sought-after witness before various committees on anti-American activities. And *her* previous husband was the Comintern agent Gerhard Eisler, whose brash, argumentative sister Ruth had also become strongly anti-Soviet. It was difficult to reconcile the eminently respectable bourgeois lifestyle of this crew with their revolutionary pasts.

Yet another former Soviet agent (and, according to some charges, hit man), Mark Zborowski, was a project director at the Bureau of Applied Social Research. He was working on a study on the use of analgesics, which he said were underused by Jews "because they loved to suffer." Mark was the co-author of what became a classic study of life in the Jewish *shtetls* of Eastern Europe.[2] His collaborator on this project, Elizabeth Herzog, married Ralph White, a social psychologist who was her colleague at the Voice of America.* Small, trim, and cheerful, Betsy departed life after she was diagnosed with cancer, with a large mailing that began, "To my nears and dears: I am committing euthanasia."

Lazarsfeld's circle was remarkable in that it bridged the business and academic worlds. Those two other fountainheads of large-scale applied social research—the Institute for Social Research at the University of Michigan and the National Opinion

---

*Ralph White became a specialist on public opinion in South Vietnam. Before the Tet offensive I asked him how it broke down. He estimated that 20 percent of the population supported the government and 20 percent the Vietcong, while the majority just wanted to be left alone.

Research Center (originally at the University of Denver and then at the University of Chicago)—focused strictly on questions of public policy. Lazarsfeld and his associates at the Bureau found pleasure and stimulation in examining business problems, and took on assignments of proprietary interest with the understanding that they would be able to squeeze the data later for information of social scientific interest.

Among the leading exponents of both the quantitative and qualitative schools of research were two other refugees from Hitler's Europe. Alfred Politz, who held a doctorate in theoretical physics, was a German who had come to the United States in 1937, switched his interest to advertising, and in 1940 was hired as a statistician by Elmo Roper. Politz had learned English quickly. He was bantam-sized, an indefatigable athlete, endowed with prodigious stamina and appetites. The research firm that he later set up got its start with a study of transportation advertising and hit the big time with a 1949 study of *Life* magazine's cumulative audience.

Since the mid-1930s, magazines had based their advertising sales pitches on surveys that demonstrated the scope and purchasing power of their audiences. The importance of these studies grew with the introduction of television. By replacing paid circulation (that is, copies sold) with a measure of the total number of people exposed to an issue of a magazine (whether purchased by them or not), the surveys generated huge numbers that compared favorably with the gigantic audiences of network TV.

Politz prided himself on his commercial applications of probability sampling, which, with its promise of greater accuracy, was especially important to the magazine business. (Two of Politz's vice presidents, Lester Frankel and J. Stevens Stock, had helped pioneer the development of this method as statisticians in the New Deal's Works Progress Administration.)

Steve Stock had a genuinely homespun manner and a good heart. Staid and conservative in manner, the widowed Steve had married a sizzling platinum-blonde airline hostess who threw roaring parties, at which she contained neither her thirst nor her language. He chain-drank cups of tea in lieu of alcohol and regaled me with tales of his research projects. He was especially proud of a study he had made for the poultry industry. This showed a widespread preference for white meat and prompted the chicken breeders to develop birds with outsize breasts.

On at least two occasions Politz hired the ballroom of the Park Lane Hotel in New York to address the assembled advertising community—once in the mid-1950s to denounce motivation research, and again in 1961 to attack the technical standards set by the Advertising Research Foundation.

The most prominent practitioner of motivation research (and a principal target of Vance Packard's influential polemic, *The Hidden Persuaders*[3]) was Ernest Dichter, originally from Vienna. Dichter's analyses were highly imaginative and drenched in quaintly orthodox Freudianism. Like Politz, he was gifted with great energy and fine speaking ability. Unlike Politz, his English had no trace of an accent. His analytical insights were penetrating, and his fruitful imagination appealed to the "creative people" who wrote copy, laid out ads, and produced commercials. (Allowing the housewife to add an egg to a prepared cake mix, for example, gave her the illusion that she was virtually baking from scratch.)

Ernest's demeanor was in fact earnest; he lacked a sense of humor. (On one occasion when he and I shared a platform as speakers at an editors' convention, he repeated one of his favorite case histories, about his services to the undertaking profession. I teased him by asking whether, with his funereal experience, he had any suggestions for the newspaper morgue [where old clippings were filed before the computer era]. He thereupon set forth on a prolonged critique of obituary pages.)

While Politz maintained a test facility and his winter residence in Tampa, Dichter ran his business from a castle on the Hudson in upper Westchester County. His former employees generally conceded that the "depth interviews" they collected served more to illustrate observations and insights that the master had spun a priori than as evidence from which to pursue a subsequent analysis. This lack of scientific procedure was what got Politz's goat. He exhorted the marketing community on the importance of solid statistical evidence to support assertions about consumer behavior. Dichter retorted that "A thousand times zero is still zero!"

Willard R. Simmons headed one of two principal firms studying magazine audiences after the death of Politz and his company. The other was the Target Group Index, which used a somewhat different method of establishing whether a respondent was a reader. Simmons, like Politz, took people through a magazine and then asked the trick question of whether they had seen that issue before. (This was called the "through-the-book" procedure.) TGI used small reproductions of the magazine's nameplate and took it from there to establish "recent reading." The two services produced numbers that were sometimes quite disparate, though neither came up consistently with larger ones. (The numbers from each service for a given magazine also varied from issue to issue, even though circulation did not.)

TGI was owned by the J. Walter Thompson agency. Its methodology had been developed by Thompson's research director in England, Timothy Joyce, who was transplanted to the United States along with his trade secrets. At Cambridge, Joyce had received a doctorate in moral sciences (a faculty that was later eliminated, presumably for lack of demand). His intellectual interests far transcended those of the usual market researcher. (For one thing, he had deciphered and transcribed illicit shorthand records of parliamentary debates on the American colonies in 1774 and 1775, and had later accumulated what may have been the world's leading collection of books about shorthand.) He narrowly missed being elected to Parliament himself as a Liberal party candidate. Amusing though sober-seeming, ingenious and ambitious, good-humored but occasionally caustic, Joyce piloted TGI through a series of owners and grew rich, like a good many other research entrepreneurs.*

While still in England, Timothy had taken issue with an essay on "The Researcher's Dilemma," in which I said that "the professional goals of a scientist include the ideal of social service and the independent search for truth, and these goals may not be altogether consistent with the researcher's assignment or motivations as a businessman." Quoting the eighteenth-century Bishop Butler, Joyce argued that there was "far too little self-love in the world."[4] He pointed to "the common interest, of those whose livelihood is research, in preventing undesirable practices because they would queer the pitch for research." "The researcher's goals should be those of his client or employer; the truth he is concerned with is the truth that will solve their problems." "Brutal simplification is sometimes necessary to get research acted on." I observed that there was no shortage of *that.*

Before the rise of syndicated studies (like Simmons's and Joyce's) that measured reading for dozens of magazines at a clip, buyers judged the merits of different media, especially competing newspapers and magazines, on the basis of the audience studies they had individually commissioned. These studies were generally unveiled in elaborate presentations delivered just before exquisite lunches in fashionable venues like the Stork Club, El Morocco, and the 21 Club. The presentations themselves were preceded by an extended cocktail hour during which the media buyers were presumably lulled into an appropriately receptive state. The *Saturday Evening Post* once changed the format, with an 8:30 breakfast accompanied by Bloody Marys.

A potent force in magazine audience research was John Maloney, the *Reader's Digest*'s modest and good-humored director of international research. In 1935 he had been George Gallup's third employee, at a salary of $26 a week, but during World War II he

---

*TGI later became Mediamark Research, Inc., or MRI.

was elevated to command of a destroyer escort. When Jack
joined the *Digest* it had just begun the postwar expansion of its
international editions. Europe was a shambles, and survey research barely existed outside the English-speaking countries.
Maloney's coordinated market and attitude survey in eight countries was a landmark in international research, the starting point
for a series of surveys he launched worldwide. They had an
important ripple effect, teaching the fundamentals of research
procedures to an expanding cadre of professionals. Maloney's
greatest achievement was to persuade his employers that the
magazine would not be destroyed by introducing advertising in
its domestic edition. This brought them and their company into a
period of incredible prosperity. Appropriately, having made
them a lot of money, Jack's final assignment was to give some of
it away, as head of the Reader's Digest Foundation.

Perhaps the most sophisticated sales use of research was
made by William Blair, the publisher of *Harper's*. (After his magazine was sold, Blair was given the unfortunate task of firing
Willie Morris, its wild and highly esteemed editor.) A blithe and
worldly Scot, Blair had also apprenticed at the Gallup organization. He had a gift for turning small numbers to large sales advantage. When an advertiser ran an ad featuring a large illustration
of a male kangaroo, *Harper's* ran it as submitted while the *New
Yorker* retouched it to eliminate the animal's scrotum. Blair disseminated a deadly poem that punctured his competitor's decorum.

The most high-powered shows were those put on for *Life*
magazine by its research director, Edward Miller. Instead of separately inviting groups of buyers from the individual agencies,
Miller entertained them collectively in a vast hotel ballroom
with slide shows of charts from the latest study made by Alfred
Politz. Miller, who later became president of the Politz organization, was stout, bespectacled, and serious in manner. He delivered his well-scripted addresses as though he himself were
astounded by the enormity of his numbers. They *were* enormous,
because *Life*, like its rivals among the great magazines, was rais-

ing its readership through giveaway promotions in an effort to match television's huge audiences. It bled to death as a result.

Life, Look, the *Saturday Evening Post,* and *Colliers* vied with one another, employing different research firms to produce studies that invariably showed their readership to be better than their rivals', if not in absolute size then in purchasing power, future buying potential, loyalty, or some other intangible quality. One magazine proclaimed its superiority in "reader heat." Wallace Wegge, the research director of *Look* magazine in the 1950s and '60s, had the countenance of a mournful beagle. He told a newcomer to magazine research, "Do something more respectable with your life! Get a job in a whorehouse!"

The advent of computers made mathematical modeling of behavior, once the exclusive domain of economists, an ever-more important part of marketing practice and of research on consumption and media use. This was especially apparent in the development of systems that sought to heighten the efficiency of media schedules. In recent decades the 15 percent commission structure, on which advertising agencies operated for a century, has eroded. But before this change, media buying had taken a growing share of agency operating costs, involving as it did tedious clerical tasks. Now agencies moved to spin off the media function and turn it into a profit center.*

An incentive to do this came as a result of competition from independent time-buying services that grew out of time-bartering

---

*The agency media department traditionally has had a number of tasks: (1) Media research evaluates the available data on different media. (2) Media planning seeks the best ways to allocate the client's budget among media, and to schedule advertisements for maximum effectiveness. (3) Media buying bargains with media and their representatives over rates and advertising positions. (4) Media relations involve the innumerable contacts about details of service, complaints, and grievances. Media contracts must constantly be renegotiated as market conditions change. In addition there is (5) verification that the ad ran as it was supposed to, and (6) all of the billing, payment, and other accounting transactions are usually handled by a separate department. In a large agency these functions are usually handled by different units.

in radio and the early days of television.* Their pitch to the client was always based on their proclaimed ability to buy more ratings points for the dollar because of their narrow focus, their cunning, and their capacity to combine buying weight to gain leverage in what was essentially a commodity auction market. Norman King, gross, sloppy looking, and foulmouthed, was perhaps the most flamboyant character in a fraternity of high-rolling, freewheeling traders. He loudly received sycophants and supplicants at his regular table in the Fountain Room of the Four Seasons restaurant. The bankruptcy of his U.S. Media International caused a sensation.

In the mid-1970s a new type of time-buying service emerged, attracting some clients of larger agencies who thought they could get more personal service from a small organization. Most of these companies were bought by large European "buying centrals," which had flourished in a climate of loose controls and looser morals as commercial television replaced state-operated systems. (The head of one of the largest services, Zenith, kept costs to a minimum by "filling half-empty bottles of Perrier with tap water and putting them back in the fridge.") Faced with this new competition, the large agencies set up or bought up buying services as a substitute for their own media departments. In the twenty-first century, this has become general practice.

Buying services originally began with the premise that they were uniquely skilled at bargaining down rates, but their main selling point shifted to the claim that they selected media with highly sophisticated skill. They developed "optimization models" that stressed "accountability"† and performance rather than

---

*A time broker would offer an advertiser a certain amount of air time in exchange for merchandise which could be sold to a third party. (The precedent had been set in the newspaper business with "due bills" for transportation services, restaurants, and hotels.) As middlemen, brokers ended up with substantial amounts of time, inexpensively purchased, which they could resell at a substantial profit, still at a cut-rate price for the buyer.

†This term was first applied to advertising by Marion Harper, Jr. It implies that tangible results of a given strategy can be identified and measured—a difficult and often impossible objective.

cost efficiency. Similar models had been used—and abandoned—by agencies thirty years earlier.

The simplest optimization model might be a table ranking different media options in terms of only two variables: the cost of an advertisement and the size of the audience each would deliver—or, putting the two together, the cost-per-thousand gross rating points or "impressions" a given investment would buy. By adding information about the composition of the audience, the comparison could be refined further to the cost of reaching people of a certain kind who might be customers for a particular product—men aged eighteen to thirty-four,* mothers of children under six, professionals and managers. With the aid of a computer, alternative schedules could be quickly compared by any desired criteria; the effects of shifting budgets or revising schedules could be calculated almost instantly.

When comparing schedules that combined different media and involved repeated advertisements, the model became more complicated, because it added the dimensions of reach and frequency over the life of the campaign. It was possible to set an "optimum" frequency, like three exposures per person, and assign less value to impressions that fell above or below that level.

"Optimization" models commonly carried the built-in premise that three broadcasts of a commercial were the optimum "effective frequency." This followed from an observation by Herb Krugman. He proposed that the first time a viewer saw a television commercial, the reaction was, "What is it?"; the second time it was, "What of it?"; the third exposure was a useful reminder of what had already been learned; further exposures might not be

---

*Young adults have become the dream target of most advertisers, in spite of their modest disposable income, compared with older age groups. They are more elusive targets, since their crowded lives leave less time for television. Since they are more fickle in their purchasing habits, the conventional advertising wisdom is that their brand preferences are more malleable than those of older consumers. In fact, impressions of a product's merits can be influenced at any age, and people beyond the first blush of youth make the bulk of most consumer purchases. The willingness of many advertisers to pay a heavy premium for messages delivered to the post-teen generation illustrates herd behavior rather than marketing wisdom.

very helpful. Media planners latched on to this observation to formulate "the rule of three," which confused the diffusion of messages with their reception and disregarded the fact that advertisements carry different meanings and have different objectives.

The audience measurement services fed this development, by supplying lots and lots of numbers to crank into the models. As the analysis of media schedules grew more complex, the large agencies and buying services had a further advantage, because they could afford the necessary technology and professional talent.

More research data and more complex ways of manipulating them on the computer made media buyers better informed but not more intelligent. Planners might switch from one yardstick, like cost per thousand, to another, like cost per reach point, but to make either the number of impressions or the number of people reached the sole criterion for evaluating media, or media schedules, was to fall into a fatal error. My studies taught me that in advertising there were simply no universal rules, no sure formulas for marketing success. There was, however, a formula for failure, and that was a reliance on formulas. I began to learn this lesson when I worked in the agency business.

Decision models based on survey data take the accuracy of the data as a given, but this assumption is not always warranted. As telephone interviewing has replaced home visits, the rate of cooperation with surveys has dropped precipitously. A typical survey in 2002 may get completed interviews with no more than one-sixth of a sample of individuals picked by pure probability. The people who are hard to reach differ in many respects from those who are easily contacted. Survey researchers have met this challenge with the help of the computer, which enables them to weight their results according to the characteristics of the respondents. This means that the percentages shown in a survey report are rarely identical to those that might come as raw data from the people originally interviewed. Half a century ago, in the precomputer era, such adjustments could only be done crudely, if at all.

Researchers not only face greater difficulty in contacting people in today's more mobile society; they also find it harder to get people to sit still as they make greater demands upon them. Syndicated studies that serve many different clients crowd more and more questions, often on unrelated topics, into longer and longer questionnaires.

I encountered the aftermath of this development as one of my first assignments at McCann-Erickson. Marion Harper had just purchased the rights to the Brand Index, developed by Cornelius and Louise Du Bois. Neil Du Bois, a mild-mannered Harvard man of soft and hesitant speech, was a writer of promotional copy who became the research director of *Life* magazine. He had left to start the Brand Index, unsuccessfully, as an independent entrepreneur.*

The Brand Index included an exhaustive set of questions on each respondent's use of all major media as well as on the use of products in dozens of categories of merchandise and services; it also measured awareness, opinion, and the purchase of individual brands. One complete survey using this method had been made. My job was to see how the resulting mountain of tabulations could be put to work on behalf of the agency's existing clients, or as a promotional tool to attract new ones. My initial approach was to take a number of product fields and examine how people who were frequent, occasional, light, or nonusers of a product differed in their social characteristics and in their response to individual brands. (Although this may seem surprising now, such information was then not generally available.) The results of this analysis seemed both puzzling and bizarre until I discovered striking variations in the proportions of respondents who had been coded as "don't know" or "no answer" on different questions. The reason soon became clear: less than half of

*He later became research director of the Foote, Cone & Belding agency.

those who started out had been willing to slog all the way through the lengthy interview. The whole costly effort had to be abandoned, though today's sophisticated computer technology could probably have solved the problem by eliminating the dropouts and rebalancing the sample. (Years later, Du Bois's original concept became wildly popular again as advertisers sought a "single source" for data to be used in media planning with the help of computer models.* The problems of retaining respondents' cooperation were no different than before.)

The problems of the Brand Index were egregious, but audience surveys were, and are, just as imprecise as other forms of survey research. The proof is in the instability of statistics that measure the readership of the same publications over time, even when they continue to sell the same number of copies. It is also demonstrated in the great disparity often found among the projections offered by different research organizations measuring readership of the same publications at the same point in time. Similar variability occurred in the program ratings produced by different broadcast measurement services.

When I arrived at McCann-Erickson in 1952, its research department in Radio City was housed in a series of small windowed offices for the executives and a central bull pen of desks for clerks and junior personnel. Guarding the entrance to this labyrinth, with the pugnacious scowl of a bull terrier, was the office manager, Ernest Lamoureux (known as "Lammy"), resplendent in a double-breasted sharkskin suit. (An officious martinet by day, Lammy had a nocturnal career as a cabaret performer in New Jersey, reciting arch and clever monologues to his own tuneful piano accompaniment.) As temperatures and humidity rose during the summer, Lammy distributed fresh towels with which we could sop the perspiration from our brows and necks.

---

*The idea was partly embodied in the syndicated surveys launched by W. R. Simmons, Target Group Index, and Scarborough Research.

The clerks who spent their days adding up numbers and computing percentages on mechanical calculators or with slide rules included two categories of the agency's trainees. "A" trainees were Ivy League college graduates who were exposed to various departments before being elevated to the rank of junior account executives and sent on to greatness. (One was the son of a leading officer of McCann's client, Chrysler. When I had occasion to summon him to my glass-enclosed office, he would fly across the floor, still seated in his armchair on rollers.) "B" trainees were poor creatures of less privileged origins, with degrees from lesser institutions, who remained stuck in their jobs until they won a promotion within the research department. The trainees were all men, but secretaries, clerks, and a few analysts brought the sexes into balance. A network of after-hours partying and surreptitious romances held this miscellaneous assortment of young people together.

Only a handful of women had attained executive rank in the advertising agency business. Nowhere did they deal as primary contacts with clients in account service. At our shop, Dorothy K. McCann, Harrison's wife, moved in a stratosphere of her own, as producer of a radio show, Twenty Mule Team Borax's "Death Valley Days." A handful of female copywriters had achieved the rank of vice president. Women held only low-level time-buying positions in the media department, a field they have since come to dominate. In the research department, talent was recognized.* As research director, Harper broke through an otherwise universal barrier by hiring Jews; still, there were limits. ("You will never be research director of McCann-Erickson," Herta Herzog told me, and paused. "Because you are a Jew.") Blacks were nowhere to be seen. When I tried to hire one, I was told I

---

*Attempts to admit women to the prestigious Market Research Council were always met with contemptuous laughter and voted down by secret ballot. As in other gentlemen's clubs, the presence of "the ladies" was considered to inhibit candor of expression. Instead of pursuing the battle on general principles, I nominated Babette Jackson, an outstanding agency research director, for membership in 1974, and shamed the group into letting her in.

couldn't. When I persisted, Bob Healy, the executive vice president, descended from his Olympian suite to confront me in my humble cubicle. "What will the clients say?" he demanded. I told him I had never seen a client on our floor. He switched to the argument that the candidate would be unbearably uncomfortable. "Where will he eat?" When I told him where, he brought out the sharpest arrow in his quiver. "I'm the president of the New York Urban League!" Indeed he was. I refused to fill the opening, but unheroically, I didn't quit.*

The research department moved from crisis to crisis, sometimes working through the night to meet arbitrary and often unnecessary deadlines. There was a general sense of excitement. Something new could be expected each day. One of my projects was to produce a large series of trend charts on the growing economy. Harper had forecast what he named and indeed turned out to be "The Soaring Sixties." The charts were installed for potential clients' inspection on a vacant floor of McCann's new headquarters building. (Foreseeing expansion, Harper leased far more space than was immediately needed.)

One of my responsibilities at the agency was media research. We did no original studies but monitored and evaluated those made by individual periodicals and broadcasting organizations. This required close coordination with the agency's media department, which did the actual planning and buying of advertising schedules. On the broadcast side, the task required a feverish negotiation of rates, which were flexible, to say the least.

McCann's media director, Bill Decker, trembled in a perpetual state of unwarranted high anxiety. His acolytes were equally Dickensian characters. The purchase of different media was handled by specialists. The principal time buyer, Thaddeus Kelly, kept in his head an encyclopedic catalog of radio and television schedules and ratings, which he cited in order to whittle prices

---

*Several years later, when Lionel C. Barrow, Jr., joined me at the Bureau of Advertising, he became, as far as I know, the first black professional employed in a major advertising organization. He later became the dean of the journalism school at Howard University.

down to their bare minimum. The buyers of print, with less bargaining room, generally accepted publications' readership claims as the literal truth. After all, they needed to cite statistics to justify the plans they prepared for clients.

Some of our original research was undertaken to help in the selection of advertising themes and to evaluate alternative ad headlines or plots for radio and television commercials. Harper's wife, Virginia, who had worked with him in the research department, had devised a procedure for testing prototype ads. This "Relative Sales Conviction Test" was heavily touted for its predictive infallibility in every presentation to a prospective client. The test employed a battery of questions, along the lines of "Which of these ads most makes you feel like buying?" The answers were weighted by a formula so secret that it was considered to be endowed with magical powers.

The section of McCann's research department that tested radio and television commercials was headed by William Millard, an always-worried-looking Texan whom Lazarsfeld had earlier sent to study radio listening in the Middle East, on behalf of the Voice of America. One of the project directors was Frank Orenstein, who had previously been employed at the Department of State, investigating whether foreign visitors they had brought over to taste the American Way of Life really learned to like it. (He later was my colleague at the Bureau of Advertising, where he was research director.) Orenstein had a breezy wit, a marvelous knack for staying out of trouble, great skill as a survey analyst, and a delightful writing style. He retired to churn forth a series of polished mystery novels, in which an ad agency research director was the heroic sleuth and the assorted suspects were thinly masked former colleagues.

Also evaluating commercials was a former associate of Bob Bower's in Washington—Harold Mendelsohn, roly-poly, droll, and jolly. Mendelsohn commuted to Manhattan from a remote residential area in Queens near Idlewild (now John F. Kennedy) airport. He was undecided about accepting a professorship at the University of Denver because it was so far away. I told him that he was halfway there already; he said this convinced him. When AAPOR held its annual meeting at the Claremont Hotel near Berkeley, the facilities were shared with another convention, that of the American Simian Society. Mendelsohn claimed never to have recovered from the shock of getting into the elevator and finding himself face-to-face with a chimpanzee.

The study of how advertising works was stimulated by the postwar expansion of consumer marketing and of advertising budgets, especially after the emergence of television. Research that predicted the performance of individual advertisements had been practiced since the 1920s, and George Gallup's employment at the Young and Rubicam advertising agency (between 1932 and 1947) demonstrated its growing importance.

Gallup practiced advertising research at the same time he pursued his wider interests in opinion polling through the American Institute of Public Opinion, which he had founded in 1935. He followed the valuable practice of asking the same questions over and over, so that changes in public opinion could be accurately traced through time and related back to world events. He built a large international network of affiliates that used his name; thus it became synonymous with polling around the world. His opinion polls, reported in newspapers across the United States, were not a moneymaker, but they provided the priceless publicity that brought in commercial market research clients. Gallup's easygoing manner disguised his great energy and organizing ability.

Gallup was not alone in the ad-testing field. Copy tests had evolved to include the performance of "concepts" and themes, of print ad layouts and television commercials. Such research, like the related testing of consumer products, did not require the massive national samples conventionally employed in market surveys. This type of study generally went beyond asking people to make simple choices among different versions of the same ad or different versions of the same product, to open-ended questions about their reasons for liking or disliking what they saw or used.

Success in selling seems to correlate strongly with an individual's height, and this is also true in selling research, where many, though not all, of the individuals who have made the greatest mark have been of large stature. Horace Schwerin was one of the first to devise a procedure to test television commercials, both before and after they reached finished form. Schwerin was not merely tall, optimistic, and extroverted; he was a showman who spoke with powerful self-assurance. He combined the art of presenting data simply and clearly with a willingness to pass personal judgment on creative ideas and executions. In this he exemplified the attributes of many of the most renowned practitioners. Their skill lay, and still lies, not in their technical expertise or their ability to analyze the results of surveys but in their willingness to stick their necks out and tell the clients what they should do. In 2000, corporate executives whom the Advertising Research Foundation asked what they wanted from research overwhelmingly said they wanted to be told what to do! As with earlier generations, the validity of the advice they received seemed subordinate to the air of assurance with which it was uttered.

Reliance on subjective judgment rather than on evidence is particularly noticeable in those realms of research that involve the creation of messages—the selection of themes, the casting of commercials, the phrasing of copy, the choice of spokesmen, the management of their appearance.

Research techniques originally developed to study advertising appeals and product preferences came to be applied to political campaigning and to the law. In the early 1970s, Jay Schulman, a shaggy, black-bearded sociologist, who had been blackballed by the City University of New York for his aggressive anti-war activities, began to study public opinion about such widely publicized trials as those of the Berrigan brothers—priests who engaged in militant acts of civil disobedience.[5] Schulman used the findings to offer advice to the defendants' attorneys on the selection of jurors in the *voir-dire* process. Others followed, like Martin Herbst, an advertising media researcher skilled in profiling television audiences. This evolved into a substantial subspecialty of opinion research, in which jury consultants used their accumulated knowledge and insight, rather than original research, to assess what kinds of people were more or less likely to favor one side or the other in a particular case.

Similarly, in the domain of politics, consultants relied increasingly on their personal judgments rather than on direct investigation and evidence. It became standard procedure in significant races for candidates to undergo survey research on their name recognition, "image," and points of likability or weakness, and on the voter appeal of different themes and messages. More and more, under the pressure of time and budgets, this kind of original research has been supplemented or even bypassed in favor of straightforward advice backed only by the presumed know-how and authority of the adviser. Thus the trade of political consultancy, emerging from research, was taken over by a new breed of smooth operators, like President Bill Clinton's friend Dick Morris, who counseled him to take his vacation in Montana because this would sway "swing" (late-deciding) voters attracted to horseback-riding and the Marlboro Man.

The deadliest phrase in the advertising business was "The client wants. . . ." There were no appeals from this dread mandate. Harper sprang into action when the president of Nabisco, an important account, called to express his concern over a sudden drop in his Ritz brand's share of the dry cracker market on the West Coast. High-powered executives flew out to California to investigate the sudden shift in consumer preferences. The incriminating data were not just squiggles on a work sheet. They were embodied in a handsome, very official-looking bar chart that carried the name of A. C. Nielsen, the uncontested provider of supermarket sales statistics. We never did find out what had caused the squiggle, but it *was* a squiggle, not a real change in the brand's market position. Whatever had gone wrong in that inexplicable variation in the trend line had caused a lot of highly paid grown-ups to waste their time on a fool's errand.

This was an unusual case. Most market research on consumer activities and preferences was done at the client's request. Since such studies were not covered by the agency's 15 percent commission, they could be billed to the client.* This made research a profit center, so projects had to be dreamed up and sold. The successful market researcher, I learned, was good at selling—a skill not always joined to the ability to dream up ideas, write questionnaires, analyze and interpret data, and prepare readable reports.

At McCann-Erickson it was understood that employees would use only our clients' products. A colleague who was assigned to the Chesterfield cigarette account avoided a fiasco when he was observed opening a package of Lucky Strikes at a client meeting. He quickly explained that he was conducting a product taste test. I dutifully purchased a Plymouth, made by Chrysler, when the time came to trade in my Chevrolet. But I persisted in buying private labels of products that I knew to be identical to the higher-priced name brands. This got me into trouble with the assistant to the chairman of Schenley's, after he told me what a high proportion of their distillery production went to stores like Macy's that had their own private labels. "We just slap on their labels and ship them," he revealed. At a later point in the conversation he asked me what brand of blended whiskey I bought. When I foolishly said that I generally bought Macy's house brands, he became enraged and told me that he would fire any agency that didn't require its employees to use the client's products.

The advertising business lived in uncertainty. A McCann copywriter who started his own agency received a new business lead regarding a huge Japanese conglomerate that owned a large

---

*Harper even established a new subsidiary for this purpose, the Market Planning Corporation (later Marplan).

chewing gum company among its many enterprises. At the time, Japanese manufacturers were just beginning to enter the American market, and the chewing gum business was a promising opening into what might expand into a substantial account. An unsmiling senior executive of the company arrived at the office of the new agency to look around, accompanied by a hotshot young interpreter. The advertising man, after providing evidence of his agency's qualifications and accomplishments, offered a brief presentation on the size of the American chewing gum market, explaining that Wrigley's had 85 percent of the business and Chiclets most of the remainder. The Japanese executive, listening gravely to the interpreter's translation, kept nodding his head and finally broke forth into a ponderously delivered statement. It ran as follows: "I understand. Situation very difficult. Will take long time to establish position. First year, only 10 percent market share. Second year, 25 percent. Third year, number *one*!"

To extrapolate research findings one must be sure that the people interviewed accurately represent the population from which they are selected. The early arguments about quota and probability sampling centered on this point. In other words, quantification entails qualitative judgments. Published polls are now conventionally accompanied by a statement of statistical tolerances for a sample of the size that was employed. These "confidence levels" merely indicate the range of random variation that occurs 95 percent of the time, but news people and the public generally interpret them to express all the possible differences between the survey results and the true distribution of percentages among the sampled population. Statistical error is only one source of those differences. Faulty questionnaires, inadequate sampling procedures, poor interviewing, and mistakes in data processing provide even more reason to avoid taking survey findings as the literal truth.

I learned this lesson early when, at Standard Oil, I ordered a special set of tabulations from The Pulse, then a leading supplier of radio program ratings. The Pulse used the "roster recall" method: respondents were personally shown a list of programs for each time period in which they said they had been listening, and were asked to indicate which ones they had heard. When I examined the numbers, I discovered that there were twice as many women as men in the sample. The explanation was simple: most of the interviews were done during daytime hours, and most women of that era were housewives. Yet in the tabulation of ratings, every interview, male or female, was assigned equal weight, even though women's listening preferences were obviously different from men's. Such technicalities were not taken very seriously then. Each year The Pulse's founder, Sydney Roslow, a calm, soft-spoken psychologist, filled a hotel ballroom with the elite of the radio and advertising businesses for his presentation of a "Man [sic] of the Year" award.

A roster of program listings in personal interviews was also used in the earliest radio ratings service by Archibald Crossley. Crossley, who was small, rotund, and ever preoccupied, achieved recognition for his preelection surveys of voting intentions. But the flashiest figure in broadcast research was C. E. Hooper, a vigorous salesman whose Hooperatings were obtained by "coincidental" telephone calls that asked people to what programs, if any, they were listening. This method, with all its obvious procedural flaws, was synonymous with listening measurement during the 1930s. Albert Sindlinger, a pollster who also combined election surveys with media research, was one of the first to rely on the telephone to get information that went beyond coincidental broadcast ratings. Sindlinger, an old associate of Gallup's, sold his product with evangelical fervor. He was magnificently self-assured.

The triumphant survivor among these research pioneers was Arthur C. Nielsen, Sr. He had already established an enormously successful company that conducted drug and food store audits to measure consumption and brand market shares by checking invoices for goods received against actual counts of goods in stock. Nielsen had acquired the rights to what he called an "audimeter," a device that was attached to each stationary radio in a household and recorded the times of operation and the frequencies to which it was tuned. Both the radio and advertising industries came to regard the measurements obtained by this impersonal method as definitive. Nielsen was a brilliant organizer who built an empire through astute and meticulous generalship. A demonic tennis player, he looked schoolmasterish behind his wire-rimmed glasses. On sales calls he presented his data to clients in the form of ponderous bar charts, which showed all the percentages carried out to a precise-looking decimal point that disguised their extremely fuzzy origins. The charts were assembled on an easel, and Nielsen flipped the pages and called attention to the numbers with a pointer that he wielded like a magic wand. No one could dare question those numbers.

Advertising was often successful in getting the public to accept a brand, but it faced greater difficulty when it came up against traditions. The Corn Products Company was going nowhere with a brand of shortening it had introduced in Mexico. The vital ingredient in Mexican cuisine, it seemed, was lard. In the central markets of the towns I visited, large open vats of dirt-laced lard attracted swarms of flies and a procession of housewives, whose purchases were doled out with a wooden ladle and wrapped in old newspapers. The client's local manager shook his head in bewildered frustration. "Our product is sanitary; it's packaged nicely and in a standard weight." But, said the Mexicans, it lacked *sabor*. The solution didn't seem to require much research. The creative department advised the client to add lard flavoring and to have a large pig's head pictured on the package. This was done, but the product still didn't sell.

My former employer, Jersey Standard, was now a major client. When the agency launched a new campaign for Esso gasoline, we sought as always to find something new to say. The great creative minds interrogated representatives of the company about the characteristics of the same old gasoline. There were, it turned out, various chemicals added, besides lead, including one that reportedly had a cleansing effect in the engine. Of course, every other brand had the same cocktail of ingredients, but we gave this one a name, a name that sparkled with life and scored high in copy tests. "Vitane" was promoted for years.

Former Jersey associates took on a different and sometimes wary stance when I tried to sell them research projects. One proposal, which never came to fruition, was to study the receptivity of Western Europeans to the kind of centralized home heating that had long become almost universal in the United States. With the impetus of the Marshall Plan, the postwar recovery of Europe had greatly increased the number of motor vehicles on the roads. The oil companies had responded to the resulting demand for gasoline by increasing their capacity to refine crude oil. As the refineries "cracked" the raw product to produce light fuels, they were left with large quantities of heavier grades. In the United States these would have found their way into the market for home heating oil. In Europe such a market barely existed, since individual rooms were usually heated by coal stoves, charcoal burners, or wood-burning fireplaces. Central heating would be more comfortable, safe, and economical, but Europeans generally scoffed at the idea, sneered at what they considered the overheating of American houses, and preferred the spartan frigidity to which they had always been accustomed in the winter months.

The challenge was not merely to gain acceptance of a not-so-new invention but to change an ancient pattern of culture. To help formulate the right questions, and if possible even to suggest strategies, I organized a day-long discussion that included several Standard Oil executives, Herta Herzog, and an improbable combination of three outsiders: Margaret Mead, Charles Winick, and Leo Lowenthal (of whom I shall say more). Mead's reputation was already at its height, and no perturbing questions had yet been raised about the authenticity of her field work in the South Seas. She was no-nonsense but had lots of insights and ideas, on all of which she expounded at some length. (Evidently she found the day interesting, because soon afterward she readily agreed to speak at a session I chaired for the American Marketing Association. In introducing her, I was reminded of an answer Louis Wirth had once given to a student who asked him to explain the difference between sociology and anthropology. He said that there used to be a difference, with sociologists studying contemporary society and anthropologists studying primitive ones. There were, however, no primitive societies left to study, because Margaret Mead had visited them all. He paused and added, "With the result that they are no longer primitive." I suddenly remembered the afterthought while in the middle of telling this story and managed to stop myself from delivering the punch line. Mead took it as a compliment, which I meant it to be.)

Winick, then teaching at Syracuse University, was one of those rare social scientists who could claim to be not only an anthropologist *and* a sociologist, but a psychologist as well. He had been a military intelligence officer during World War II, remaining in the reserve through the cold war. His scholarly interests embraced the mass media, drug addiction, and the legal process. He had a wry wit, an air of constant surprise, an amazing memory, and an acquaintanceship with a broad range of subjects and people.

The Standard Oil executives sat stolidly through this imaginative discussion, which evidently convinced them that their imposing task went well beyond the preparation of a good advertising campaign. Lowenthal even evoked the brothers Grimm as he expatiated on the importance of the glowing hearth as an archetypal symbol of warm ties to home and family. I was impressed by how many good ideas could come forth through the interplay of intelligent conversation on a serious topic—and yet of how necessary it was to put those ideas to some kind of empirical test.

This problem-solving exercise had only a superficial resemblance to the kind of group interviewing that takes place when small numbers of people are asked about their experiences with consumer products or their reactions to political candidates. In these cases the purpose is to gain insight into the public's attitudes. In proper practice this means that the right questions can later be asked of a true sampling of the population. In bad and more common practice, what the atypical members of "focus groups" say is taken literally, as universal.

International research was one of my responsibilities at McCann-Erickson. (I was told that this was because I spoke Spanish; I retorted that I also knew shorthand but didn't expect to be used as a secretary.) The work required frequent travel throughout Latin America, where most of the surveys were confined to urban areas, and often to the middle and upper classes. Social position was commonly defined, as it had been in the United States in the 1930s, by the designations A, B, C, and D. This simplistic practice, arising from the necessities of quota sampling, continues to this day.

My trips to Latin America usually were on specific projects but demanded considerable counseling, hand-holding, and client contact work that went well beyond research.

In the mid-1950s, Bogotá was not yet the vast metropolis it has become, and its streets were safe for the foreign visitor. Heading McCann's office was a courtly Venezuelan of German antecedents who snapped his heels on being introduced and pronounced himself "Christian Hamann, *á sus órdenes!*" (at your orders). The titular head of the company was an elderly (or so I perceived him) Colombian gentleman of patrician lineage, Joaquín Samper, who bore a striking resemblance to Don Quixote. Don Joaquín had been a cabinet minister and was a master of genial small talk, though devoid of either experience or aptitude for the advertising business. He had been recruited because of what were thought to be his excellent connections with the political and business elite. His elegant wife, Nina, was the driving force in his household, but her remarkable wiles could not compensate for his ineptitude, and he was reluctantly fired by Art Grimes, who ran the international division. When this happened she wrote asking me to intervene with Marion Harper. (Joaquín had already sent off a long document detailing the injustices that had been done to him.) He was shown no mercy.

The country had one television station, which operated in only one studio with a single camera. A quiz show featuring a panel of distinguished citizens was followed by a program that provided entertainment by reviewing the hard-luck stories of a selection of especially pitiable charity cases. Between shows the camera turned to the wall to film a succession of still commercial messages and announcements, while the learned doctors rushed out of the single exit to make way for large families of barefoot Indians simultaneously rushing in to do their stint.

Although Bogotá was calm, except at the bullring on Sundays, much of Colombia was being devastated by the endless civil war known as *La Violencia*, which had originated in the political struggles between Liberals and Conservatives and had degenerated into mere banditry. The countryside was bristling with troops. They stopped us in a remote stretch of the Cauca Valley when I took a long bus ride from Bogotá to Cali, and made all of the passengers get off for a weapons search. One of the peasants among my fellow travelers tried to lighten matters by saying, "*Somos todos pacíficos aquí*" (We're all pacific [peaceful] here). A soldier replied grimly. "*Pero son los atlánticos que buscamos!*" (But we're looking for the atlantics).

Cali had not yet become the capital of the drug trade, but it was already a major manufacturing center and home for the head offices of many of the international companies that were our principal clients. I was briefed on the intricacies of Latin American economics by an imposing Swiss executive who ran Nestlé's Colombian operations and had wide experience throughout the hemisphere. He held up Cuba as a model and contrasted the attitude, lifestyle, and wages of a Havana taxi driver with those of his Colombian counterpart. Batista's Cuba understood the dynamic force of capitalism, he said. It was making enormous strides toward developing a modern consumer economy. (This stimulating conversation occurred about two years before Castro and his small band of guerrillas came down from the Sierra Maestra.)

One day when I was preparing to make a presentation, a young, recently hired office boy showed some initiative in setting things up. Stefan Riess, the manager of the Cali office, gave him a raise on the spot, which impressed me. Stefan was a good manager, a European sophisticate stuck in a provincial backwater with no fellow spirits for company and no connections to the life he should have led. He was short, stocky, and bald, with a squared-off brown brush of a mustache, and spoke excellent English with a German accent. His mother lived on the Upper West Side of Manhattan, and I figured out that he was a German Jew who had managed to make his way to Colombia at the outset of the war. He knew that I knew this, though I never alluded to it. Years later he told me that I was the only person who knew his secret. He identified himself to the Colombians as a German. Neither his wife nor his children ever knew any more than that about his origins.

The woman whom Stefan married (some years after my regular visits to Colombia ended) was a tall dark beauty with long ruby-red fingernails and a languid air. She was one of two Leonoras who worked as secretaries in McCann's office. Their work was a sign of emancipation from their upper-crust backgrounds. Poor Colombian women worked out of necessity; middle-class wives tended house; only those few of the rich whose social status was secure were self-confident enough to pursue careers. On Sundays, after Mass, the two Leonoras could be found lounging beside the pool at one of the "Countries," the suburban tennis and swim clubs around which the social life of Bogotá's elite revolved. The other Leonora was not quite as pretty as Stefan's, but she was bright and outgoing, and was promoted (by Stefan) to the rank of account executive. A decade passed, and I encountered her, out of any context with Colombia or McCann, at a New

York party. She was wearing expensive jewelry and a coat made of jaguar skins. She was now, according to gossip, the mistress of an older married tycoon, who kept her in a Miami apartment.

In the 1950s television was already well established in the United States, but it was just being introduced in Cuba. Havana was an ideal place to recapture the sense of what people did with their evenings before TV. I roamed through its neighborhoods, peering at lighted living rooms through their wide-open windows. Many people sat listening to popular music on the radio. Some engaged in conversation or played cards. But most of them were just sitting, doing nothing. Only a few years later, television had taken over, and black-and-white sets were flickering beyond every window. Gaspar Pumarejo, the amply proportioned host of a program called "*Hogar* (Home) *Club*," held housewives spellbound every morning as he gave away fabulous prizes.

Bizarre research practices were taken for granted in Cuba. A company could buy a handsome plaque attesting to its high standing before "The Court of Public Opinion" without the bothersome necessity of conducting a survey to support its claim.

Havana in the 1950s was a popular American tourist destination. The glittering Tropicana nightclub produced spectacular nonstop shows that outdid anything in Las Vegas. Off the palm-bedecked first-floor corridor of the Hotel Nacional, the casino's slot machines clattered continuously, but the Mafiosi who ran them were invisible. At the racetrack the gamblers looked up from the roulette tables only briefly to eye the winners of the last race and the changing odds on the next. At the Círculo Vasco on Sunday afternoons, a well-dressed crowd danced slow, traditional Spanish sarabandes. I was taken there by McCann's main man in Havana, Raúl Barrios. Barrios had a narrow black mustache and thinning slick black hair. Dapper and highly convivial, he dispensed generous tips from an enormous stack of peso notes. Like everyone else I knew in Havana, he longed for the end of the corrupt Batista regime. As the political situation grew tense and as the tourists disappeared, Raúl conspiratorially showed me how on the pages of the Caribbean's leading magazine, *Bohemia*, coded colors appeared each month to signal support for Fidel Castro, still holed up in the eastern mountains.

Barrios accompanied me on a visit to the office of one of Cuba's richest men, Julio Lobo, who reportedly controlled the world's sugar market. Lobo's sanctum was sumptuous; on its walls were a number of portrait paintings by Joshua Reynolds and his contemporaries. The tycoon remained phlegmatic while an associate explained why we had been summoned. He was concerned about his "image," which had suffered from unfavorable publicity in *Time* and other American publications. He wanted McCann's public relations subsidiary to design a campaign to burnish his reputation. I asked whether Señor Lobo had any public-spirited or charitable endeavors that might be worth publicizing. Lobo went blank. After a moment's hesitation, the associate however spoke up. "He has a very large collection of Napoleoniana."*

Without Barrios's prior knowledge or approval, McCann-Erickson had taken on the account of promoting Cuban tourism, which was, understandably, languishing as the country became more unsettled. The job was entrusted to Bill Bray, a breezy old Latin American hand, born in Chile of an American mother and a British father. Bray was flawlessly trilingual—in Spanish, American, and British English. His eyes glittered as he explained that he always added at least a 15 percent personal commission to his expense statements.

I was shocked to find that Harper was tying the agency to the discredited Batista government. I learned, however, that he had been asked to do so by the U.S. State Department. Frank Kenyon, a kind little elderly gentleman who was one of Harper's lightning-quick personnel acquisitions, explained to me in hushed tones that Fidel and Raúl Castro were Communists. I

---

*Lobo's surreptitious financial support of Castro went unrewarded. He fled Cuba soon after the revolution.

found this preposterous. The charge was less difficult to believe when I returned to Cuba on a private visit in 1959, just before the break in diplomatic relations, and saw one of Fidel's endless harangues on TV.* (Hitler at least had known when to stop.) Castro was still having a honeymoon with the Cuban public, and his bearded, fatigue-clad warriors (or those who masqueraded as such) were everybody's heroes.

McCann's principal Venezuelan client was Jersey Standard's subsidiary, the Creole Petroleum Corporation. Its presence occasioned constant leftist and nationalist agitation. Responding to political pressures, Creole put its advertising account (which McCann had had from the start) up for review. Our principal rival was a locally owned agency whose executives had not so subtly manifested their patriotic credentials by appearing before the Creole board in a traditional costume, the *liki liki*. (This was a kind of Nehru jacket well before its brief appearance on the international fashion scene.) I flew down from New York with my merry associate David Thomas to make the case for McCann. We jokingly toyed with the idea of donning *liki likis* ourselves, but I did the next best thing, delivering my presentation in Spanish to the directors, who were all Americans except for a token Venezuelan or two. We kept the account. (Years afterward, Creole was taken over by the government, with disastrous consequences for its efficiency and productivity.)

Our Caracas office was largely staffed by expatriates from other Spanish-speaking countries. The manager was a Spanish Republican soldier who had managed to make his way to South America after Franco's victory. Incongruously, Don Antonio enjoyed all the perquisites of his new life to the full. He dressed in

---

*Viewers were still following his every word, but not every Communist dictator had Castro's showmanship. In the mid-1980s I stopped in a Bucharest department store to watch Nicolae Ceausescu address his Parliament in wooden style and at interminable length. None of the hundreds of shoppers paid the slightest attention.

well-tailored double-breasted suits and drove about town in an enormous silver Lincoln.

The creative director was an Argentine poet of fine sensibility and extremely doleful appearance. He had left his family in Buenos Aires for what he undoubtedly had thought of as a lucrative but brief diversion from his literary career, but found it impossible to extricate himself from this dreary lotusland of perpetual spring. He wrote much advertising copy but no more poems and died very young.

In Argentina, McCann's research operation consisted of a youthful trio who were especially welcome to new ideas and introduced me to the tango bars that then still enlivened the capital. Two of these researchers, Miguel Gorfinkiel and Carmen Zayuelas, had been recently married. Miguel, a psychologist, chuckled delightedly over orthodox psychoanalytic interpretations of the data he collected about consumer preferences. He spoke Spanish with a slight Polish-Jewish accent, was animated, rumpled, and several inches shorter than his slender, dark-haired wife.

Gorfinkiel had an entrepreneurial streak and decided to start a research company of his own, with Carmen as his partner. Since his special interest was in the popular field of motivational research, he came to New York to meet with Ernest Dichter, who offered him the franchise of using his name in return for a 50 percent share in the company's profits. I suggested that instead he should see Solomon Dutka, who, with Politz's former associate, Lester Frankel, had set up Audits and Surveys, a company that checked the movement of merchandise through retail stores and also conducted consumer surveys.* Gorfinkiel struck a deal with Dutka and went back with the capital to begin store auditing and a television rating service. He was a great success, establishing companies in Brazil and Peru.

As the terrorizing colonels tightened their grip on Argentina,

---

*In the small world department, they had been bankrolled in their new venture by Elmo Roper.

all social scientists, especially psychologists, were suspect, and
many began to disappear, dropped from military airplanes into
the sea. Miguel left Carmen in charge in Buenos Aires and
moved to São Paulo to run the flourishing Brazilian company.
There he lived like a magnate in a gigantic apartment overlooking the brightly lit racetrack from a great height. He had several
refrigerators, one stuffed entirely with jeroboams of Coca-Cola.
On weekends he retreated to a well-staffed *fazenda* in the country. His firm's ratings dominated Brazil's television world until
the insatiable A. C. Nielsen Company arrived on the scene.

Suddenly Miguel's empire collapsed. The usually commu-
nicative Dutka only shook his head sadly when asked what had
happened. Gorfinkiel's name vanished from telephone directo-
ries in São Paulo, Rio, and Buenos Aires, where Carmen's company continued to flourish.

As one of his extracurricular interests, Harper was on the advisory board to the newly established U.S. Information Agency.
(USIA replaced the International Information Agency, which had
been part of the State Department.*) Harper's connections to USIA
may have come about as a result of McCann-Erickson's work for
political candidates, starting with Nelson Rockefeller.

In 1956, McCann-Erickson was one of the agencies supporting the Goldwater presidential campaign, whose vice-
presidential candidate was a conservative upstate New York
Republican congressman, William Miller. Coming back from a
late dinner to my hotel in a gritty Midwestern industrial city, I
came upon Miller returning from the last campaign rally of the
day. He trudged along, hunched over, a picture of fatigue and de-
spondency. Six paces behind, sagging under the weight of an
oversized dispatch case, came the ex-trainee assigned as the ex-

---

*It brought together several organizations that had formerly operated sepa-
rately: the overseas libraries operated by the U.S. Information Service, the publications programs of the International Information Agency, the Voice of America, and
the State Department's exchange-of-persons program.

ecutive on the account, looking equally glum. Not a word passed between them.

Throughout the past half-century, as television commercials have become the most visible element in political campaigns, the uncontested impression has been created that advertising techniques can readily be transferred from the sale of goods and services to the promotion of personalities, causes, and ideas. Not by accident, J. Walter Thompson's H. R. Haldeman became Richard Nixon's confidant and criminal accomplice in the Watergate cover-up. Agency heads who have served successful candidates have received ambassadorships (Young and Rubicam's Edward Ney as the first Bush's ambassador to Canada, Backer Spielvogel Bates's Carl Spielvogel* as Clinton's ambassador to Slovakia).

It was always assumed that Harper had political ambitions, but pursuing an international agenda also fitted well with his goal of making the company truly global. Congress was under the illusion at that time (as often since) that problems of international political communication could be dealt with best by harnessing the talents of America's advertising and public relations professionals.

The notion that ideological propaganda could be propagated by the same rules that govern the promotion of toothpaste and deodorants seemed absurd to me (and still does). Yet through the years, advertising executives have been given key positions in directing American propaganda. Several have headed the Voice of America, and in 2001 Ogilvy and Mather's former chairman, Charlotte Beers, was named assistant secretary of state in charge of worldwide information activities. She said, "I'd be happier if my real enemy was dandruff."

In 1952, at Harper's behest, the USIA had assigned McCann-Erickson to prepare a series of fourteen newspaper ads and a booklet intended to convert war-ravaged Greece into a bastion of

---

*A former advertising reporter for the *New York Times*, Spielvogel had been recruited by Harper. He became a powerful hirer and firer of Interpublic executives and then turned on his benefactor when the time came to depose him.

the Free World. (Greece had just suffered through a fierce civil war in which the American-supported side had defeated the Soviet-backed ELAS guerrillas.) The size and styling of the ads made them stand out in the very thin newspapers of Salonica, the city selected for a test. The four dailies claimed a combined total daily circulation of only about fifty thousand. But each copy reached a number of people as a result of pass-along readership; some paid the news vendor a small sum just to look at the paper.

The ads aimed to create or reinforce the conviction that the United States and Greece had common ideals embodied in the Universal Declaration of Human Rights. Citizens' rights were visualized with large photographs as "the rights of children." A thirty-two-page booklet, "The March of Freedom," showed significant stages in the development of human rights. Like the ads, it contained no direct references to communism.

Harper had committed the agency to evaluate the effects of this advertising. Although there was an obvious conflict of interest in having an organization pass judgment on its own handiwork, the practice was not uncommon then in the advertising business. The study was planned by Herta Herzog and McCann's research director, Don Armstrong, a dashing, hardworking, chain-smoking fellow who had been a conscientious objector in World War II. Don was, as the expression went, "good with clients." Lazarsfeld's influence was apparent in the design of the research, with its experimental features and its use of a panel (involving repeated interviews with the same people).

The research was organized and timed as an integral part of the campaign itself. The objectives were to determine (1) whether or not the ads attracted the attention of a wide popular audience; (2) what kinds of people they reached; (3) what the readers thought of them; (4) what kinds of information they conveyed; and (5) what political attitudes they modified, if any.

A cross section of adults in Salonica was interviewed shortly before and again immediately after the advertisements appeared. To overcome any possible "panel effect" (the influence of the interviews in sensitizing readers to the subject), the second wave of interviews (after the ad campaign) was conducted not only with the *same* people as in the original sample, but also with *another* parallel cross section of the population who had not been interviewed previously.

Changes in opinion between the first and second surveys could have occurred quite independently of the advertising campaign, through the impact of world events or of political developments in Greece.* For example, attitudes toward the United States could have grown more favorable between the first and second wave of the study because opinion throughout the country had generally improved rather than because of the ad campaign. Or opinion could have remained about the same in Salonica while it became less favorable elsewhere in Greece. (That is, the ads may have produced their effect not by improving attitudes but by preventing a decline that was evident elsewhere.)

To take these possibilities into account, a simultaneous before-after survey had to be run in *another* Greek city in which no advertising or information campaign had been conducted. In the control city, Patras, two identical random samples of people were interviewed in two waves corresponding to those of the Salonica survey. The study was completed with a special sample of persons in Salonica who had asked for the booklet. Altogether, 2,238 interviews were conducted.

The field work in Greece had been entrusted to a wild-eyed and scatterbrained character, Bill Reynolds, recently hired from another agency. He came back with a large stack of completed interviews which were duly coded and translated into punch cards for data processing. Apparently his adventures in postwar Greece had been less than triumphant, and he soon left the scene.

---

*During this period, elections were held both in Greece and in the United States, truce negotiations were bogged down in the Korean War, and the Soviet bloc continued to spar with the West in the UN General Assembly.

When I looked at the preliminary tabulations, it was clear that the field staff had met the same problem as The Pulse: the interviews were disproportionately with women, even though men were the primary political target. To compensate for this I did two separate sets of tabulations, one for each sex, within the limits of an already complex sampling design, and then used the averages in my analysis and presentation of the results. Of course the whole project could have been junked. But that would have abandoned another demonstration of the difficulty of assessing the effects of mass communication!

MEASURING THE EFFECTIVENESS OF AN OVERSEAS INFORMATION CAMPAIGN: A CASE HISTORY (1953)[6]

Questions about political convictions and sympathies could not be raised directly, but Greeks thought communism had grown because of economic conditions rather than because of Russian influence. The United States was the most popular and respected nation while the Soviet Union was widely criticized and disliked; its power was generally believed to be on the wane. The key right of citizens in a free country was considered to be freedom of opinion and expression. The Universal Declaration of Human Rights was unknown to all but a tiny minority.

The ads were seen by a large proportion of the reading public.* For a good many of those who saw them, attention was drawn from the *ultimate* point (U.S.-Greek unity in support of universal human rights) to the *immediate* appeal—children's rights. The ads were liked precisely because their readers accepted them at face value: they were *not* thought

---

*Their readership was estimated in two ways: (1) by asking respondents directly how many ads they had seen, and (2) by taking them through the ads one by one.

of as propaganda serving a selfish interest. Their purpose was seen in their literal message rather than with any sophisticated inferences about their underlying political objectives.

A majority of those who saw the ads had the impression of having been influenced (whether or not they actually were). Since attitudes were so predominantly favorable to begin with, the major potential for change was on the part of a small minority of critics.

The study design made it possible to look for effects in three distinct ways: (1) by comparing results before and after, for the test and control cities; (2) by comparing results, before and after, for exposed and unexposed groups within the test city; and (3) by internal analysis of changes within the test city panel.

Opinion did not significantly shift in either city in the proportions who felt very favorably toward the U.S., or thought that: the U.S. was interested in dominating Greece; Russia was the country most guilty of meddling in Greek affairs; the U.S. was doing all it could to help Greece; or communism was mainly caused by economic conditions.

Apparently as the result of attitude trends throughout Greece, opinions changed the same way in *both* Salonica and Patras in the proportions who felt that the U.S. was sincerely concerned with the freedom of its citizens, and that the U.S. would raise its following among nations within the next ten years while Russia would decrease its following.

In both cities there was an increase in the percentage mentioning free elections among the rights and freedoms that citizens enjoy in a democracy. This was understandable in the light of the interest generated by the election campaigns.

Although there was no change in either city in the proportion who said the U.S. was sincerely interested in keeping Greece free and independent, the proportion able to support this point of view

with *reasons* increased enormously in Salonica while
it remained the same in Patras.

Opinions underwent only slight changes in
Salonica, compared with Patras, while *knowledge* of
the subjects stressed in the ads underwent major
increases. Were these changes due to the direct
influence of the campaign, or did they occur
independently?

The greater the exposure to the ads in
Salonica, the more familiar respondents at every
social level were with the rights of citizens in a
democracy. The campaign tended to select for its
audience people who were more articulate and
already predisposed to be favorable toward its
objectives. Among those who at the start believed
that Greece's attitude mattered a great deal in
shaping international events, more subsequently
read the ads or the booklet.

Of those who claimed to have heard of the
Declaration of Human Rights on the first wave of
interviews, only a minority were actually able to
explain what it was. These few became a very highly
exposed group.

Did exposure *change* information or attitudes?
The less the exposure, the less favorable the
original attitude. Among those who had read the ads
or the booklet, a smaller percentage (about a
third) shifted opinion than among those who were
less exposed (about half).

In spite of the fairly large fluctuation of
opinion within the panel, shifts in one direction
canceled out shifts in the other direction—except
in the case of those who were completely unexposed.
This group was less favorable in the postcampaign
survey, suggesting that exposure to the campaign
offset a generally unfavorable trend.

Readers accepted the ads and the booklet at
face value, as a genuine attempt to inform people
about rights and freedoms, rather than to preach at
them or to change their views. The fact that the
ads and the booklet were not directly perceived as
"propaganda" is as important as the fact that the

motives behind them were seen as worthwhile or
disinterested.

In Salonica the campaign increased public
knowledge of the subject on which it was focused,
the Declaration of Human Rights, and raised
familiarity with democratic rights and freedoms.
The gain was greatest among those who were most
highly exposed, and it took place among those
exposed within every element of the population. No
increase in knowledge took place in the control
city, Patras.

It is easier to convey information than to
change attitudes. There was only a small residue of
individuals with a neutral, suspicious, or critical
view of the United States who might have been
considered primary targets, but they were harder
than average to reach through conventional
channels.

Although no change due to the campaign took
place in fundamental attitudes, a *simpler* study
design might have suggested major shifts on a
number of points. In some cases opinions became
more favorable in Salonica, but also became more
favorable in Patras. On the second wave in
Salonica, the exposed were more favorable than the
nonexposed, but the same individuals were also more
favorable to begin with.

Only one facet of opinion appears to have been
influenced as the direct result of the campaign: it
made people better able to give reasons in support
of their existing conviction that the United States
wanted Greece to remain free and independent. This
demonstrates how the campaign's effects in
conveying information may have been translated into
attitudes. The campaign confirmed already favorable
opinion by giving it a supporting argument.

Changes in public opinion come about slowly,
and international propaganda always functions
within the context of world events. Apart from
political acts, which may have an immediate effect,
attempts to influence opinion through words and
images must be carried on consistently and over a

```
period of time before any major shifts are
detectable.
```

I was skeptical of the underlying assumption in the Greek advertising campaign: that ideological persuasion was essentially no
different from any other kind. (Nearly twenty years later, in the
early 1970s, I was horrified when Charles Ramond, the very
bright editor of the *Journal of Advertising Research*, just returned
from a whirlwind trip to Saigon, gave a speech on "The Vietnam
War as a Marketing Problem." And forty years later, after the col-
lapse of the Soviet Union, I was equally horrified to see the enormous banner that the Freedom Forum Foundation had strung up
in Red Square on the façade of the State History Museum, notorious for its falsified photographs of the Revolution. Its message, of
equal magnitude in Russian and English: "Freedom Works!")

If clever ads could heighten awareness of a brand name and
its estimable properties, why couldn't they also convert believers
in the coming triumph of the proletariat to acolytes of Free Enterprise and the American Way of Life? Because consumer product
claims involve no deep-seated commitments, while political beliefs, like those of religion, express an individual's identity and
are embedded in emotional attachments to family, friends, and
the surrounding culture. The difficulty of surmounting these attachments is illustrated by the irrational persistence in Eastern
Europe of strong support for leaders and parties originally imposed by Soviet arms.

To get people to change their impressions of the United
States demanded that they be made to think and talk among
themselves. This might come about as a result of American government actions on the world stage. It might stem from the em-
pathic attraction of an American spokesman with the authority
and personal appeal of John F. Kennedy. But it seemed unlikely
to me that a series of informational advertisements could speak
more loudly and convincingly than the innumerable subtle messages disseminated through American films and consumer products—both attractive and repellent to many.

Harper was a member of the USIA's advisory committee on research, headed by Wilbur L. Schramm, dean of the journalism school at the University of Illinois. Schramm was a gifted novelist and journalist who had acquired broader interests in the study of mass communication and its effects. He was a prodigious and productive worker. Bill stammered, but his sweet and diffident manner generated good feelings in others.

The committee had determined that a proper program of research for the USIA should start with fundamentals, first by determining what assumptions underlay the organization's operations, and second by assembling and distilling available knowledge about effective communications. When the two were put together, the committee believed, mistaken assumptions could be corrected and assumptions unsupported by evidence could be tested. Schramm agreed to produce the desired compendium of all human wisdom, which he eventually published as an academic text.[7] Harper acquired for McCann-Erickson the contract to study the assumptions, and I was assigned to carry it out.

President Eisenhower had appointed as director of the USIA Theodore Streibert, a large, friendly advertising salesman who had been president of a waning radio network, the Mutual Broadcasting System. (Streibert was out of his depth and disappeared before my study was completed.) At this time Senator McCarthy was at the height of his power, directing his simulated rage particularly at the State Department and the Information Agency. He had forced the resignation of the agency's highly able and dedicated associate director, Reed Harris, who had signed some of the wrong petitions in his days as a student leader.

Since its wartime beginnings as an arm of the Office of War Information, the Voice of America had been located in New York, in rambling offices near Columbus Circle. The Voice's newly appointed director was amiable, white-haired Leonard Carlson, whom Harper had seconded from his position as the head of McCann's broadcasting department, where he oversaw the production of commercials. As part of my preliminary reconnoitering, I attended a meeting that Carlson had called of the Voice's language section chiefs. Hands quivering, he delivered a written talk bravely asserting his intention to defend their integrity against any political onslaughts. This evoked no particular enthusiasm from his blasé subordinates, many of whom continued to read their newspapers while he spoke.

The Voice's 150-person research department was almost an extension of Lazarsfeld's Columbia Bureau of Applied Social Research. The Voice's research director was Leo Lowenthal; the associate director was another Bureau alumna, Marjorie Fiske, whom Lowenthal eventually married.

Urbane, erudite, subtle-minded, and witty, exuding a world-weary irony, Lowenthal suffered no fools gladly and wielded a razor-sharp critical scalpel. After a stint in the kaiser's army, he had been the youngest staff member of the University of Frankfurt's *Institut für Sozialforschung* (Institute for Social Research), where he had written scintillating essays on the sociology of literature. When Hitler rose to power, Leo abandoned his ten-thousand-volume library and fled to America, along with Max Horkheimer, Theodor Adorno, and other luminaries of neo-Marxist critical theory. At the Columbia Bureau he studied fascist propaganda themes for the OWI and was hired to work at the Voice.

Under his guidance the Voice's research examined foreign radio listening and reading in relation to the social, political, and cultural conditions of the countries that were being addressed. The research combined a respect for scientific objectivity with a practical concern for how program producers would use the information to conduct propaganda in the most bitter years of the cold war. One of McCarthy's most zealous staff members, William F. Buckley, Jr., investigated Lowenthal but found no subversive taint. In 1968, as a professor at Berkeley, Lowenthal defended the Free Speech Movement and provided his vacation home in Carmel Valley as a hideaway for Herbert Marcuse when that guru of the New Left was being hounded by the press.

While the Voice's research program was long established and ambitious in scope, USIA was just in the process of setting up a research department. The director was Ben Gedalecia, a re-treaded journalist who had switched to research at the OWI and briefly worked for the newly established ABC radio network.* From his relatively modest quarters in Washington, Gedalecia regarded Lowenthal's empire with envy, though this empire later disintegrated when the Voice was moved to Washington.

My interviewing for the "assumption" study (as it was called by all, with guffaws about its theological overtones) required frequent travel to Washington. I juggled this with my regular routine at McCann-Erickson, where we were required to fill out time sheets, assigning our hours to specific accounts. To avoid exceeding the limit set by McCann's modest $10,000 contract with USIA, I charged my time in Robin Hood style to big clients whose account executives would never notice.

The assignment required security clearance, which, in the McCarthy era, was especially stringent, if not paranoid. I chose to carry over my "Secret" clearance from the Korean War at the lower "Confidential" level rather than go through a time-consuming review of all my youthful acquaintanceships.

As in Aruba, I was struck by the readiness with which people opened up in conversation about their work and its frustrations, even when I was copying down what they said in shorthand. The only uncooperative informant, among the 142 I talked to at length, was Andrew Berding, then a policy officer, later an assistant secretary of state. He evidently thought the entire exercise was a waste of time.

Perhaps it was. Although Harper claimed he had read "every fucking word" of my six-volume report, his interests turned elsewhere. The Schramm Committee dissolved when a new director took over the USIA. The report, with its Confidential designation, languished in the USIA's files. According to Leo Crespi, a later re-

---

*Gedalecia's second-in-command, Melvin Goldberg, also an old OWI hand, was to become one of television research's pioneers at the DuMont Network and research director of the National Association of Broadcasters. He was yet another student of Lazarsfeld's. Gedalecia cultivated his relationship with Harper and became research director of the BBDO advertising agency.

search director there, it contained too much material that exposed the weaknesses of the American propaganda effort.

Of course it was precisely the Schramm Committee's objective to identify those shortcomings, to clarify contradictions in
philosophy and practice. The librarians' aim in life was to lead
the world's less fortunate to good books; the Russian exiles at the
Voice were out to overthrow the Soviet tyranny. As I learned, the
theory of propaganda could not be considered separate from its
practice. The grievances, antagonisms, and power politics of the
staff were infused into the content of what they sent out.

527147
693604
411082
354755
102986

BEAUTY AND THE BEASTS

■ Sooner or later, all communications research, whether on great matters (like America's struggle to "win hearts and minds") or minor ones (like Jersey Standard's mailings to educators) came down to the evaluation of what was achieved.

In the psychological laboratory, an experimenter can trace how communications of one kind or another register with the audience and how long their effects last. It is a different and more difficult matter to track awareness of the news or responses to it. Survey analysts typically work over their data to capture the details of a particular historical moment. Interpretations of the evidence must be tempered by awareness that the measurements reflect a fleeting combination of events that can never be exactly duplicated at another point in time. It is lucky if the same questions can be repeated to the same population after an interval. The analysis of opinion trends is preoccupied with understanding patterns of influence, with the reasons for change in the public's "definition of the situation."

Even in the heat of a major election campaign, when polls succeed each other thick and fast, it is rarely possible to reason back, with acceptable validity, from specific effects to specific causes. Too many complex interacting forces are generally at work to blur the exact relationship of cause and effect, especially when weeks or even months pass between one wave of interviews and the next—as they did until fairly recently.

The study of the USIA's information campaign in Greece illustrates the problem of measuring the impact of propaganda on advertising amidst the normal tumult of the marketplace. In the 1950s the task was slow and time-consuming. Half a century later, Internet surveys (of unrepresentative samples) are increasingly being used (as telephone surveys have been for many years) to capture the public's immediate reactions to presidential speeches and debates as well as to breaking news events. The feedback can be instantaneous.

The 1959 Congressional hearings on the rigging of TV quiz shows presented an unusual opportunity to trace the development of public opinion in response to an ongoing news event. By that time I had left McCann-Erickson to become the first market research director of Revlon, whose corporate history was closely linked to the quiz show phenomenon.

Revlon's president, Charles Revson, was one of three brothers who began their business as itinerant peddlers of lipsticks and nail polish and steadily expanded into all aspects of the cosmetics business. Charles, the creative force, had an uncanny sensitivity to feminine tastes in a market that was as volatile as the fashion industry of which he fancied himself a part. He had an eye for the most gorgeous models and an ear for product names like "Ultima" and "Fire and Ice" that captured attention and evoked fantasy. He built the company ruthlessly, buying out his brothers in the process.

Charles ("Mr. Charles" to the rank and file) flashed a vulpine smirk. He was a perfectionist who demanded long hours of his executives and asked them to spend their Saturdays prowling around competitors' counters in department stores. To those who said they needed their weekends to mow the lawn, he retorted that they would soon be making so much money that they could hire platoons of gardeners to handle such menial tasks. He favored a dress code that mirrored his own: black or grey suits, black shoes, white (preferably white-on-white) shirts, chunky cuff links, and white, silver, or grey ties. Women employees, by contrast, were expected to be colorful and dramatic in their dress, to wear rich garlands of costume jewelry in the office, embellish long fingernails in exotic shades, and be walking specimens of the company's line of perfumes and *eaux de cologne.*

When he hired me (on Alfred Politz's recommendation), Revson told me that Procter and Gamble was his model. As the world's largest advertiser of packaged goods, that company was generally regarded with awe, and its research and media practices were accepted as the standard for the advertising business. Necessarily so, because the P&G account was the keystone for its agencies, each of which was always eager to grab one of the company's constant output of new products. P&G had its own well-defined notions of how media should be evaluated, and its own criteria for what constituted acceptable research. Its agencies, having adopted these standards, tended to impose them on their other clients. P&G had pioneered in the creation of radio soap operas and had its own production house to create their television counterparts. Its formulaic approach had become a major influence on American culture.

To ape P&G may indeed have been Charles's aspiration, but where P&G was staid, systematic, and bureaucratic, Revlon was frantic and chaotic. Decisions were made and quickly canceled, executives and departments jockeyed for advantage in the eyes of the autocratic ruler, and every action was driven by the need to "make the numbers," to fill the sales quotas that had been set to meet the incessant growth that Wall Street expected. "This is the firing line of marketing!" I was told when I came aboard.

Revson held business lunches in his office. His secretary would call two weeks ahead of time to ask what I wanted to eat—but then invariably cancel a half hour ahead of the appointment. The executive ranks of the company were constantly being pruned. The search for replacements was the task of two of the company's highest-paid managers, the vice president of employee relations and the director of personnel. One of their principal functions was to convey the orders of execution to the victims, usually late on Friday afternoon after Charles had left the office and all avenues of appeal had been effectively cut off. Settlements were generous, and apparently ironclad employment contracts were easily disposed of. The unfortunate chosen were usually asked to clean out their desks and go forth immediately, leaving their chairs warm for successors who had already been hired. The executive staff's active social life centered on lavish farewell parties for the departed, always held on neutral ground. It was a camaraderie of the damned.

The company's products spanned a broad range; lowly hair sprays and deodorants were sold in supermarkets and variety stores, creams and unguents in exclusive department stores. The department stores gave Revlon products their cachet, but drugstores were the main channel of distribution. They were called on by a large national sales force led by George Kirk. Kirk was unassuming in private conversation but rose to spellbinding heights of oratory when he urged his troops on to ever-greater achievement, in the style of General George Patton (or at least of George C. Scott playing Patton).

The company's annual sales meeting took over the ballroom of the Hotel Waldorf Astoria and was crammed with inspiring speeches. It featured a kind of *tableau vivant*, in which each department head carried the *papier-mâché* limb of a body which, after a moment of darkness, turned into a lovely lady who symbolized our corporate unity of purpose and action. The climax of the event came with Revson's speech, in which he delivered a diatribe against his twelve-year-old son (who was present) for not paying proper attention to his homework. There was a lesson for all of us in this, he insisted.

Distribution was critical for success in the toiletries business. I discovered that no one at Revlon had a clue as to the characteristics of drugstores, their size, sales volume, workforce, shelf space devoted to cosmetics and toiletries, and other information that I considered essential. I designed a questionnaire to supply this vital information, with the hope that the salesmen (there were no women in this army) would fill it in. I quickly learned that this was not part of their job description.

I learned another lesson when I tried to professionalize the company's product testing. Revlon's product research laboratory was in an ancient and decrepit factory building in the South Bronx, a world away from the gleaming headquarters high above Fifth Avenue. The laboratory was run by one of Charles's original associates, and product testing was under the supervision of an ill-groomed crone whose dowdy appearance was in sharp contrast to the chic and heavily made-up product managers in the main office. Her testing procedure was to offer samples of new shades, textures, or scents to half a dozen of her best friends and to report back on their preferences, which were duly followed. When I suggested that this procedure did not meet acceptable methodological criteria, I was told that this was the way it had always been done and that Charles liked it. I was able to set up a separate product research unit to do independent testing, but the laboratory regarded this activity with contempt and considered it mere empire-building.

The female side of the sales force was made up of "consultants," the elegantly dressed ladies who presided over Revlon's booths on the main floors of department stores. Their guru was a makeup artist with a French name and a German accent, fetching bangs, and an extraordinary gift for transforming even the most unpromising of customers into a sexpot, at least in appearance.

Revlon taught me a valuable lesson about corporate finance. I had written about what I called a kind of "pathetic fallacy" in the world of media research, in which projected estimates of market or audience size based on surveys were imbued with the genuineness of the numbers produced by a company's accounting department in making up a payroll or calculating a profit or loss. Those, I thought, were really *hard* and reliable numbers. But at Revlon, office employees were called to the New Jersey factory to work late over the year-end holidays, right up to midnight on New Year's Eve, placing product shipments in the mail so that they would show up as sales in the year-end statement and make the numbers look good for Wall Street's analysts. If the goods were returned unsold, we could worry about that next year. Hard numbers indeed!

My first boss at Revlon was Jack Kauffman, who had been a sales executive at Procter and Gamble and later headed a new and quickly abandoned consumer products division of the cotton factors Anderson Clayton, which owned a large vegetable oil processing company in Texas. Kauffman's wife was from Louisville. On its outskirts her father owned a horse farm that the city had gradually enveloped. The main annual event on the couple's calendar was the Kentucky Derby, for which they departed one Thursday afternoon in May. The following day Revson could not find his marketing vice president, and Kauffman was sacked soon afterward, with the usual generous termination pay. He was followed by the smart and furiously energetic Henry Tavs, always elegantly attired in the company uniform of black, grey, and white, with silver cuff links. His motto was, "When you want to get something done, give it to a busy man," and he certainly kept very busy. Tavs jotted down ideas all day long on miscellaneous scraps of paper and telephone message pads. He reviewed them at a staff meeting each morning, like a field marshal assigning orders to his commanders. (When I left he told me, "The light is always burning in the window.")

In the few years before I came to Revlon, the company had undergone a period of extraordinary growth, spurred by its sponsorship of "The $64,000 Question," one of two highly popular quiz shows that were enjoying an extraordinary success on prime-time television in the 1957 and 1958 broadcast seasons. The quiz sponsorship multiplied Revlon's sales, escalated the value of its stock, and permitted it to make a number of foolish acquisitions.

Television had almost reached the level of universal saturation. In its brief life it had become the major element of leisure time, an important source of public information, and the preeminent force in politics. The quiz or information game show had been a staple item of radio programming in the United States and elsewhere before World War II. It appeared under a variety of formats using both "naïve" contestants (presumably selected at random from the studio audience, the telephone directory, or the ranks of the general public) or "expert" contestants (selected because of their unusual memories, their specialized knowledge, or their interesting or appealing personalities).[1]

During the 1950s the quiz format was revived for television; it achieved almost instant popularity. Quiz shows offering very high prizes were featured in prime evening viewing time by all three television networks under the sponsorship of a considerable number of leading companies. (At this point in television's history, advertisers did not scatter their commercials widely among programs as they generally do today; they sought to identify themselves with particular shows. The practice changed when the cost of sponsorship became prohibitive.)

"Twenty-One" and "The $64,000 Question" completely dominated the attention of the vast television audience at their broadcast hours. On at least one occasion one of these shows achieved a Nielsen rating of 53, which meant, if you took the number literally, that over half the TV homes in the nation were tuned in. Outstanding contestants became widely known public personalities, and their fortunes were followed from week to week with considerable suspense.

In the broadcasting and advertising world it was common knowledge that prospective participants in the leading quiz shows were put through a careful screening procedure that left the program producers with few doubts as to the subjects on which they were well informed and ignorant. By the late fall of 1958 the vogue had already run its course, and the principal programs went off the air. At this relatively late date the press reported charges by an unsuccessful contestant that the producers of his show had tried to "fix" his quiz responses. Other similar accusations followed. A New York grand jury investigating the matter found some contestants who acknowledged that they had been coached by the producers, either by being given the correct answers or by being ordered to give incorrect answers to make way for a contestant with greater audience appeal. In an atmosphere of growing press attention, a House subcommittee scheduled public hearings.

In defiance of all odds, I was acquainted with three of the big winners on "Twenty One." Two of them admitted that they had been given the answers. The third, a rare exception among the contestants, was the polymath Joseph H. Spigelman, who knew his game was up when he was asked—and correctly answered— a question about baseball. (He had told the producers that his two weak categories were sports and popular entertainment.)*

Quiz shows were rarely mentioned during the first eleven months of my employment at Revlon, though the story of Revson's micromanagement of "The $64,000 Question"—deciding which contestants would survive and which would perish—had already been described in a novel, Robert Foreman's *The Hot Half Hour*.[2] Then, late one Friday afternoon, October 30, 1959, I received a telephone call from Evan ("Bill") Mandel, Charles Revson's executive assistant. "The shit is about to hit the fan," he announced, referring to the congressional hearings on the quiz shows, which were scheduled to begin in Washington the following Monday. Revson wanted to know, "What is this going to do to us?"

There was little time to answer the question and no existing facility to get information fast. At that time, telephone interviewing was not customary. Because of high long-distance rates, there

---

*At the time he appeared on the program, Spigelman liked to describe himself as a laborer on the docks, consorting with strong-arm men and racketeers. Actually he was a shipping clerk for a freight forwarding firm whose owner, a gambling enthusiast, had set him to work tracing the bloodlines of winning race horses. His career up to that point had been varied: instructor in English literature at the City College of New York at the age of nineteen; protegé of Henry Luce as a staff writer at *Fortune*; recipient of an award by Harry Truman for his work as a planner for the War Production Board; encyclopedia editor; professor of physiological optics and dean of humanities at the New York Institute of Optics. Joe splurged his quiz show money on a deluxe grand tour of Europe and then settled into a new career as an acclaimed financial analyst. His abiding interest, throughout these vicissitudes of fortune, was in theoretical physics.

was no way (as there is today) to conduct national surveys from a central phone room with computer-assisted interviews. There were no overnight mail services, no fax machines to send instructions or questionnaires to interviewers or get results back from them. There were no mechanisms for speedy assembly and processing of data. Local interviewers shipped their completed questionnaires back to headquarters to be edited and key-punched.

We needed a national telephone sample and a way to collect the data immediately. I called on Don Cahalan, who headed ARB surveys, a subsidiary of the American Research Bureau (later renamed Arbitron), one of the two leading radio and television ratings services.* Arbitron was uniquely equipped to do the job. The firm placed tens of thousands of listener and viewer diaries in households that were first contacted on the telephone by local interviewers throughout the country, asking them to cooperate. Cahalan met the challenge with enthusiasm. The decision to conduct the research was made on Friday evening. That night the interview schedule was drafted, the sampling plan prepared, and the interviewers alerted. On Saturday the schedule was pretested and transmitted to the field by telegram, and a tabulation plan was set up.

The initial survey took place on the eve of the hearings, Sunday, November 1. On Monday the nation's evening papers emblazoned the story in huge headlines announcing contestants' confessions that the popular shows had been rigged. Repeat surveys were conducted that evening and again on Tuesday, Wednesday, and Thursday of that week, with a final follow-up two weeks later. Each wave of interviews covered a comparable national probability sample of five hundred telephone households in metropolitan areas. Alternate interviews were conducted with adult men and women. To conserve time, each interviewer tabulated replies on completion of the daily assign-

*Cahalan, who was passionate on the subject of research ethics and standards, later became a professor of sociology at the University of California, Berkeley, and an authority on drug and alcohol addiction.

ment and telephoned them to headquarters for collation. By 7
a.m. each morning a complete national tabulation of the previous
evening's interviewing was phoned to me. I had my analysis prepared in time for Revson's 9:30 arrival at work.

REACTIONS TO THE TV QUIZ SHOW SCANDAL (1959)

Even before the quiz show hearings began, the first
survey showed an already near-universal awareness
of them and a high level of public discussion. (A
fourth of the men and a third of the women had
talked about the programs with someone in the past
twenty-four hours.)

In retrospect, most people expressed a kind of
bemused tolerance for the quiz shows. A majority
agreed that they were enjoyable and that no great
harm had been done by them. Few believed that *all*
the programs had been fixed. A majority of those
who had been viewers of any one of five leading
quiz shows believed that the problem centered only
on some (rather than all or none) of that show's
contestants.

A substantial minority agreed that the programs
had to be fixed to make them more dramatic and
interesting. A majority felt that the story had
been blown out of all proportions and disagreed
with the charge that "it was criminal to try to put
this over on the public." Most people (especially
men) agreed that "the contestants who were fixed
just did what any average person would have done in
their place." Blame was placed overwhelmingly on
the producers of the shows rather than on the
quizmasters, the networks, advertisers, or
agencies.

On Monday, the first day of the hearings, came
the admissions of Charles Van Doren, a popular quiz
winner (and scion of a renowned academic family)
who had earlier denied all charges before a grand
jury. On the following three days there was

testimony from other former contestants and from executives of the sponsors.

The full impact of the Van Doren testimony was not registered until Tuesday night. On that evening and the next two nights, two of three respondents reported fresh conversations on the subject.

Although references to the hearings continued to appear in national magazines and intermittently in news reports, the quiz shows had faded from the headlines by the time of the final survey. By that date, conversation about the shows had fallen back to about the same level (reported by one person in four) that preceded the first day of the hearings.

The public seems to have interpreted the week's revelations in the light of already well-established expectations. The attitudes that stood up during the hearings also persisted for several weeks after they ended. Opinions remained generally stable throughout the entire period, though a few shifts did occur on Monday, after the drama of the Van Doren testimony. There was a small rise in the minority who felt "it was criminal to put this over on the public," but by Tuesday this wave of anger had dissipated. There was also on Monday a small drop in the majority who defined the quiz fixes as relatively harmless and the shows as enjoyable; this effect persisted throughout the remaining surveys.

On Tuesday the hearings shifted their emphasis to the testimony of producers and sponsors, who told their side of the story. There was now a rise in the proportion who felt "the programs had to be fixed to make them more dramatic and interesting." More people agreed that "the contestants who were fixed just did what any average person would have done in their place." (Two weeks later, opinion on both these points had shifted back to about where it was before the hearings began.) As the hearings continued to dominate the headlines on Wednesday and Thursday, an increased proportion believed the publicity was excessive. Basic attitudes remained relatively stable in the face of a steadily growing disenchantment. The proportion believing that *all* quiz shows were fixed grew steadily (from 16 percent to 30 percent) during the week, though it fell back to 20 percent two weeks later, after the topic faded from the news.

Van Doren had been a contestant on "Twenty One." By the evening of the day after his testimony, the proportion of former "Twenty One" viewers who thought *none* of the contestants on that program had been fixed had declined to 4 percent from a level of 15 percent before the hearings began. There was also a rise in the percentage who said *all* had been fixed. But this momentary reaction was gone by the following day.

The hearings increased the public's belief that responsibility was a many-sided affair. Before the start, the producers of the shows were considered "really responsible" by almost three of four. While there was no lessening of that judgment, there were substantial increases in the proportion who felt that responsibility also fell on other people and on the institutions involved. Much of this widening of the blame took place on Monday after Van Doren shattered illusions. All the way through, about three in five said the contestants themselves were really responsible. Later in the week the sponsors, TV networks, and advertising agencies were increasingly considered responsible.

Van Doren emerged as the outstanding individual personality associated with the scandal, and had the sympathy of a majority, especially of women. He was perceived not as a confidence man cheating a gullible public but as a double victim, first of the dimly defined "fixers," and second of the busybody investigators who were stirring up trouble where none existed before. [This closely parallels the public's reaction to the impeachment of President Bill Clinton forty years later.]

While the quiz shows carried the advertising of many leading corporations, some were more closely identified with the programs during the hearings than others were. On the eve of the hearings, many

viewers were unable to correctly connect the quiz
shows they had watched with the names of their
sponsors. The sponsor of one show was correctly
identified by three-tenths of its former viewers,
that of another by almost half. The two sponsors of
another show were recalled by relatively few.
Attitudes toward the companies remained very
stable. (The explanation was apparent from a
separate analysis of forty-four intensive personal
interviews. People did not associate advertisers'
managements with the actions discussed in the
hearings. Their opinions seemed to reflect their
own self-interest as consumers of a company's
products rather than broad, general judgments about
its advertising practices.)

Just as viewers did not clearly distinguish
among the individual programs or their sponsors,
they did not differentiate among degrees of
"fixing" or distinguish among the varying kinds of
control over contestants that different program
formats made possible.

Quiz shows have attained enormous popularity
because of the empathy viewers feel toward the
contestants; only for this reason was public
disenchantment so directly and broadly translated
into indignation and concern. Viewers were
indignant not only about the original deception
involved in the "fixing," but also about the mere
fact that the hearings had stirred up otherwise
calm waters. They did not like to be reminded that
in the first instance they had been delightfully
credulous of the contestants' prodigious feats of
memory. Mixed with these unpleasant feelings was a
sense of glee and relief. Since the contestants
were, after all, not as smart as they had
originally appeared to be, the viewers' own self-
esteem was reaffirmed.

During the week of the hearings, public opinion
on the subject of quiz shows found a voice, but the
opinions themselves seem to have been shaped long
in advance. Although they changed during the
hearings, they largely returned to their previous

```
state after two weeks. People respond to events in
terms of their existing predispositions, and their
views are not easily shifted from one day to the
next.*
```

On the morning after the first day of hearings, Revson called to find out what I had learned. When I launched into an exposition of the findings, he cut me off quickly. "Just give me the net net!" I said, "It's not going to hurt the company." "Okay, thanks." He hung up. That taught me that brevity and conclusiveness are essential to successful presentation of research to any client who accepts the technical competence of the researcher but is interested only in formulating his own course of action.

Indeed, the quiz show hearings did not hurt the company's sales, and its stock value recovered quickly.

---

*A curious by-product of this study was the discovery that in a dispute between an industry and the government (in this case between the cosmetics industry and the Food and Drug Administration), the public was more inclined to accept the industry's word, though not that of individual company spokesmen.

FROM RADIO TO TELEVISION

■ By the time of the quiz show scandals, television had firmly established itself as the dominant form of national advertising and the nation's principal source of entertainment. It had also become a major source of news, since, from the start, it had the potential to combine the best elements of two important news conveyors—radio and films.

Radio's brief bulletins had more immediacy than the afternoon papers with their constantly updated editions. But throughout my childhood, movie newsreels had given me a greater sense of direct contact with distant settings of great events and with the world's leading political personalities. At the movies I vicariously experienced the Nazis' Nuremberg rallies, parades in Red Square, battles in Spain and China, Haile Selassie's futile address to the League of Nations. The "news" in newsreels was always a week or two out of date and was smothered in vapid features about pie-eating contests and the Iowa Hog of the Year. Yet they made me feel connected to history.

I had first seen television at the 1939 World's Fair, but its flickering images were an unreal part of the fair's "World of Tomorrow" and seemed remote from the realities of everyday American life. At Pilot Radio, where I worked before entering the army, the entire factory had supposedly been converted to the production of military radio transmitters, but a small team of reclusive engineers somewhat furtively designed TV receivers. When television finally emerged into the market, after the war, its audiences were tiny at first. Saloon keepers were among the first to purchase sets, and they attracted substantial patronage. Wrestling matches were a major attraction.

Even as television became something more than a curiosity, radio retained its hold over Americans' free time. The Philharmonic radio broadcasts represented Jersey Standard's premiere venture into institutional advertising, but Esso, Jersey's principal domestic refining and marketing subsidiary, had for some time sponsored an early evening radio newscast, "The Esso Reporter." It was produced to a standardized format by the news departments of local radio stations in the states where products could be sold under the Esso name.

The broadcast news of that 1950's era was strikingly different from today's. There are now a handful of twenty-four-hour all-news radio stations, but everywhere else on the spectrum even the five-minute radio news bulletins "on the hour" have almost vanished. In its heyday, radio news adhered mainly to a skeleton format in which events were reduced to "news items" and rarely seen as incidents in a long, complex, and continuing story. A handful of commentators (Lowell Thomas, Quincy Howe, John Cameron Swayze, Gabriel Heatter*) made the reading of the news entertaining. Listeners tuned in to "Lowell Thomas," not to the news, just as more recently they have tuned in to "Peter Jennings," "Tom Brokaw," or "Dan Rather." "The Esso Reporter" lacked such a central personality; it was impersonal by design.

After the "Reporter" expanded into television in 1950, I analyzed the content of one week's broadcasts in twenty different cities and found no difference between big- and small-city sta-

---

*In 1936, Heatter's report on the execution of Bruno Hauptmann, killer of the Lindbergh baby, was an unforgettable *tour de force*, creating high drama out of a non-event.

tions in the distribution of air time to local and world news. The small-city stations made relatively greater use of film. The big-city stations were more likely to give the latest bulletins even without film footage, but filmed items were given more air time than news for which no visuals were available. I noted that "the recent perfection of a television tape recorder will permit news film to be played over the air by local stations almost as quickly as it is in New York." (What I did not foresee were inventions that make possible the worldwide on-scene broadcasting of live events.) "In their selection of the principal stories each day, the individual television news editors showed a remarkable similarity of judgment. Local news reported most often dealt with disasters or natural catastrophes." Today, on local TV news, the formula remains the same.

Television's dominance over radio as a news source came rapidly. By 1956 it was "by far the preferred medium of information and entertainment."* News ranked second only to drama as the most popular type of TV program. About half the public said they would prefer to keep TV if they could have only one medium; a third chose newspapers. Television made the news "most interesting," but newspapers held a substantial lead as the best source of "news of what [was] happening in the world." I observed that "young people are most apt to select television and least apt to select newspapers. This may perhaps swell into a significant trend, as a new generation grows up in the television age." (This prognosis was correct, and its consequences were to become disturbingly evident a generation later. They became a major preoccupation of my later work for the newspaper business.)

There were ten news shows on the air in New York at that time. Only a small percentage of those who had watched any television on the previous evening had not watched one of them; over half of this viewing was purposeful rather than accidental

*This was in a study I directed, which interviewed 4,500 persons in New York, Philadelphia, and Charlotte.

or a carryover from a preceding program. I found these findings "startling, since the television viewer can see only a limited number of news programs in the course of the day, whereas the radio listener can hear news every half hour. The explanation lies in the average person's changed leisure habits—the fact that far more time is now spent watching television than listening to the radio." Radio was mentioned less often than television as the medium that "brings the news most quickly." (Only three years earlier, a survey had asked people where they would turn if they heard a rumor that war had broken out; 55 percent had then said radio and only 15 percent TV.)

By 1956 television was reaching the point of saturation. Only 3 percent of the nation's households were beyond reach of a TV signal, and three of four owned a set, which on average could pick up four channels and was on for five hours a day. Although "the bulk of air time is taken up with entertainment programs," I wrote then, "television has quickly become a major vehicle of conveying news and information." This took place through four functions: direct eyewitness reporting (like "the dramatic arrival of the survivors of the *Andrea Doria*"), documentary programs ("the direct offspring of radio or film documentaries"), planned events ("a speech, interview, or panel discussion involving an important political figure whose pronouncements are inherently newsworthy") and news programs ("usually of ten or fifteen minutes' duration, which corresponds to the familiar radio news report. Here the newscaster reads the bulletins and whenever possible the camera shifts from him to motion pictures of the events he talks about").

Today's television news audience watches primarily local news shows, but in 1956 only one in ten preferred to see programs consisting mainly of local news.* "The minority who prefer local news are most often found at the bottom of the social scale, and among the young. They are the very people who rely

---

*Five in ten preferred a concentration of national and world news, and four volunteered that they wanted equal attention to both local and world news.

most strongly on television as their major source of information."
One person in four preferred the latest news bulletins read by an
announcer, but two of three preferred films showing the actual
events, even if they were a day or two old. I commented,

> The television newscaster is a familiar human bridge between
> the audience and the unfamiliar subject matter of the news. . . .
> He is a public personality . . . the more popular ones tend to be
> colorful individuals who add interpretations to the wire dis-
> patches and who may even take sides on controversial matters,
> as Edward R. Murrow did. . . . The newscaster's personality
> may be the most important factor in determining the success or
> failure of the program. News programs broadcast on different
> stations at the same time show considerable differences in au-
> dience size even though they draw on much the same press as-
> sociation and news film services. Minute-by-minute analyses of
> audience reactions show that the same news item may evoke
> very different degrees of interest and approval when read on
> two different programs.

Word of the bombardment of Fort Sumter on April 12, 1861,
reached the American public on the following day through tele-
graphic reports in the press. On December 7, 1941, my listening
to the New York Philharmonic Symphony radio broadcast was
interrupted by a news bulletin reporting the attack on Pearl Harbor. On September 11, 2001, horrified viewers throughout the
world watched the collapsing twin towers of the World Trade
Center in real time. We have all become witnesses to history as it
unfolds.

The viewing public now takes it for granted that television
will offer live coverage of news in the making on distant battle-
fields and disaster sites. This is made possible by miniaturized
cameras, recording equipment, computers, satellite transmis-
sion, cellular phones—technology that is relatively new. The
spread of cable and the creation of vigorously competing twenty-
four-hour cable news networks have brought intimacy and immediacy to what were formerly remote events, places, and

people. Even as recently as in the Vietnam War, television's field
reporters traveled with camera crews and heavy equipment that
limited their mobility. Reels of film were shipped by plane to
New York, so footage was several days out of date by the time it
went on the air. Even with these limitations, the imagery was
powerful and shocking, in contrast to the filmed newsreels of
previous conflicts.

Vietnam showed the power of television to transform public
opinion. At the height of domestic controversy over the war, and
shortly before the radical student takeover of Columbia University, I talked to Louis Cowan's seminar on media management at
the Columbia Graduate School of Journalism. (Cowan was a former president of CBS Television who had adapted the radio quiz
show format to television as producer of the enormously successful "Twenty One." Gracious, cultivated, and intellectually
astute, he seemed an unlikely originator of a game show popular
with the masses.) According to the transcript of the recorded session, he asked, "Why has so little been done about measuring the
real impact of the media? The war in Vietnam is reported every
single day—in color. What is the effect of this, night after night,
drenching a society that sees it by the millions? Why is it that
this impact is not studied, not measured?" This was my answer:

TELEVISION NEWS (1968)

With $30 billion a year being spent on the Vietnam
War, plus countless hundreds of millions by the
networks and advertisers to support presentation of
the TV newscasts that have brought the realities of
the war home to the American public, maybe it would
be worth $150,000 to investigate the real effect of
television on so vital a subject. Why isn't it
being done? Because there's no immediate payoff.
There's much more payoff for someone to compare
audience size for the newscasts of Networks A and
B, and thereby to demonstrate to a prospective
advertiser that Huntley and Brinkley have a higher
rating than Cronkite, or vice versa.

A couple of years ago I posed a problem to a sociologist in Russia. A guy works all day in a factory. He comes home tired and worn out. He turns on the radio to Tchaikovsky. He turns on the television set to a performance of Chekhov. If he goes to a bookstore, apart from Marxist tracts, all the books for sale are on a high cultural level. There are no detective stories, romances, or mysteries, no comic books. He's too exhausted and bored at that particular moment to want to indulge in any of the higher art forms. What does he do?" The sociologist answered, "Well, he can go walk in the park, in a cultural atmosphere."

This exchange came in the context of a discussion of what people make of the opportunities provided for them. The prevailing philosophy in the socialist countries is that all the junk should be eliminated from the popular culture. The government does not permit self-consciously bad material either in print or on the air. The program director must not give people music that he thinks is bad, that he knows to be bad. The publisher must not give them cheap "True Romance" magazines or books, or any kind of sensational reading matter that serves only as a pastime and has no artistic merit. If he gives them entertainment, it must raise their cultural level at the same time. In the Soviet Union they sell editions of Jack London in the millions, they create tremendous mass markets for good music, and they elevate what here would be considered high culture to the status of popular culture.

The size of the broadcast audience is almost inelastic. At seven o'clock this evening a certain number of people in this country will flick on their television sets. Plus or minus a few percent, the same number will turn them on if they can watch one channel, two channels, or seven, unless there are extraordinary changes in the programming. For example, if the president is going to deliver a major address and all three networks broadcast it, audience share will soar for the occasional

independent station that runs a rerun of an old
movie, and the total level of viewing may drop
somewhat, unless the occasion is a national
emergency.

The bad will always drive out the good, because
the bad is always easier to take than the good. If
there's a Professor George Kennan show and a rerun
of the "I Love Lucy" show, most people will choose
Lucy. If there is no choice, or if the choice is
between the Professor Kennan show and the Professor
Cowan show, the choices are raised to a higher
level, but the audience size stays the same.

The solution here would be collusion between
competing broadcast networks, which is unthinkable
from any practical standpoint. I can't imagine the
networks agreeing to the proposal that on Sunday
afternoon they put on nothing but good programs,
with no regard for the sponsors. If all the
networks were striving for excellence, how would
anyone get to watch the football game? This is the
essential dilemma for our broadcast system. This is
why public broadcasting is so essential—to provide
at least one source of programming with high
aspirations.

Aspirations and achievements rarely match, but
if the aspirations are at least consistently high,
then the option to achieve will be there. Public
broadcasting is different from educational
television, which has a didactic purpose. The
objective of public broadcasting should be simply
to have the broadcaster's own judgment about what
he wants to communicate be the guide as to what
gets on the air, rather than the arbitrary
criterion of audience size. There is no such thing
as an educational or public television audience per
se. The people who watch those channels also watch
commercial TV.

The economics of commercial television do not
make possible the same kind of advertising support
for limited-appeal vehicles that exists in print.
The range of choice is more restricted; it is
controlled by the time of the broadcast, the size

of the available viewing public, and the competition, which determines what the alternatives are at that point in time. In print, people can be defined as the *Scientific American* type or the *Playboy* type. On television, it's just impossible to zero in so narrowly. There are bound to be more people in the hopper who don't meet that fine distinction.

All the institutions of broadcasting we talk about today are very transitory. If we take a twenty-five-year perspective, the range of choice is going to be quite different. New possibilities are going to come, for delaying, freezing, compacting, scanning, and programming communications.

None of the major media gives adequate coverage to subjects like the war in Biafra.* Why aren't there more correspondents? The answer is simple: it costs a lot of money to maintain them. A broader question relates to the coverage of world affairs in general, the low level of sophistication that is brought to bear on the interpretation of news trends and developments, the failure to use scholarly know-how about the remote areas where things happen out of the blue. Most of the crises of our recent history have come from obscure places. Who knows where they're likely to come from in the future? †

In spite of the excellent public affairs and news staffs of the networks, the amount of money they spend on their Vietnam coverage is not proportionate in relation to the total spectrum of world events. They aren't covering Nigeria, they're not covering Guatemala.

People have a high level of interest in foreign news coverage, but the big events are those they associate with dramatic episodes that lend themselves to television portrayal: President

*This was the murderous Nigerian civil war occasioned by the attempted seces-
sion of the Ibo people in the country's southeastern region.
† From a cave in Afghanistan!

Johnson shaking hands with the South Korean
ambassador outside the White House. "Today, Viet
Cong guerrillas invaded the embassy compound in
Saigon." Flash to action shots of troops firing on
the Viet Cong inside the compound. Shots of Marine
guards moving up at the ready. Now we've had it.
We've seen the picture. We know it all. Not the
current state of the political balance among the
parties in South Vietnam, or the status of secret
negotiations now under way with Hanoi, or the long-
term trends developing in Laos that will get us
into trouble in the next six months.

News is being reduced more and more to the
illusion of knowing it because we've seen it—that
moving picture that conveys a feeling of
familiarity which is not really warranted by any
depth of understanding of what lies behind it.
People are interested in the big news—the Viet Cong
breaking into the embassy compound, the
negotiations for the release of the *Pueblo*.* Are
they interested in the provincial elections in
Colombia? No, they couldn't care less. But if the
Communists suddenly moved in, in force, in the
hills of Colombia and started kidnaping provincial
officials and shooting up army posts, then they'd
surely be interested.† How do you alert them to the
fact that the provincial elections in Colombia may
have a greater significance for them than the
shooting up of the compound in Saigon?

More and more television news coverage in the
future will be documentary reportage. Over the long
term, more of the content is going to be, "We
switch you now to Newark for the riot," or "We take
you now to the embassy for the assault." If we say
that this sort of thing can't be shown, it would be
like saying, "We shouldn't have seen the death of
[Lee Harvey] Oswald." The camera was there. It

*The USS *Pueblo*, an intelligence-gathering ship, was captured in international
waters by North Korean gunboats. Her crew faced an uncertain fate, though they were
released after thirteen months.
†I was wrong about this.

would be losing television's greatest opportunity
to communicate.

Television shows things that most Americans
have been shielded from until now. I had a feeling
during the Pueblo crisis that a very profound
change is just beginning to take place in this
country—a recognition of the realities of the
twentieth century. It is absolutely impossible for
anyone to grasp those realities who has not been
part of them, the experience of being in a city
under bombardment and seeing windows shatter around
you. You can describe it, but it isn't the same.
You can see newsreels, but it isn't the same.

What we're suddenly encountering is the sense
of participation in this Vietnam War, along with
the feeling that there really are limitations to
what we can do about it. As long as we were
omnipotent, as we have been throughout our history
up to this time, we had the illusion that we could
cope with all the fairy tales that occurred in
distant places. Now they are no longer fairy tales.
Television has played a very important role in this
transformation.

We don't know whether those eighty-three guys
who were on the *Pueblo* are going to be lined up
against the wall and shot. Fifteen years ago we'd
have known that the U.S. Marines were going to land
and get them out of there. Now we don't know that.
We're faced with the same uncertainty that people
in Europe felt when they saw planes overhead and
didn't know whether their homes were going to be
bombed or not. This immediacy in reportage
introduces a totally new dimension into the
national experience.

While I tracked the growth of television at McCann-Erickson in
the early 1950s, I was fascinated by its impact on everyday life.
When a publisher proposed that I write a text about radio ratings,
I convinced him that television was the coming thing and that
ratings were less important than what the new medium was

doing to society.[1] It was already too late to discover all the details of what life had been like before television. There was, to be sure, considerable evidence on media habits, political beliefs, and buying habits, but very little nuanced information on the interpersonal relationships, conversational patterns, and personal values that would be affected by television viewing. Because people who owned sets were different from those who did not, they could not be compared directly after television's arrival. My attention was attracted to situations where the advent of TV could really be looked at before and after. With every passing year, the number of such places became fewer. One was South Africa.

I made two trips to that country in the shadow of an impending event: the introduction of television, which had already arrived in almost every other nation in the world. I regarded its coming to South Africa as inevitable and felt that it would be cataclysmic in its political and social consequences. The second though not the first part of that judgment was shared by the Afrikaner masters of that country, who had kept out television in fear of the disturbing impact of its images. (Albert Hertzog, the redoubtable minister of posts and telegraphs, called it "The Devil's Box.") Their rationale was that television would be dominated by the prurience and violence of American programming. But what they really feared was the exposure of their nonwhite population to unpredictable and disturbing scenes of international news, to intimate details of domestic life in more permissive and democratic societies, and to enticing and envy-arousing displays of material culture.

But it was precisely the power of that material culture that made the arrival of television inexorable. South African industry was too closely bound to international marketing to forgo the energies of television advertising as a stimulus to sales. The pressures were building fast. Between my first trip in 1970, when television was still unthinkable, and the second in 1973, the government was wearily and warily succumbing to them. The head of the South African Broadcasting Corporation switched his public position from anti- to pro-TV after a new minister of posts and telegraphs was appointed, and at the start of 1976 television was finally introduced.

When I addressed the South African Marketing Association on my second trip, the question was no longer whether but when. I chose to summarize "What would I like to have known before TV came along?"

LESSONS FROM A QUARTER-CENTURY OF U.S. TELEVISION EXPERIENCE (1973)

1. Television opens a new era of competition. Media compete for the advertiser's budget but serve different functions for the audience and therefore for the advertiser. On balance, the size of the budget and creative skill are more important than the selection of media. All media can claim to be competitive in their cost efficiency. What is important is to understand the differences in their capacities to communicate.

2. Existing media survive when television comes, but they change. Television redefines the geographic boundaries of markets. It generates new funding for advertising at the expense of other forms of selling. Other media adapt their content and become more specialized. Television changes too. It has its own life cycle, starting with the initial phase as an object of curiosity to its primacy as an instrument of family cohesion and finally to its transformation into a personal medium.

3. For advertisers, the range of performance among vehicles within any medium is greater than the range among media. Everything hinges on the creative element.

4. Advertisers follow the leader, but innovation pays off. There is steady concentration in decision making among advertisers and agencies.

Small individual decisions add up to momentous
social policies. Small audience losses for a medium
are translated into large advertising losses.

5.Capturing attention is not an end in itself.
Television is used to build brand image for
products that are virtually identical. It
emphasizes technique over substance. In the context
of entertainment, commercials must be entertaining,
but memorability is not to be equated with sales
results.

6. Broadcast and print work differently. The
reader is in control and can conduct an active
search. The viewer must accept the flow of messages
as the broadcaster transmits them. Print offers
specificity, tangibility, utility, the capacity for
abstraction and reference. Broadcast offers mood,
engagement, and the facility for demonstration.

7. What the advertiser transmits is not what
the viewer experiences. What the viewer sees at
home is not what the client sees in the viewing
room. Commercials are experienced in context.

8. People who have the most time to spend spend
it with a medium that takes up time. Television's
audience profile is skewed to the low end of the
social scale. People make time for television, and
change their life routine.

9.The big questions about television are the
perennial questions in communication and
persuasion.

These conclusions have held up, though I did not foresee the
evolution of cable; the multiplication of channels; the VCR and
the almost universal use of the handheld remote control to mute
sound and switch viewing choices constantly; interactivity and
the eventual convergence of the TV set with the yet-to-be-
invented personal computer.

A year later, in 1974, I submitted a research proposal pre-
dicting that television penetration in South Africa would very
rapidly become almost universal among the white population

and also become a significant medium among the colored and Asian populations and some sectors of the Bantu population.*

The unique multi-racial and multi-lingual character of South Africa, with its highly disparate levels of income, social development, and living standards, offered an extraordinary microcosmic opportunity to study television's effects. It was also the last chance to do a true "before and after" study, incorporating all the afterthoughts and second guesses that had not been accounted for in the many pre/post researches undertaken in Europe and the United States as the medium was introduced and grew to maturity. Important benchmark measurements had not been taken before television appeared, not for lack of interest but because of the difficulty of getting financial support; in and of themselves—and without the follow-up—the data would have little value.

In the case of South Africa, an important set of measurements concerned expectations about television. How much exposure had the public already had through trips abroad, closed-circuit television events, scenes in motion pictures, and textual descriptions and reports? How did people expect it to affect their own lives and the country? I wanted to record their opinions about television advertising, about the balance among different types of programs, about the social responsibility of the broadcasting service. I offered a detailed plan for a benchmark study of how time was spent, of media exposure, shopping, and interpersonal contacts. I urged the study of attitudes toward advertising and consumption, community involvement, personal values, sexual mores, and political knowledge and beliefs, including those about the country's various ethnic groups. I proposed collecting data on children's school grades and

*The South African Human Science Research Council was already gearing up to study the effects of TV, but only among whites, and in a far less ambitious way than I proposed. Baseline data were being collected from six thousand adults, about their expectations and their present leisure-time activities. Twenty-one thousand white school children were undergoing tests. Other racial groups were excluded from the study for political reasons.

achievement, time spent on homework and academic interests. For the population as a whole, familiarity with current events as well as the sense of involvement or participation in current events should be measured with respect to the local community, the nation, and the world. How did various sectors of the population (a euphemism for racial and ethnic groups) rate both the importance and the merits of the various controversies in which the country had become involved, principally in connection with its racial policies? An archive of benchmark data would also have to include statistics from nonsurvey sources, on crime, mental health, and library and media use.

The premise, of course, was that all this information would provide a base for comparison with studies repeated over time. Such an ambitious program of research would have required a substantial budget as well as acquiescence, if not support, from the apartheid government. Neither was forthcoming, and so passed the last opportunity for systematic study of the way in which television changed all aspects of life in a complex contemporary society.

The subject of media violence had first come to the fore when I was studying newspaper comics. The war years had seen the rise of comic books. These featured an assortment of imaginary heroes like Superman, Spiderman, and Batman, endowed with powers of the kind that could well have been used to defeat the nation's evil wartime enemies. Comic books had a youthful male audience, sharply distinguished from the broad range of people who read newspaper comics. The mayhem depicted in the books attracted concern and condemnation, led by a psychiatrist, Frederick W. Wertham, who was a highly vocal and prolific author and activist.

Even earlier, films had brought similar reactions. As they came to represent a good chunk of television content, the outcry began again. I had taken note of this in my study of television, and in 1968 I was asked to testify before the President's Commission on the Control and Prevention of Violence, chaired by Milton Eisenhower. My testimony deplored the commercial pressures that led to the exploitation of violent content but argued against any attempt to limit it by government review or censorship. It concluded, "Who will guard the guards?" Staring down intimidatingly from their Olympian heights, the commissioners were more intent on querying me about the possibility of licensing journalists than about the matter at hand.

Not long after the commission completed its inquiry, Senator John Pastore suggested that television violence should be examined by the surgeon general, William Stewart. Stewart wrote the networks and the National Association of Broadcasters with a list of forty social scientists, asking them to indicate any who could not be objective members of an advisory committee. CBS wisely declined the offer. The other broadcasters blackballed a number of social psychologists who were the leading experts on the link between media violence and aggressive behavior in children, including Albert Bandura, Leonard Berkowitz, Otto Larsen, and Percy Tannenbaum. (They also had me on their list.)

In defending the blackballing procedure, Stewart's boss, Health, Education and Welfare Secretary Robert Finch, raised the First Amendment issue. He said it was "essential that the government be protected from any possible charge that it was intimidating the broadcasting industry." (Finch was close to President Nixon, who soon afterward threatened the Washington Post Company with the loss of its television station licenses, because of its reports on Watergate.)

Of the twelve members of the surgeon general's advisory committee, four were affiliated with CBS as consultants (my old friends Cisin, Wiebe, Klapper, and Mendelsohn). Another was NBC's research director, Thomas Coffin. Needless to say, all were highly qualified, if not altogether disinterested. *Newsweek* reported that "the most ardent defender of the industry was CBS research director Joseph Klapper, who lobbied for the inclusion of a plethora of 'howevers' in the report." The advisory committee released its findings in 1972, clearly indicating a connection between exposure to televised violence and anti-social behavior in children.[2] But the "howevers" had their consequences. The *New York Times* headlined its story on the report, "TV Violence Held Unharmful to Youth."

After the scandal that followed disclosure of the broadcasters' veto of proposed members of the advisory committee, Pastore called a hearing of his Senate subcommittee. His colleague, Alaska's Senator Ted Stevens, noted that I was identified as a sociologist and asked if that was like a socialist. In my testimony, I asked:

"Does this mean that the government is to reject all independent experts as authorities on controversial matters except those acceptable to one side, and that the side with the greatest burden of proof upon it?"

The great commotion was all about violence in cartoons and other programming directed to children. But, as I pointed out, most of the viewing done by children was of adult programs. My statement continued:

THE SURGEON GENERAL'S REPORT (1972)

```
If I take issue with the report it is not because
of what it says, but what it does not say. From
the beginning, the program seems to have been
designed with a cause-and-effect, stimulus-and-
response theory in mind. Violent messages go out
and a bad, mean, aggressive act follows.
Communication in context doesn't work that way. It
is extraordinarily difficult to tease out specific
effects from the tissue of surrounding social
influences. The absence of conclusive results, by
rigorous statistical criteria, reflects the
limitations of the survey method more than a
genuine absence of forces at work.
    What the press, and perhaps this committee,
perceive as a weak, shilly-shallying statement,
surrounded by ifs, ands, and buts, comes as close
to representing a solid inference as most social
```

scientists are apt to come upon in most studies of this kind. Public officials tend to think of the issue as either proving a case or failing to prove it, in legal terms. The legal analogy simply does not apply to science, social or otherwise, in which we come ever closer to an elusive truth by constantly reexamining our evidence, where what is most interesting is often precisely the unique exception to our generalizations and where the quality of almost any study is not only in its findings but in the new questions it throws up for further research.

The real issue is not the relationship between television violence and aggression or other behavioral problems in children. Rather it is whether such violence has any long-run consequences in the shaping of our national character. How do you measure the forces that shape character? I don't think anyone knows, but our society, in its finest expressions, understands what makes for good character, and I don't think that includes violence in symbolic fantasy. A Congress that fails to enact gun control laws is not in a strong moral position to lecture the television industry about the bloodthirsty appetites of its viewing public. Violence in the mass media is merely a tawdry commercial expression of anxieties and rages that suffuse wide areas of our national life. It is fatuous to argue that these forces would abate if the media were to ban all showings of *Macbeth* and confine newscasts to the happy side of life, as some have already done.

Are there not other far more pressing problems that demand the same large-scale funding, sense of urgency, collaborative effort, and variety of research techniques? What kind of a social research budget would be appropriate, relative to the $1 million spent on TV violence, to get findings of equivalent authority and utility on the drug problem? The great lesson to be drawn from the report is not that media violence contributes to the real-life violence of our age. We knew that all

along, didn't we? The real lesson is that we can
learn very fast, and at modest expense, a great
many specific and practical and useful things about
ourselves and our institutions to help us decide
how to shape them to meet our needs and our ideals.

The subject of television violence became front-page news again
in 1984, when the National Institute of Mental Health released a
report that examined some 2,500 research papers. These by no
means covered the full worldwide array of studies of television's
content, audiences, effects, and economic functions. (By contrast, when I first tried to assess "The Age of Television" in 1955,
it was still possible to be comprehensive, to examine and summarize every shred of evidence on viewing habits and the
medium's social impact.*) I set down some reflections on television research for the preface to a never-issued commercial edition of the NIMH report:

REFLECTIONS ON TELEVISION RESEARCH (1985)

More empirical research has been done on television
than on other great inventions, from fire-making to
the computer. The airplane and the telephone have
probably had greater consequences, yet neither has
received equivalent attention from social
scientists.
     It would be difficult to think of another
contemporary institution that has been the subject
of as much social science investigation in such a
concentrated period. Before television came along,
radio listening occupied two-thirds as much time
for the average family as television does today,
and yet radio never prompted more than a fraction
of the studies that television does.

---

*Even then my own effort was incomplete, because it was largely limited to the
North American experience and did not venture into the area of instructional television, which was already becoming a highly specialized subject.

There are a number of explanations for the extraordinary interest in television on the part of social scientists. First is its rapid rise to dominance in the promotion and advertising of nationally marketed products. This was accompanied by a vast amount of routine research on audience flow, size, and composition, which stimulated analysis. Great efforts were made to track television's effects on sales, and there was a heavy investment in research techniques to evaluate both programs and commercial messages. Even if there had been no independent incentive to examine television's effects on social behavior, the existence of such a vast body of data would have prompted academic interest.

Another reason why television has attracted so much research interest is that it is a regulated industry whose political influence has been apparent almost from the start. There always has been a public concern—occasionally manifested in uneasiness on the part of legislators—about how to maintain social control over an institution so powerful that it often appears to be operating under its own rules.

The periodic clamor about violence and sex on television is in a long tradition that probably goes back to the day when Gutenberg turned from the Bible to the printing of secular literature. Censorship of the press has always been an acknowledgment of its ability to influence behavior. In recent times, anguish over the moral impact of the media has focused in turn on "penny dreadfuls," on motion pictures, and on comic books. Not surprisingly, the focus has been on the impressionable juvenile audience, and inquiries into television's links to violence have reflected and also encouraged this concern.

The studies commissioned by the Eisenhower Commission on the Causes and Prevention of Violence[3] and for the Surgeon General's Report on Television and Social Behavior prompted a substantial amount of defensive research by the

television business. They also stimulated
foundation-sponsored and independently initiated
research at universities. Inevitably, some of the
resulting studies went off at a tangent through
clever exercise of grantsmanship. The availability
of funding permitted a variety of interesting
theoretical questions in social psychology to be
pursued under the pretense of studying television's
influence on the young.

The flowering of television research also came
about because television's growth coincided with
that of survey research and the social sciences.
The people and the organizations were in place,
thanks both to the postwar rise of marketing in
American business and to the explosion of
university enrollments and faculties and the
resulting cascade of publications essential to
academic careers.

The age of television has been one of enormous
political turmoil and excitement. World War II and
the ensuing cold war prompted what was first called
"propaganda analysis" and became the systematic
study of communications content. The study of
public opinion intensified and increasingly focused
on the influence of mass media on public
perceptions of issues and political candidates. The
media and their personalities became a matter of
widespread discussion. Mass communications became a
particular popular field of study because it is
closely linked to the basic processes that control
human behavior and therefore hold theoretical
interest.

Could the same scholarly resources have been
better applied to more pressing social issues? No
doubt they could have been, but there is no
assurance that equivalent budgets would have been
found for alternate subjects if there had not been
substantial government, foundation, and corporate
funding for the study of television.

There is one probable advantage in the fact
that such a sharply directed effort has been made
to examine a single well-defined subject. The

result is a body of information that (with all the qualifications and caveats that are a necessary part of scientific discourse) leads to some clear-cut conclusions about television's impact on American society. For example, the papers commissioned for the 1984 NIMH report (an eclectic assortment in tone, sources, methods, and theoretical orientations) demonstrate how a focused, funded program of research can enrich the literature in many fields beyond the one in which its efforts are concentrated. They contribute to the understanding of child development, the sociology of knowledge, imitative behavior, the American power structure, educational technology, and the relationship between immediate sensory perceptions and the realms of stored learning experience and of the imagination.

Like every previous synthesis of the research on how television affects what people do, this report met stiff resistance from the industry, on the grounds that no perfect link had been established between televised violence and juvenile aggression. The protests illuminate a fundamental difference between social science and applied social research.

Social science is a dynamic body of knowledge and theory that represents the current state of understanding of human beings and their relationships. It must constantly confront new evidence that appears inconsistent with what is already known or believed, and assimilate that new evidence by refining its theories or improving its methods. By contrast, applied social research is always conducted with pragmatic ends in view; it is intended to guide the decision maker. In social science no statements can ever be accepted as final; in policymaking they must be, as a basis for taking action.

527147
693604
411082
354755
102986

SELLING NEWSPAPERS

■ Television's remarkable persuasive powers transformed the marketing of consumer products. While I continued to be fascinated by its social consequences, the next job I took after Revlon forced me to concentrate on its limitations. I had gone to work for a competing medium.

My arrival at the Bureau of Advertising of the American Newspaper Publishers Association (ANPA) in 1960 coincided with the beginning of a new sales program led by its president, Charles T. Lipscomb, Jr. The Bureau's principal mission, since its founding in 1913, was to promote the sale of national advertising,* which had been steadily eroded by radio and then television. In spite of its name, the Bureau was never part of the ANPA, though it maintained a close working relationship and the same leading publishers were recycled through the boards of the two organizations. For half the Bureau's existence it was headed by a remarkable man named William A. Thomson, who introduced an extravagant style of entertaining leading advertisers with $3.50(!) luncheons at the Waldorf-Astoria hotel. While the Bureau used the immense editorial power of the press to gain a

---

*Advertising of branded goods and services that are sold in more than a single market.

hearing for its sales messages, some advertisers demanded a quid pro quo. A corset manufacturer, Thomson reported, "poured out his heart in a long statement assailing newspaper fashion writers' 'thoughtless' propaganda of the so-called 'corsetless' mode." The maker of a "new and startling auto horn" suggested that reports of motor accidents should show that these were due to "inadequate horn-honking," and promised a paid ad in exchange for every such news item.

Charlie Lipscomb was a salesman of the old school, when a steady gaze, a bright greeting, and a very firm handshake mattered more than a mastery of marketing theory. He had a good salesman's acute ability to connect names and faces, yet at newspaper conventions, where everyone knew him and assumed that he knew them equally well, his standing rule was that associates should walk behind rather than beside him as he strode through the halls, to avoid the embarrassing necessity of making introductions. He greeted the hordes of nameless faces with hearty backslaps and cries of "Hiya, boy!"

Lipscomb's new executive vice president and designated successor was the same Jack Kauffman who had fleetingly been my boss at Revlon. Charlie and Jack shared enthusiasms for golf, gin rummy,* and good living, with all of which my own experience was extremely limited. The publishers who hired them had wisely decided that the Bureau should be led by managers who brought an advertiser's perspective to the sale of advertising, rather than from the ranks of the industry's own weary sales force.

A newspaper reporter goes into the field today armed with a laptop computer on which his story, once written, is downloaded through the Internet to the work station of a copy editor. It is as-

---

*At one January convention in Chicago's lakeside Edgewater Beach Hotel, the outside temperature stood for days at 20 below. In their suite, Lipscomb and Kauffman stolidly played gin rummy, huddled in overcoats and thick layers of blankets.

sembled by computer with other stories, illustrations, and ads into a page layout and transferred directly to a plastic plate that fits on a printing press roller.

Soon after I joined the Bureau in 1960, I toured the plant of the *New York World-Telegram and Sun*, an afternoon daily. The ebullient and feisty general manager, Jacques Caldwell, escorted me into the composing room, where rows of clacking linotype machines translated hand-edited typewritten copy into one-line leaden slugs of type. Caldwell proudly showed me his latest high-tech innovation, which speeded up the time-consuming process of resetting the stock tables for each successive edition. Instead of using the line-set slugs, his tables were set character by character, so that the compositor could quickly substitute a quote of 15-1/4 for one of 14-7/8 as the price went down or up. It was, unchanged, the technology of Gutenberg.

Newspapers were a cumbersome manufacturing business, constricted not only by the cost of newsprint and ink but by the work rules that their powerful specialized craft unions imposed. These unions passed their memberships on from father to son, engaged in notorious featherbedding, and maintained a defiant solidarity in resisting devices or rules that might introduce change and limit their powers. And Powers, Bertram Powers, was the name of one of their most militant officials, who headed Typographical Union Number 6 in New York. His intransigeance led in 1965 to a long and disastrous strike that permanently altered New Yorkers' reading habits and caused three papers to merge and then give up the ghost entirely. Twenty years later, when the unions were resisting New York newspaper publishers' attempts to introduce color (which was by then universal everywhere else in the country), Powers was among a group of labor leaders the *Daily News*'s publisher James Hoge assembled to hear me repeat a presentation I had made to the Bureau board. This showed the discouraging trends in newspapers' position in the advertising market and reviewed advertisers' complaints about their cost efficiency relative to other media. At one point I mentioned the momentous shift to preprinted advertising inserts, away from ROP (run-of-press) ads in the body of the paper. Powers interrupted me. "What's ROP?"*

My first prototypical images of media tycoons probably came from the newspaper publishers depicted in the country-house novels of P. G. Wodehouse. I delighted in the antics of the *New York Evening Graphic*'s Bernarr Macfadden, who also successfully published a string of pulp magazines, including *True Story* and several devoted to what he called Physical Culture. In his eighties, Macfadden was famous for his escapades with very young women, and was always photographed flexing his biceps and sporting a leotard of imitation leopard skin. In 1936, long before William Randolph Hearst was immortalized by Orson Welles in *Citizen Kane*, I read Ferdinand Lundberg's biography, which made him appear both repellent and fascinating.

Such early impressions of publishers made them seem remote and superhuman, like foreign potentates or figures in history. Hearst was reduced to human dimensions for me many years later when his son and namesake unburdened himself on a cross-continental plane ride. "Dad" was for him still a living and demanding presence. (Bill Junior was in an emotional state, his mood shuttling between euphoria and lachrymose self-pity.)

"Hap" Kern, the longtime publisher of the elder Hearst's *Boston Record-American*, described the experience of being summoned to San Simeon, presumably for a top-of-the mountain review of his business. Crossing the country in a Pullman sleeper on the four-and-a-half-day journey, he would arrive in Los Angeles, where a private railroad car took him and a handful of other company executives up the coast to the chief's estate. Dinner was at the long medieval refectory table (still on view in what is now a state museum), with Hearst's mistress, the film actress Marion Davies, acting as hostess. After dinner a new movie was shown,

---

*The analogy might be an electrician asking, "What's a volt?" or a senator asking, "What's a quorum?"

and then all went to bed. The following day the publishers disported themselves around the grounds, awaiting a private audience. After two or three days they might get one, or maybe not, and be told that they could go home, back on the long train ride.

Kern was in his seventies when I knew him; he was six feet two inches, ramrod straight, and dressed in the fashion of the early 1920s, complete with a stiff rounded white collar. His office in the ancient *Record* building appeared to have been furnished in the same period. When he opened several drawers of the imposing dark wood cabinets behind his desk, in a search for old photographs, they turned out to be empty. The office shook whenever the presses (probably also contemporaneous with the collar and the cabinets) were rolling.

At the Bureau's annual dinner in the ballroom of the Waldorf-Astoria, board members on the dais wore white ties and tails; the crowd below was in tuxedos and ball gowns. The West Point glee club sang "Dixie," prompting Southern publishers to mount their chairs, hurling fierce rebel yells.

While most of the publishers brought their wives to such industry affairs, some who traveled solo found the steady flow of free booze impossible to resist. At dinner a nodding head might topple perilously close to the soup. Occasionally voices grew strident and argumentative. When the *New York Times* and the *Washington Post* published the Pentagon Papers in 1971, Frank Warren, the usually quiet publisher of the *Houston Chronicle*, angrily condemned their treachery. He had refused to publish excerpts in his paper. Would it have been a legitimate news story, I asked, if they had first been published in *The Village Voice* or if Daniel Ellsberg had simply distributed copies to everyone? No matter how many people had the documents, he insisted loftily, reporting on what they contained was treason.

It came as no surprise, then, that some weeks after the *Washington Post* began digging into the Watergate story, the press was still treating the break-in as an ordinary burglary. Katharine Graham was puzzled and saddened. "Why don't they understand that this is important?" she asked, rhetorically, because both of us knew the answer. (Almost twenty years after his resignation, Nixon made a triumphant appearance at a publishers' luncheon, flashing one of his victory smiles and ostentatiously kissing Graham, who was seated on the dais.)

The publishers of the old type were strong and self-confident personalities, used to command. One was Irwin Maier of the *Milwaukee Journal*, an outsize version of Teddy Roosevelt without the mustache. A vigorous defender of press freedom, Maier could break his usual reserve to deliver an impassioned attack on the cultural depravity of network television. Another leonine figure was the *Denver Post*'s Palmer ("Ep") Hoyt, a grizzled, growling old editor who was privately thoughtful and warm. When I gave him a candid and dismal appraisal of the quality of most newspapers, he challenged me to name one I respected. I answered, "The *New York Times*." "And what percentage of the people in New York read the *Times*?" "Maybe 20 percent." "Do you think I could publish a paper that was read by only 20 percent of the people in Denver?" It was an upsetting but eye-opening response.

Other publishers were notable for their unusual interests.[1] There was Britt Brown of the *Wichita Eagle-Beacon*, whose view of humanity was expressed in the shrunken head of an Amazonian Indian, hung on the wall behind his desk. Brown was, however, not unique in his fascination with taxidermy. The *Los Angeles Times*'s Otis Chandler kept in his office suite the stuffed carcasses of a grizzly and a polar bear, each rearing ferociously to a ten-foot height.

There was Darrow ("Duke") Tully of the *Phoenix Republic* and *Arizona Gazette*, trim, vigorous, and outspoken at board meetings. A lieutenant colonel in the air force reserve, he wore his uniform back home on all possible occasions, complete with a chestful of medals won as a flying ace in Korea and Vietnam— or so he said until his own newspapers exposed him as a phony and banished him.

Amon Carter, publisher of the *Fort Worth Star-Telegram*, carried a quarter-inch-thick notebook labeled "Texas Scratch Pad" on its embossed leather cover. Each of its pages was made up of four uncut $100 bills.

The publishers and their wives instinctively gravitated into social groupings defined primarily by their wealth, though levels of age and sophistication also came into play. In 1960 most newspapers, including the chains, were still family businesses run by strong-minded men. A handful (like Maier and Hoyt—or Tully, for that matter) had made their own way, but most had come to their power by inheritance. In large cities, fiercely competitive dynasties fought over readers and advertisers. Sales representatives spent most of their time puffing their own papers and denigrating their rivals. They paid little attention to selling the generic qualities of the press. The Bureau was supposed to speak as the industry's unified voice. It was the only institution that brought competitors together and fought their collective battle with other media. Publishers of rival papers, whose ad salesmen on the street were tearing each other apart, sat together on the Bureau's board, comporting themselves with exquisite courtesy. Many of them were also proprietors of television stations that were far more profitable than their newspapers, but it was as press lords that they commanded social prestige and political power.

Since that time the newspaper business, like most others, has seen a steady winnowing of unprofitable enterprises. Ownership has been concentrated in giant corporations under professional managers typically driven to maximize profit and stock values rather than journalistic or civic values. The era of proud and colorful press tycoons has faded into history.

The Bureau strove to provide newspapers with a common front, but this was not easily achieved in a heterogeneous business. There were independently owned and chain newspapers; morning dailies, afternoon dailies, and combinations; big, medium, and small papers; papers with and without broadcast interests; and papers wedded to a vast array of page dimensions, production systems, and research procedures.

In media selling, the prevailing idea was that advertising

decisions would be strongly affected, if not determined, by personal relationships cultivated at social occasions. Media organizations vied with each other in lavish potlatches at conventions of the American Association of Advertising Agencies and of the Association of National Advertisers, held at expensive and isolated resorts like the Greenbrier in White Sulphur Springs, West Virginia. Hearty fellowship on the golf course was expected to give easy access to the client's attention and to the corporate wallet.

Golf was important to the Bureau too. Like other trade associations, we retained the loyalty of the industry's most powerful members by involving them in conventions, client contacts, and meetings that became coveted social events. Publishers newly elected to the board sometimes felt impelled to take golfing lessons to prepare them for the principal activity in the afternoons after the directors' morning meetings.

Lipscomb's favorite sales tool was the award (pronounced *awawhed*), which he bestowed liberally upon the presidents and advertising directors of major advertisers. Some were made the occasion for public ceremonies, others were delivered in the office of the honoree. Samuel Rosenstiel (a.k.a. "Mr. Sam"), the short and notoriously ill-tempered chairman of Schenley's, appeared nonplussed when Charlie and a small delegation of newspaper luminaries trooped into his headquarters to deliver a very large and beautifully framed certificate that attested to his company's cunning use of newspaper advertising.

At the Bureau, Lipscomb had initiated a program of "target account selling," which focused sales efforts on a limited number of large advertisers. We began in each case with an exhaustive study of the targeted company and the industry, developed a modest piece of market research (at a time when many companies did little or none*), and used the findings to demonstrate

---

*The chairman of Sony, on a visit to the United States to introduce a new product, was asked what kind of market research had been done on it. He tapped his skull and replied, "Market research in *here!*"

how a newspaper campaign could be mounted. We even developed prototype ads, prefacing them (to insure against the agency's jealous hostility) with a disclaimer that said these were merely our amateurish efforts and that their own agency's creative staff could do much better.

A presentation to the leading company in an industry would be followed by adaptations for its major competitors and later showings to lower echelons, to the agencies, and often (with much hoopla and a two-screen projection of slides) to national industry conventions.

The higher up one went in the business world, the more considerate and courteous was the reception. At the lower levels of an advertising agency media department, appointments were easily broken, telephone calls went unreturned, and boredom was more visibly expressed.

We concentrated, naturally, on industries that were putting their advertising money into other media. As an example, the toy industry primarily used Saturday morning television to reach children. We did a survey of how toys were bought. It showed that a large proportion were not demanded by a child who had seen it demonstrated on TV, but were purchased by parents and grandparents as birthday gifts, at holidays, or just for the pleasure of giving. These adults weren't watching the kiddie shows, but they could be reached through newspaper ads.

Our research tracked changes in American drinking habits as whiskies fell to vodka and hard drinks gave way to wine and beer. Local independent breweries were steadily losing out to the nationally distributed giants and closing down. At the Wiedemann Brewing Company in Cincinnati, our meeting with top management was at 8 a.m. in a small glass-enclosed cubicle off the employee cafeteria. The company's president asked whether we wanted some coffee or a beer. "A beer," said Jack Kauffman, assuming that this would ingratiate himself with the audience, all of whom ordered coffee, as I did. His early-morning beer arrived; he took a hearty sip and turned his sincere smile to the president: "Say! This is *delicious!*"

Since the Bureau represented the entire North American newspaper industry, and its mission was to influence advertisers of all kinds, my job entailed a good deal of travel to places that only politicians and traveling salesmen are apt to visit. Dayton, Ohio, for instance, was the headquarters of the National Cash Register Company, on whose advertising department I called with a presentation. I was not invited to lunch, but I was told that I could use the company's eating facility. This turned out to be as close as I have ever come to the spirit of "1984." After filling my luncheon tray, I entered a dining hall the size of a great auditorium. It was filled with a subdued murmur. On the main floor, thousands of employees reminiscent of Orwell's proles ate their meals cafeteria-style. At one end of the hall, the corporate executives sat arrayed at a long table on a dais, like the Soviet Politburo at a state banquet. At the other end, on a gigantic screen, was a display of inspirational film shorts. There was also a short inspirational address delivered from the head table by the chief executive officer. In forty-five minutes the meal session had ended and a second shift of workers went through the cafeteria line. This was the apotheosis of corporate efficiency.

While many of our market surveys dealt with transient situations of little applicability today, our research sometimes delved into more important social phenomena. Surveys done at the beginning and again at the end of the 1970s tracked the movement of women into the workforce, the consequent changes in feminine self-image, and the remarkable transformation of family life and consumption habits. Advertisers typically responded to these findings with indifference or denial.

We tackled large issues also in a series of studies that used the Delphi method of forecasting to predict forthcoming changes in general merchandise retailing, in the food business, and in advertising.* In each case, a group of about a dozen leading execu-

---

*My collaborator in these projects was Patrick Robinson, whom I first met when he was the brilliant market research director of Jersey Standard's Canadian subsidiary.

tives in the industry were brought together at an isolated conference center and subjected to a day and a half of intense interaction in which they speculated about the trends already under
way in the society, technology, and their own particular domain.
A questionnaire based on these discussions was then sent to a
larger panel of experts in the same field, and the findings tabulated. These forecasts, it turned out, were for the most part quite
accurate, perhaps because they mainly extrapolated from already
well-established tendencies. But many important technological
innovations could not have been imagined, nor could foreign political crises and the turns of the business cycle.

To get the attention of corporate managements, we enlisted the
newspaper publisher members of our board of directors, who
knew their opposite numbers in hometown industries. For a
while we were quite successful at this, though the leading executives to whom we talked rarely sullied themselves with marketing decisions, let alone the trivial matter of selecting media.
William Knowland, the publisher of the *Oakland Tribune*, just
retired from the U.S. Senate and a recent contender for the Republican presidential nomination, set up a meeting with the top
brass at Crown Zellerbach, the San Francisco–based paper giant.
The presentation centered on research we had done on the consumption of household paper products. As I went through a series of charts that dealt with habits of toilet paper use* I became
aware that Knowland, seated in the front row, was gravely nodding his head as if to confirm what I was saying.

Bill Knowland was large, stately, and kindly. He later committed suicide, trapped in an illicit romance. While his heirs
continued to reign in the rickety Tribune Tower, Oakland and the
Tribune sadly declined. The paper never seized the opportunity
to expand its readership to nearby suburban Contra Costa

---

*Ours was not the pathbreaking study on this vital aspect of human activity.
Ernest Dichter had already divided humanity into "folders" and "crinklers."

County, which was growing fast. There a new competitor appeared in the form of a free-distribution semi-weekly, which became a very prosperous paid daily, the *Contra Costa Times*. The *Times* was owned by Dean Lesher, an elderly attorney whose attractive young widow later sold it to the Knight Ridder chain. She quickly remarried a rodeo performer and died mysteriously soon after, leaving him in a legal battle with Lesher's children over the publisher's large fortune. The *Tribune* itself passed out of the hands of the Knowland family and ultimately became part of a string of East Bay dailies owned by a fresh and rising newspaper tycoon, Dean Singleton. Such dramas seemed endemic to the newspaper business.

As I took on additional tasks, I could rarely continue firsthand involvement in field research. Small, personally conducted studies would in any case not pass muster with the big advertisers to whom we addressed our presentations. Interviewing and fieldwork for large-scale studies had to be farmed out. Data were fed to us through a chain of intermediaries, obliterating the direct connection with respondents that I had always enjoyed and considered essential.

In all my previous employment, the goals of the organization had been different from those I held as a research professional, but they were not incompatible. At the Bureau I was to be an advocate, engaged in selling not just research projects, as I had done at McCann-Erickson, but a particular form of advertising with deficiencies as well as merits. Advocacy without credibility could serve no purpose, but credibility required an adherence to proper professional practices. I resolved the ambiguities by setting up a new marketing group parallel to the research department. The researchers were to do what researchers should do, with complete objectivity. The marketing managers were to define the requirements for research that met the sales needs of the industry, so that a good presentation could be developed from the results. They were to work in tandem with the salesmen ("account executives," we called them) who cultivated client contacts, looked for sales opportunities, and set up meetings.

The Bureau's sales staff (all male) included a curious assortment of personalities. A dazzling speaker, retail vice president
Mark Arnold, enraptured merchants with a demonstration of the
Magic Slate, from which an advertisement disappeared after
thirty seconds "just like a broadcast commercial." Marketing vice
president Charles Kinsolving, Jr., who had worked at NBC, could
infuriate a hall filled with newspaper sales representatives as he
nonchalantly impersonated a network television vice president.
(Kinsolving had been my assistant on the study of the USIA. An irrepressible raconteur and an intrepid world traveler, he combined his daytime job with even more strenuous activity as a
district leader of the Democratic party.)

At the opposite political pole was the dashing Howard
Keefe, who maintained, uncontaminated by the passage of time,
the philosophical outlook of his former boss, the *Chicago Tribune's* Colonel Robert McCormick. Keefe, a former navy pilot,
spent his weekends dangerously racing his P-51 Mustang fighter
plane, "Miss America," at air shows around the country. On occasion, at Bureau board meetings, he would take a passenger
along for a terrifying ride, looping the loop, performing Immelmann maneuvers, and buzzing closely above publishers' wives
lazing by the swimming pool. I returned to Palm Springs from
one such excursion to be told that I had missed all the excitement. "Some maniac was dive-bombing the hotel!"

Another salesman had been a colleague of "Dutch" Reagan
as a radio announcer in Iowa; yet another was writing a biography of Horace Greeley, a collateral ancestor; two others left the
Bureau to become evangelical ministers. Uldis Grava, our marketing manager, led a double life as a leader of the movement to
free the Baltic nations from the Soviet yoke. (He was apologetically expelled from Finland after he confronted Foreign Minister
Andrei Gromyko at an international meeting in Helsinki.*)

---

*Grava found a second career with RFE/RL, and a third as head of Latvian public television.

The physical production of the presentations was done by the creative department, which wrote scripts, prepared storyboards and artwork, and handled the mechanics of slides, films, and audio recordings. A perennial difficulty in producing research presentations and booklets was to get the art department to recognize that the primary job was not to produce aesthetically pleasing designs but to communicate what we had learned.

Lipscomb believed in face-to-face intimacy with clients and feared they would fall asleep in a darkened room. So in the early days of target account selling, presentations were hand-lettered on cardboard panels and carried in backbreaking custom-made black cases. (We switched to slides because projectors were lighter to carry.) Major presentations were made to large audiences at trade association conventions, and some of our most ambitious shows were put on for gatherings within the newspaper industry itself.

Ed Falasca, the Bureau's creative director when I first arrived, was the organization's flaming soul. His stirring speeches, corny art, and clichéd copy gave him an instinctive rapport with the cultural values of Middle American ad directors, numerically the Bureau's principal constituents. Falasca's appetite for work was prodigious; he drove through the night along winding mountain roads to get from a dinner speaking engagement in one small town to a breakfast meeting hundreds of miles away. He clashed with Kauffman, and when he left, spurned the inscribed silver bowl that Lipscomb tried to present to him. "Find someone else named Ed Falasca and give it to *him*!" he snarled. (He became a suburban librarian.) Falasca's successor, who strutted about like a proud pigeon, promised to bring a "touch of humanity" to our presentations. He left precipitously when he was discovered to be double-dipping, turning freelance assignments over to a dummy company he had set up at home.

The Bureau's most flamboyant creative director was Steve Sohmer, who achieved that position while still in his twenties. He had written a successful coming-of-age novel and reveled in the Yippie political slogan, "Never trust anyone over thirty!" But he soon became thirty himself. Sohmer emblazoned his personal stationery with the two lightning flashes of the Nazi SS. He had a gift for producing well-crafted and exciting presentations and an equally great talent for spending money. He lived in a state of constant agitation but was fearless in handling business magnates like the chairman and president of General Motors, whom he induced to star in a funny film short destined to be shown only once, at a meeting with the publishers.

Sohmer went on to become, briefly, the president of Columbia Pictures. When I finished an exhausting two-hour meeting with him and his staff at six o'clock one evening, after a day of back-to-back presentations at three other studios, he ushered me into his corner office, called on his secretary to get him a whiskey, and then asked whether I wanted a cup of coffee. Unrelentingly aspiring, Steve went on to acquire a doctorate from Oxford with a dissertation on Shakespeare's hidden Catholicism, and was sued by a former professor who claimed he had stolen her ideas.

Much of the humor in our presentations was the work of Steve's successor, Henry Simons, who kept a large collection of old joke books from which he culled evergreen specimens to serve up along with incongruous photographs in our slide shows. He would show a picture of the gangster Al Capone, to whom he attributed the saying, "You can get far with a kind word, but a kind word and a gun will get you even farther."

Our presentations to the movie studios sought to convince them that newspapers still deserved an important place in their advertising schedules, though they had turned increasingly to television commercials to promote new productions. But our research went well beyond the subject of advertising.

The rise of television and the decline of urban centers had brought annual per capita film attendance down from twenty-nine times in 1946 to five times in 1985. In a nationwide survey we found that nearly three of four people over fifty had not gone to the movies in a year. Adolescents eager to get out of the house and young adults dating accounted for a disproportionate share of theatrical filmgoing; the content and tone of Hollywood's output was geared to that youthful audience. In an earlier study we had seen that youthful moviegoers were attracted to "vivid horror scenes" and "vivid sex scenes," "wounding and killing scenes," and scenes of fires, explosions, and crashes. The film industry had not neglected these interests.

Most filmgoers went to the movies with another member of the household and went out for a meal or refreshment before or after the show. They were drawn to the movies not merely to be entertained, informed, amused, or aroused by the actual content of the film but as an occasion for conversation, shared emotions, and diversion from the regular daily routine.

But increasingly the audience for movies was not to be found in the theater; it was in the home, on cable (especially pay cable) channels and on videocassettes. In its composition, this home audience was the same mass public that Hollywood had drawn before television forced it to change. As the process continued, the consequences might be a reversal of the trend for fewer films to be produced, a broadened range of choice, and a strengthened appeal of film as a shared family experience for children and adults. This would mean not necessarily a return to the innocuous formulas of Hollywood's Golden Era but a shift away from the images and techniques that the filmmakers adopted to defend their domain during the years of television's ascendancy.

The message of our study was that Hollywood would have to rethink the assumption that its audience was people in their teens and twenties; it would again have to seek out a larger mass audience. The presentation was made to the movie moguls, after their leading lights, Lew Wasserman and the Motion Picture Association of America's honey-voiced Jack Valenti, had harangued the publishers about their industry's problems. Sidney Sheinberg, Wasserman's next-in-line at Universal Studios, disputed my basic point. "The kids are the ones who go to the movies!" he insisted. Several other moguls spoke up from the floor to complain about newspaper movie critics. What they wanted, in exchange for all the advertising they placed in the press, was only favorable reviews.

Our original research was especially welcome in industries that had no substantial market studies of their own, but we also ventured into fields on which a substantial amount of information was already being churned out. Our studies of car-buying preferences showed a shift toward smaller cars while Detroit was still producing great finned monsters and well before the Japanese made heavy inroads into the market. I discussed this at a lunch with Tom Staudt, a former business school professor who was now the marketing director of General Motors' Chevrolet Division.

The Bureau board had recently met with the directors of the American Petroleum Institute. As a quid pro quo for our sales presentation to them, the heads of three of the largest oil companies had offered a masterful overview of the world's energy problems. They cited the country's growing dependence on imports from the politically unstable Middle East and stressed the need for conservation. I played back the gist of their message to Staudt and asked how much of his company's engineering research was being directed to improve fuel efficiency. None, he said. General Motors' huge product research facility was preoccupied with the subject of product safety in the aftermath of Ralph Nader's book *Unsafe at Any Speed*.

The pseudo-anthropological term "corporate culture" had not yet come into vogue, but there were distinct differences in style among the men (all men!) who ran the various automobile companies. Ford executives were bright and convivial. The General Motors crew tended to be stolid, humorless, and extremely formal. With the Japanese on the West Coast, relations were stiff, even though they handed out nifty pocket calculators to everyone.

At Chrysler, two vice presidents arrived a few minutes late for an 8:30 a.m. meeting and were viciously dressed down by the company's president, Lynn Townsend. Townsend, tall, stern, and pompous, harangued the publishers with lengthy monologues about the constrictive policies and miscellaneous misdeeds of the Washington bureaucrats.

By contrast, his successor, Lee Iacocca, sounded many of the same themes entertainingly and with great vigor. The man who had fired him, Henry Ford II, also enjoyed delivering lengthy off-the-cuff comments on the state of the world. After our evening dinners, speeches, presentations, and liqueurs, he would join the publishers in our hospitality suite—one of the boys, though not joining the late-into-the-night poker games. Once, after a beer too many, he began to fulminate against the "damn Jews" in the presence of the *Washington Post*'s Katharine Meyer Graham. The *Worcester Telegram*'s gracious publisher Dick Steele later apologized to her for the offensive remarks. She replied, "Oh, he's such a naughty boy!"

At McCann-Erickson a magazine salesman had arrived at my office unannounced to tell me magisterially that he had been given the agency as his full-time assignment at an annual salary of $30,000 (twice mine), and that I was to be his principal preoccupation. Another magazine representative with no particular story to tell invited me to a lunch, which he preceded with three martinis, accompanied with a bottle of wine, and followed with a couple of brandies. Another ever-jolly fellow periodically invited media buyers (then still mostly male) to swinging parties with airline hostesses at his duplex apartment.

As time passed I became a student, even a connoisseur, of effective salesmanship. In the face of television's mounting offensive, the Radio Advertising Bureau's Kevin Sweeney dressed up in a Confederate uniform, brandished a saber, and cried out to the faithful, "The battle is not lost!" *Parade*'s "Red" Motley transfixed audiences with the fervid cadences of an old-time preacher. He advised me, "Make your point and then just walk away from it. Just walk away!" The ever-jaunty and debonair Ed Crimmins, a thwarted thespian, used his considerable talent as a sales representative for the Advertising Checking Bureau, which provided advertisers with proof that newspapers were actually running their ads. A different kind of actor, who affected Western costumes, was a sales manager for a Sunday magazine. Known as "the sagebrush horse-shit artist," he preached the merits of "targeting," counseling customers, "Don't use a blunderbuss! Use only a long rifle!"

There was no scarcity of colorful individuals within the newspaper business itself. The *Chicago Tribune*'s flamboyant promotion director, Pierre Martineau, was one of two supersalesmen who used research ingeniously to sell newspaper advertising. Martineau had the battered features of an old pugilist. Gruff and tireless, he remained perfectly lucid after six dry martinis. He was an avid exponent and proselytizer for Warner and Gardner's Social Research, Inc., and used their consumer research with great effect to open advertising clients' doors by giving them information about their own customers.

The other great newspaper salesman was Alan Donnahoe, the research director of the Richmond newspapers. (Like many morning-evening combinations under the same ownership, they pursued independent and different editorial policies. One of their editors explained that his own paper was "reactionary" while the other was "extremely reactionary.") Donnahoe used coincidental telephone interviews to demonstrate the meager size of the broadcast audience in comparison with the broad reach of his own medium. Austere and solemn, he talked to agency media buyers with the passion of a trial attorney (which he had originally been) addressing a jury, marshaling his facts so relentlessly that his spellbound listeners could raise no questions. Donnahoe was fiercely loyal to his publisher, J. Tennant Bryan, a Virginia aristocrat of great gentility who peered at interlocutors over half-glasses and who, with the addition of a wig, would have fit easily into any group portrait of the Republic's Founding Fathers. Donnahoe masterminded the expansion of the company into a substantial publicly held corporation, Media General, from which he retired as president.

When I joined the Bureau in 1960, newspapers' share of all U.S. advertising was equivalent to that of television, radio, and magazines put together. This fact became a standing sales point in our presentations, on the premise that the judgment of the marketplace reflected the true value of the medium. But television kept adding to its share of national advertising. With the growth of chain retailing, it became a force in retail advertising as well. Our claims to supremacy therefore demanded periodic revision.

In one respect, newspapers had a clear advantage over the broadcast media. Their readership was highest among the better-educated, higher-income people who were the best prospects for most goods and services. (Paradoxically, this tilt became more pronounced as daily readership lost the near-universality that it once enjoyed, falling from 80 percent in 1960 to 50 percent in 2002.) By contrast, television viewing was and remains most popular among people with the most time on their hands and least likely to read for either information or pleasure.

Foolishly, the president of NBC, Julian Goodman, a newsman in his earlier career, chose to highlight television's virtues in a keynote address to the Association of National Advertisers in 1968, asserting that its "heavy viewers" (this was the operative phrase in advertising researchspeak) were the most prosperous members of the public. Since this directly contradicted our own sales mantra, as well as the facts, I issued a rebuttal at the next conference of newspaper advertising executives, and fortified it with an offer of $10,000 to anyone who could provide evidence to support Goodman's statement.

The following week I entered a crowded elevator and was shocked to notice that the man next to me was wearing a button proclaiming, "Leo Bogart Is a Heavy Viewer." These buttons, it turned out, were being worn by television sales people all over town. They were the creation of Paul Klein, NBC's marketing director, a big, loud, clever cynic who later became the network's head of programming on the West Coast. Klein followed this promotional blitz with a letter published in *Sponsor* magazine, in which he compared me to Joseph Goebbels.

Klein distributed to agencies and advertisers a "memorandum" addressed to me, pointing out that "Cadillac division will be taking its story to TV for the first time. (Nice to know that your message is getting across, isn't it?)" Tom Coffin, NBC's research director, forwarded this to me with a dry handwritten note: "Leo, My people are getting restive."* The episode was especially painful for Coffin, who was required to prepare a strange statement attempting to rationalize Goodman's false claim. The television people played rough, but then, there was a lot of money at stake. Klein later left NBC to start a company that supplied pornographic and other pay videos to hotel guests.

Shortly before I arrived at the Bureau, Charlie Lipscomb had orchestrated what he hoped would be a major research enterprise. He had been approached by the Harvard Business School to support an ambitious study of the value of repetition in advertising, to be conducted by a doctoral candidate, John M. Stewart. Stewart's thesis adviser, and the prime mover in the project's design, was my old friend Raymond Bauer, a social psychologist with a keen intelligence and catholic interests. (He had been interviewing Soviet defectors in Germany before taking the post at Harvard.)

Coincidentally Lipscomb had been talking to executives of a leading public relations firm, Hill and Knowlton, which had a group of Canadian newsprint manufacturers as a client. After repeatedly raising the price of their product, the members of this Newsprint Information Committee were anxious to repair frayed

---

*Coffin, a mild-mannered man whose sailboat was the joy of his life, had been a psychology professor at Hofstra College on Long Island. In television's early days he compared the buying habits of television owners and their neighbors. This ingenious piece of research, known as the "Hofstra Study," clearly demonstrated television's power to sell branded goods and became the cornerstone of the television industry's advertising sales promotion. Coffin was brought to NBC by its research eminence, Hugh ("Mal") Beville, an important figure in the development of radio research.

ties to their customers, American publishers. At Lipscomb's urging, the Canadians had funded "the Harvard project" (as it was called), which the Bureau was to monitor and, if things worked out, exploit to promote newspaper advertising. Lipscomb had obtained cooperation from the managers of two consumer brands (Sara Lee frozen chicken and Lestare bleach) and had also persuaded the Fort Wayne newspapers to provide free advertising space. The study was complex, with the city divided into matched districts; one area carried no ads, another had ads for four weeks, a third for eight weeks, and a fourth for twenty weeks. Altogether, 6,200 people were interviewed in successive waves.

Hill and Knowlton considered that their valuable account was at stake in the project's successful outcome. Hopefully, it would demonstrate that sustained newspaper advertising paid off in additional sales. Unfortunately, unforeseen complications arose. Since the Harvard Business School prided itself on being in the technological avant-garde, the tabulations were to be done on a mainframe computer. This was somewhat daring, since there was little experience to draw upon. Weeks and months dragged on while programs were debugged and data unsuccessfully run and rerun. These delays threatened to impede the funding I was hoping to get from the Canadians for the project I considered to be of highest priority—a national study of newspaper readership. Happily, they were persuaded to go ahead on this new front while maintaining their support for the Harvard study. After more than a year passed, I had to insist that Bauer and Stewart run the most critical statistical tables on an old-fashioned IBM machine, and I put together a joint presentation to an audience of agency research directors. (Stewart eventually got his computer to work; his report was published several years later.[2])

The study produced mixed results. It showed that repetition increased buying and buying intentions up to a point, but that the effects then leveled off. The most striking inference I drew was that it demonstrated the importance of changing the outer form of messages in the course of an advertising campaign rather than repeating the same ad again and again. This conclusion has apparently still not sunk in. Because of the high cost of producing television commercials, they are typically run over and over, deadening the audience's response.

Over the next twenty years the Canadians funded a number of large research projects that investigated reading and other uses of media, the intricate workings of advertising, and consumer buying habits.

The newsprint executives exuded black pin-striped conservatism. Some were highly personable, as befitted men who routinely negotiated multi-million-dollar contracts. Their meetings were held in high-ceilinged rooms with Edwardian furnishings in luxurious but gloomy Montreal hotels. Although their initial objective was to win the publishers' goodwill, I tried to convince them (and did) that their interests were also being served directly by research that helped sell more advertising pages and thus raised the demand for paper. They in turn convinced me that they were engaged in a precarious business that demanded very long-range planning. The hugely expensive machinery in their mills required years to manufacture, so that a miscalculation of future paper demand could have grievous consequences. (In Jonkoping, Sweden, I once toured a plant that housed a totally automated machine a city block long. Logs went in at one end, rolls of newsprint emerged at the other. The only human intervention was that of an enormous muscular Valkyrie wearing a leather apron. Wielding a mallet, she knocked the rolls apart as they came off the line.)

In 1960, paid and audited circulation was the accepted measurement of newspaper size. I considered it essential for newspapers to demonstrate their full impact by showing their total readership rather than the number of copies they printed and sold. A few large papers had already done this kind of survey, but they had used different research companies and different methods.

I recognized, however, that the concept of audience, so useful to magazines, had less utility to newspapers. A single issue of *Life*, with a circulation of six million at its peak, generated a total audience of thirty million readers over the course of a month. This prodigious figure was still only a fraction of the total public. By contrast, a single issue of a daily newspaper published every day and subscribed to by 75 percent of the households in its market could never accumulate a similarly high proportion of "pass-along" readers.

Our first national audience study, "The Daily Newspaper and Its Reading Public," underwent technical review by the Advertising Research Foundation, which represented agencies, advertisers, and media. The presentation that resulted from it was widely promoted, and stimulated metropolitan dailies to conduct audience research of their own. I wanted newspapers to follow this model, "bringing them into the nineteenth century," I told Lipscomb.*

As the stock of publicly listed newspaper corporations soared, publishers squeezed expenses and were reluctant to make what I considered to be necessary long-term investments in research and development. This was illustrated by my experience with ten newspapers that were induced to cooperate in a one-year experiment to place their classified advertising on-line through CompuServe, a pioneer Internet service provider. By the mid-1980s almost all newspapers were setting type by computer and

---

*The Bureau had been an important force in advertising research for a long time before my arrival. Its most important effort, which continued between the 1930s and 1950s, was a "Continuing Study of Newspaper Readership," an aggregation of studies done for individual papers. In these studies an interviewer took each reader through the paper, asking what items had been "noted" and "read" on the original reading. It was demonstrable that big ads were "noted" better than small ads, ads with color better than those in black and white, ads with big pictures better than those that were cluttered in appearance, and so on. The Bureau's presentations to agencies exploited this trove of information, particularly in encouraging copywriters and art directors to follow the principles that led to success.

could readily convert their texts into a transmittable electronic format. My hope was to combine electronic classified ads from many papers and make them accessible to people outside each paper's home market. (A job seeker in Boston might be able to see what was available in Houston or San José, or even what had been advertised within the past two weeks.) At the end of the year, several of the papers still had not ironed out the technical problems of putting their text on-line. There was as yet no cash flow to offset the modest costs of the project. The publishers demanded instant gratification. One by one they pulled out, leaving the way open for new outside organizations to capture a significant chunk of newspapers' valuable advertising business in the 1990s. Classified advertising represented a growing part of the industry's income as the traditional mainstay—retail advertising—weakened.

Although retailers had been reliable clients of newspapers, they were increasingly experimenting with television and with magazines. Compared with the national manufacturers of branded goods, they had done very little research on their customers. I developed the thesis that many retail buying decisions were made without forethought, and that newspaper advertising could prompt such decisions because of its near-universal daily exposure. (At that time three of four adults read a newspaper every day.) Several large-scale studies supported this premise.

The first one, in 1965, was conducted among 10,382 women in five localities.* They were asked to report in detail on all the items they had shopped for in the past week (other than groceries, toilet articles, and drugs), what stores they had visited, and whether or not they had bought the item. They were also asked what items they planned to buy soon, and to name the store or stores where they planned to shop. Seven days later the same questions were repeated.†

---

*Cleveland, Little Rock, Sioux Falls, Eureka, and Rutland, Vermont.

†When an item had been mentioned in the first interview as an intended purchase, but was not mentioned a week later as bought or as a planned purchase, a direct question was asked about it.

In the second study, conducted in the spring of 1974,* 5,900 female heads of households were contacted three times each, twice by telephone and once with a mail questionnaire. They also kept a diary to record all their shopping over a three-day period. Twenty-seven hundred of their husbands also filled in a mail questionnaire.

Because the respondents were questioned about their visits to specific stores in identifiable geographic locations, both studies were confined to individual metropolitan areas, selected to represent a variety of marketing situations. The findings were remarkably consistent from market to market.

The following paper distills the findings of this research on the dynamics of buying decisions.

THE CONSUMER AS A MOVING TARGET (1985)

Most research into consumer behavior concerns either the motivations and decisions of individual buyers or the market trends that represent the sum total of their actions. There is a third way of looking at what consumers do: to regard their buying interests as transient, what they buy as inseparable from where they buy it, and their actions as individually somewhat unpredictable. Consider the two usual approaches first:

1. *Buying Decisions.* Studies of the *process* by which individuals decide what to buy analyze the cross-pressure of forces that influence them. Such research may describe subtypes of consumer behavior or variations from the general pattern. The objective is to show what leads to a particular purchase.

2. *Market Analysis.* The second and more common type of research deals with the aggregate effect of all the individual purchase decisions. These

---

*The fieldwork was conducted by Audits and Surveys, Inc. It should be noted that this followed the energy crisis caused by the Arab oil embargo, which reduced automobile use.

studies describe the market and identify the most
promising potential customers. Surveys reveal how
much merchandise of a particular type is purchased
and how much consumed, in different types of
stores, by different kinds of people.

Research of the first type is diagnostic. It
concentrates on the dynamics of the *individual*
purchase decision. Research of the second type is
descriptive; it provides a static snapshot of the
market as a whole. Market segmentation studies
(which divide consumers into categories) must
assemble data in such a way as to freeze them for
dissection.

An alternate perspective considers a customer
as an elusive, moving target undergoing continuous
transformation. It is a target moving both in time
(as priorities, needs, and interests shift under
competitive and environmental pressures) and also
in space (as different stores and shopping
locations offer contending attractions). The
connection between these two kinds of movement is
illuminated by the survey findings.

For two of three customers, shopping for items
other than food and drugs is apt to take them some
distance from home. In the preceding month, over
half have shopped for general merchandise only or
mostly outside their own neighborhoods. A sizable
part of all retail business is done in shopping
centers, as distinct from the traditional urban
centers or neighborhood shopping districts or
streets.*

For food and drugs, three of four shopping
trips are made within the home neighborhood or
area. For general merchandise, people are willing
to travel much farther.† Low-income shoppers (who

---

*In 1999 two-thirds of the people interviewed by my longtime colleague Stuart
Tolley said they did most of their shopping in malls.

†This merely verified a commonplace of retailing theory known as Reilly's Law.
For inexpensive items, about half went to a location five or more miles away from
home and over a fifth traveled at least ten miles. For big-ticket items, like furniture
and major appliances, three-fifths traveled five miles or more and three in ten went
ten miles or more.

also tend to be older) venture out for shorter distances than high-income (and younger) shoppers.

Why do women go to a particular shopping area? Nearly half mention factors directly related to the location: closeness to home or to work, convenience; some were already drawn to the area for another reason. Only in two of five cases does a typical shopping trip for general merchandise lead the consumer from home to a shopping area and back home again.

Why did they go to that particular shopping area on that day? Over half refer to an immediate need; they had to have something right away, or it was their last chance to buy an item. A substantial proportion of all the purchases made had not been planned or previously thought of. "Big-ticket" [costly] purchases are more likely to result from needs perceived well in advance; the amount of money involved calls for reflection or family discussion. When the expenditure is small, the consumer is more likely to make what retailers call an "impulse purchase."

But most purchases are purposeful rather than impulsive, and so is most shopping activity. Conversion from search or shopping into actual purchasing varies substantially from one type of article to another. For inexpensive items like lingerie and men's underwear, seven of ten shopping visits to a store result in a purchase. Expensive items like furniture and major appliances are carefully comparison-shopped over a period of time, and seven of ten trips to a store to look at these items do *not* result in a purchase. Shopping is cautious when fashion, taste, styling, and color scheme enter into the decision.

The average woman mentions 1.7 items of general merchandise that she plans to buy. Only a very small percentage report purchase plans for any particular item. Shoppers for dresses, furniture, rugs, and draperies crowd the stores and represent aggregate annual sales in the billions of dollars. Yet those shoppers are only a tiny fraction of the

population. On any given day the market for even
the most widely purchased item must be regarded as
extremely thin.*

The percentage who actually shop and *buy* is
smaller still. Indeed, the individuals who plan "to
buy soon" account for only one-fourth of the next
week's purchases. The vast majority of dresses sold
in any given week are sold to customers who would
not have said a week earlier that they planned to
buy a dress. The same holds true for virtually
every other kind of merchandise.

In spite of all this volatility, the percentage
who plan to buy any given item and the percentage
who shopped for it and bought it are practically
identical. The apparent stability in the size of
the market and in the extent of consumer activity
masks a constant shifting of buying intentions and
interests. The substantial number who drop their
buying intentions is replaced by new people coming
into the market.

The total market in any given week represents a
tiny percentage of the potential customers.
Substantial effects of promotion on sales may be
reflected in the buying activity of only a small
number of people.

How does the tremendous spatial mobility of
today's shopper relate to the psychological
mobility that results in a constant revision of
purchase intentions? Merchandise is perceived,
compared, and purchased in context. The salience
and attractiveness of different potential purchases
are influenced by their prominence in the retail
store. As customers move from one shopping location
to another, and from one store to another, new
buying interests are aroused.

What the customer buys is inseparable from when

---

*With package goods as with general merchandise, the same principle applies:
markets that are huge in annual volume break down to rather small slivers of activity
on any one day. A 1969 study among 2,438 housewives in six markets found that
even for products bought often and massively advertised, only a small percentage of
the customers had an active buying interest on any given day.

and where she buys it. The selection of goods available in a specific retail location, their juxtaposition and display, present options and influences that govern the ultimate choice.

Any purchase or any sudden awareness of consumer need inevitably changes other purchase plans and priorities. A shopper is often attracted to a particular location because of one intended purchase and ends up with other purchases in hand.

The distribution of shopping among different types of stores varies from item to item and from market to market, since each has a unique mix of retail establishments. There are substantial variations in the rate of conversion from shopping to purchase for different types of stores in different markets and also for individual stores of a particular type. This translates into tremendous differences in sales and profits, even with equivalent store traffic produced by location and advertising.

The overall level of potential interest in any particular consumer item is typically very low, even though a small fraction of the public who are active prospects may be highly interested in it. Advertising and promotion are effective to the degree that they exert leverage on the relatively few people who are susceptible to persuasion at any given moment.

Advertising churns up latent buying interests and thereby stimulates the movement of customers that is essential to build store traffic. This traffic is not merely the basis of the retailer's success; it also assures the manufacturer of a continuing active demand for the product in spite of the fact that at any moment very few people are interested in it.*

Shopping by mail and phone [and now on the Internet] has increased phenomenally. But this kind

---

*A 1976 study of 1,347 shoppers found that among those who shopped for an item because they had seen it advertised, an additional dollar was spent for other merchandise for every dollar spent on the advertised item.

of purchase activity cannot substitute for the
social stimulation of the store, its endless
reminders of unfulfilled desires, and its ability
to evoke latent buying impulses.

To a certain degree, purchasing patterns can be
explained by the social or personality
characteristics of the consumer. Individual stores,
through their pricing policies, merchandise choice,
and style of presentation and service, tend to
attract customers of a certain kind. But a great
deal of shopping activity simply reflects the
enormous volatility in the market itself and the
complex and partially random interaction of
customer movement and merchandise offerings.

Market surveys inevitably tell us that a
minority of "heavy users" account for a substantial
chunk of total consumption for almost any item. But
most of the purchases for most products are made by
people who are not in the highest income bracket.
The conventional ways of "segmenting" the market
lose much of their meaning when the market is
recognized as thin and the consumer is seen as a
moving target.

This study dealt with what people do, rather than with what
they believe. As in surveys of opinion, the evidence came from
asking questions. But consumer decisions are manifested in impersonal records as well as in personal testimony. There was a
time when a manufacturer's best intelligence about what was
going on in the marketplace came from sales statistics and from
the impressions gathered by sales representatives. Any assessment of the effects of marketing actions had to rely on the manufacturer's records as sales rose and fell in response to product
and packaging changes, pricing, retailer relations, and promotion. This changed with the advent of market research that
looked at the sum total of consumption and purchasing and posi-
tioned the manufacturer's own brands within the context of the
total market. It became possible to track those factors that affected sales but over which the manufacturer had no control: sea-

sonality, general changes in the economy, and long-term changes in consumer habits.

Attention thus shifted from unit and dollar sales volume to market share as an indication of competitive position and as a basis for evaluating marketing programs. Records of orders received and factory shipments began to carry less weight than the records of sell-through (sales to the ultimate consumer), as measured in syndicated store-audit or warehouse withdrawal reports which track product shipments from wholesalers to stores. These usually show rather small changes from a given two-month or one-month reporting period to the next, either in industry sales volume or in the position of any given brand.

This kind of information was vital for the food manufacturers and retailers who were among the newspaper industry's principal clients. At the Newspaper Advertising Bureau (our organization's new name), Richard Neale developed a periodic report and presentation reviewing current trends in the grocery business. (Neale had produced this long-established report at the defunct Sunday supplement *This Week*.) He was in close contact with the food industry's leaders and highly familiar with new developments.

In the early 1980s grocery manufacturers were introducing the Universal Product Code, a bar symbol placed on packaging that could be passed over an electronic scanner at the supermarket checkout counter, automatically ringing up the price and identity of the merchandise. Sales information on individual products, brands, and package sizes was recorded as an incidental by-product, but most grocery chains were neglecting it. Neale was intrigued by the possibility of using these data to demonstrate the sales effects of newspaper advertising. He began to acquire the sales records for a few products from his friends in some of the chains, and collected a series of case histories that demonstrated that sales went up after an ad appeared. The ads were almost always associated with price reductions or coupon promotions. This made it hard to isolate the specific effects of the advertisement from the effects of pricing.

The accepted source of sales measurements in the grocery business was the Nielsen Food Index, which conducted store audits in a national sample of supermarkets. They recorded store inventory at the beginning and end of each two-month period, collected the records of the merchandise received in the interim, and calculated how many units had been sold. The resulting figures on market size and brand share were expressed in handsome, crisp charts. As I learned in the Ritz Crackers mystery case at McCann-Erickson, the industry accepted these as the literal truth.

I felt that scanner data might be more reliable than store audits. They could provide an accurate and sensitive measurement of actual consumer purchasing and provide it weekly (or even daily, if desired) if the sample of stores could be enlarged and made representative. The procedure could also be adapted for market and advertising tests.* The prospect aroused Jack Kauffman's entrepreneurial lust. As the Bureau's president, he was enthusiastic about any idea for expanding the organization's income. Despite skepticism on the part of some of our directors, a subsidiary called Nabscan was set up, and part of the Bureau's national sales staff was diverted to sell its services.

A motley assortment of grocery chains had been assembled by opportunity rather than by plan. The supermarket chains became aware that they were sitting on valuable information and began to charge heavily for it. Some of the largest ones refused to release their sales records in spite of assurances of confidentiality. I asked Jerome Greene, a well-regarded sampling statistician, to solve the problem of projecting the numbers so that they could represent the national picture. The results from the rebalanced sample provided a high degree of accuracy. But they were at odds with the accepted numbers from Nielsen. Companies

---

*Market tests are widely used to try out new products and promotional methods. These may be introduced in one or more places to gauge their success. More ambitiously, they may be matched with other markets to serve as a control (just as Patras was the control for Salonica), or different versions may be compared by introducing them in different places.

worked from a body of trend data to which they were happily accustomed, and they resisted any evidence that looked different, even if it was more reliable.

Several years before Nabscan's creation, I had brought a thick sheaf of computer printouts of supermarket sales data to a meeting of the Committee on Research Development, a small, informal discussion group of leading corporate and agency research directors and business professors.* They were uniformly unimpressed. The general reaction was, "Who's got the time to wade through all this?" I had this in mind later, when I prepared an analysis to demonstrate what scanner data could show about the dynamics of the consumer market.

THE TURBULENT DEPTHS OF MARKETING (1989)

```
In packaged goods marketing, these premises are
generally accepted and are constantly being
reinforced by the standard data sources:
    1. Changes in market size and brand position
usually occur slowly over time.
    2. Price cuts for a brand generally build
market share; price increases reduce it.
    3. Because most major packaged goods brands
compete nationally, they must analyze their markets
and plan their marketing strategies on a national
or broad regional scale.
    4. Big packaged goods advertisers expose their
messages to the public in major media most of the
time.
    5. Any substantial advertiser in any major
```

---

*The CORD group included wildly disparate personalities. Its organizer was R. D. ("Dusty") Hardesty, the research director of Johnson and Johnson, who retained the speech patterns of his native rural Arkansas and had the temperament of a dormant volcano. Disturbed by the impassioned tone of a postmidnight debate over marketing arcana, he flung an empty beer can across the room, narrowly missing the head of Francesco Nicosia, a Berkeley professor whose youth had been spent as a partisan fighter in the Tuscan hills. For some reason, the hypersensitive Nicosia never showed up for later meetings.

medium should be able to see its advertising's
immediate sales effects.

These premises were tested in twelve weeks of
Nabscan data for five packaged goods items (dry
cereals, instant coffee, margarine, paper towels,
and dishwashing detergent) in six markets, with six
stores in each. (To compensate for differences in
market size, the figures were standardized to
reflect unit sales per hundred stores.) In the
aggregate, total category sales for each product
class showed very little change from one period to
the next—the familiar pattern.

Market share was tracked for the major brands
in each category, and significant retail price
changes were noted as well as magazine, newspaper,
and television advertising for each. No instance
was found, in any category, of a brand that
steadily built its market position.

Local consumption patterns and sales in a
product category varied weekly within markets and
also from market to market within the same week,
and individual brand shares showed comparable
variability, in part because of the presence of
regional brands.

Pricing carried differing importance as a
marketing force among the five products. There was
little uniformity of price changes by more than one
brand within a market or by individual brands
across markets. (The comparative pricing of grocery
brands reflects not only the posted retail price of
each item but also the effects of whatever coupon
or price-off offer is currently being merchandised
and promoted. Consumers see a brand's comparative
price position not merely in terms of whether it
costs more or less than it did the previous week,
but relative to its competitors' prices.) Changes
in price rarely coincided for competitive brands.
There was no universal rule regarding the sales
effects of posted price changes.

Did increased advertising pressure add to total
sales of a product? In those weeks when, by chance
or for a combination of reasons, a number of

competing brands happened to step up their advertising volume, this was not clearly reflected in increased product movement.

In five such heavily advertised product fields, a lay person might suppose that every major brand maintains a continuous and ubiquitous presence through all the media. This turns out to be far from the case.

Any given ad occurs in the context of many competing messages; the effects of national advertising, retail advertising, and price changes are interrelated. The effects of advertising are always entangled and generally at cross-purposes with the effects of other advertising. What happens to a brand within a given store as a result of the store's own advertising is offset by what is happening in other stores in the same market. The pattern is complicated further when we look at brand-share fluctuations from week to week across the country, which reflect the net sum of all the local product movements.

Newspaper retail and national advertising showed immediate effects. For magazines, network TV, and spot TV, there was no consistent change. This did not mean that advertising in these media is ineffective. Its effects are usually spread through time, absorbed into the dense competitive communications environment, and untraceable, in the short run, at the point of sale.

1. What appears to be a stable national market for packaged goods is actually extremely volatile. This parallels the constant movement in consumers' buying plans and intentions, the constant switching of individual purchase preferences among brands.

2. There is great variability from market to market and from store to store. In every link of the distribution chain, the national manufacturer confronts a different competitive environment, a different mix of consumer attitudes. With more detailed Census, marketing, and media data available in every marketer's personal computer, there will be more and more reason to plan

advertising with an understanding of distinctive
local needs.

3. Pricing and promotion are two key marketing
elements under the manufacturer's control. Both
have an effect on a given brand's market position,
but rarely is the effect great enough to change the
total volume of consumption in the whole product
class.

4. In total category sales, peaks and valleys
seem to follow each other. This suggests that added
sales at any given moment are generally made at the
expense of future sales. But this is not true if a
specific brand is on the rise, and it is a strong
argument for sustained advertising pressure.

5. Price action does not lead predictably to
changes in market share, and it is most effective
when it is communicated to the consumer.

6. Dramatic changes in market share occur even
when no pricing or advertising activity takes
place. Shelf frontage, store positioning, in-store
display, and point-of-purchase promotion have a
great deal to do with product movement. These
forces are largely beyond the control of individual
manufacturers, no matter how aggressive or
effective their field forces may be.

7. All of the brands covered in this analysis
were big, well known, and heavily advertised. Yet
in most cases, in individual key markets, they had
no significant advertising support in any given
week. A substantial proportion of all ad messages
are disseminated sporadically and on a small scale.
This random diffusion of isolated messages can
hardly have a measurable effect.

Scanner data provide a picture of the market
that is infinitely richer, more detailed, and more
comprehensive than any hitherto available. As they
become available overnight and on-line, they open
up incredible opportunities to react with speed and
flexibility to competitive conditions. But
marketers will be drowned in vastly more
information than they can intelligently handle
unless they can develop systems through which the

significant can be sifted automatically from the
unimportant. A new era of marketing intelligence
has arrived, in which the traditional distinctions
between practice and research no longer apply.

Nabscan had become a drain on the Bureau's resources. It faced
powerful new competition. Before long, Nielsen abandoned national store auditing and also adopted scanner measurement. A
newcomer, Information Resources, Inc., began to use scanner
data to test advertising and promotion and went on to become
one of the world's leading research firms, with $550 million in
annual revenues. In the end Nabscan was given away, and its
new owners eventually closed up shop.

If the Bureau didn't exist, we used to say, it would have to be
reinvented. But the Bureau *did* cease to exist in 1993, several
years after my departure. In the hope of cutting costs, the publishers merged it with the American Newspaper Publishers Association and a number of other newspaper groups to form the new
Newspaper Association of America. Soon afterward, Allen
Neuharth, the wily founder of *USA Today*, stopped me to ask
what I would be doing on May 1, 1998. I consulted my pocket
calendar and told him that the date was clear. "That's good," he
said. "They'll be about ready to reestablish the Bureau by then."
Like 1984, 1998 has come and gone.

AFTERWORD

On a consulting assignment in Russia in 1997, I stopped to visit the dean of the journalism faculty at Moscow State University. It was housed in one of the original domed eighteenth-century buildings, yellow and white on the outside and cavernous within. The men's room was gigantic and appeared to have, if not the original latrine fixtures, others added soon after the invention of indoor plumbing. The washbasins were cracked and filthy; most of the faucets did not work. Another chamber was lined with urinals which appeared not to have been flushed since they were first installed. The peeling wall was festooned with graffiti; one read *"Bei Zhidov!"* (Kill the Yids!).

My explorations in social research have always been rooted in the effort to understand, and thus eventually help overcome, the irrational and bestial elements in human behavior. The research recounted in this book weaves back and forth between mundane subjects and great historical phenomena. Understanding why sales of a detergent brand go up and down may seem trivial, unworthy of serious study. But those fluctuations are indicators of how people respond to symbols; as such they illuminate more momentous matters.

I began with an examination of demagogy; I concluded with an analysis of dry sales figures that demonstrate (among other things) the power of mass media to influence what people do. Research energies and budgets today are largely preoccupied with the collection of impersonal secondary data on markets and audiences. They rely increasingly on mechanical indicators, like scanner data and television tuning and Internet log-in records, rather than on direct reports obtained in interviews. Does this activity come under the heading of applied social research, in the spirit of my adolescent observations on the persuasive powers of Father Divine?

It does, in a sense, because the seemingly abstract numbers are aggregated from many individual human consumption decisions and trace the commercial communications that affect them. Human actions, even at the trivial level of consumer choice, reflect values, beliefs, and judgments shaped by a dense web of social influences. Social science is dedicated to the systematic study of those influences, and its theory and insights are indispensable for the interpretation of data that represent what people do, think, or say.

This may seem rather obvious, but in practice the analysis of information, both in business and in politics, continues to be taken out of the hands of the researchers. In 2002 scanner data are typically scrutinized by brand managers, audience data by media planners, political data by campaign consultants. These are not (necessarily) stupid people; some have taken a course or two in market research or statistics; all have absorbed social science terms and phrases that have passed into the common vocabulary of journalism. But their attention is typically confined within a narrow utilitarian spectrum. Young and Rubicam, a leading advertising agency, had 250 researchers in a total staff of about 1,200 in its head office in 1976. In 2002, Y&R was part of the WPP conglomerate, and had 24 "planners" in its New York headquarters.

Audience ratings accounted for little more than one-fourth of a television network's research budget in 1979 but over half twenty years later.[1] During the same period, that network's research staff was reduced from 118 to 38, reflecting the decline of original studies that require diligent and expert analysis rather than a mere recording of performance.

Masters of business administration who have taken a course in sales and market analysis now consider themselves research experts and "crunch" numbers with scant regard for their origins or meaning. Large advertising agencies have abolished their research departments in favor of units that do "market planning and analysis."

Universal access to computers and the opportunity to play off different types of numbers against each other should greatly enrich the amount of information available to decision makers. Instead databases are ever further disembodied from the real phenomena they purport to represent. Just as in the programmed trading of securities on Wall Street, formula programs for market planning or media buying take one number from Group A and one from Group B and put them together. The result is gospel.

In telephone surveys, bored and indifferent interviewers race through questions with scant regard for their meaning. Questionnaires are often constructed without regard for their effect on the respondent. A confirmed Democrat, asked in a telephone poll to rate President George W. Bush on a scale of 1 to 10, said "1"—but changed his answer when the next question asked him to rate Saddam Hussein on the same scale.

Not long ago a telephone interviewer calling (as I later discovered) from a distant city spent twenty minutes asking me a repetitious series of questions that were supposed to plumb my impressions of local banks whose names I barely knew. At the end I asked if I could now ask him some questions. He had been calling numbers for three hours that evening, and I was the first person who had stayed with him to the end. I didn't explain that I had cooperated only because I am in the business myself.

That business is increasingly dominated by giant companies. The fifty largest account for about half the world's total expenditures on commercial research, and only a handful of these big firms are headed by individuals whose careers were spent in professional research practice.

As research has become the property of nonresearchers, the gap between academic and applied research has widened. Commercial researchers and their interests are no longer well represented in professional journals and conferences that once engaged them in fruitful dialogue with university scholars. Within academic scholarship, research interests have become highly specialized and segmented. The ready availability of computer-packaged statistical programs has facilitated complex analyses, but it has also spurred the disembodiment of data from the original expression of human voices. This tendency is heightened by the almost universally used procedure of weighting and adjusting results from flawed telephone or Internet samples to make them conform to population characteristics known from the Census—itself an imperfect product.

The counterpoise to this abstraction and dehumanization of survey findings has been an explosion of research using collective interviews with small groups of people unsystematically selected without reference to any randomized sampling plan. The comments and observations recorded in "focus groups" were originally intended to help researchers in the design of questionnaires and to illustrate points that arise in analyzing statistical tabulations of large amounts of data. Instead they are now commonly used as the basis for generalizations and as a substitute for more expensive large-scale studies. Group interviews are commonly conducted in rooms with two-way mirrors behind which clients can sit and draw their own instinctive conclusions about people's preferences for candidates or products. For the group's "facilitator," showmanship may be more important than analytical skill. This type of interviewing differs from the individual "depth interviews" employed in the heyday of motivation research in the 1950s and '60s, because it emphasizes the "what" rather than the "why" of opinions and tastes. The "what" makes sense only if the findings are truly representative of the larger population.

The old debates of Alfred Politz and Ernest Dichter falsely presumed that qualitative and quantitative research are incompatible. The studies to which I have referred in this book embody the philosophy that applied research involves the human contact of the researcher with unique individuals. Respecting their individuality and listening carefully to what they say is the first step to finding out what they believe and why they do what they do.

NOTES

Chapter 1. An Academic Apprenticeship

1. Alison Davis, Burleigh B. Gardner, and Mary R. Gardner, *Deep South* (Chicago: University of Chicago Press, 1941).

Chapter 2. Confronting the Unimaginable

1. Raul Hilberg, *The Destruction of the European Jews* (Chicago: Quadrangle Books, 1961).
2. Lucy Dawidowicz, *The War Against the Jews, 1933–45* (New York: Bantam Books, 1975).
3. Arthur D. Morse, *While Six Million Died: A Chronicle of American Apathy* (New York: Random House, 1968). Henry L. Feingold, *The Politics of Rescue: The Roosevelt Administration and the Holocaust, 1938–1945* (New York: Schocken Books, 1980). Peter Novick, *The Holocaust in American Life* (Boston: Houghton Mifflin, 1999).
4. Deborah E. Lipstadt, *Beyond Belief: The American Press and the Coming of the Holocaust 1933–1945* (New York: Free Press, 1986). Walter Laqueur, *The Terrible Secret: Suppression of the Truth About Hitler's "Final Solution"* (Boston: Little Brown, 1980).
5. Louis Wirth, *The Ghetto* (Chicago: University of Chicago Press, 1928).
6. Henry L. Feingold, *Bearing Witness: How America and Its Jews Responded to the Holocaust* (Syracuse: Syracuse University Press, 1995), p. 144.
7. This contrasts with the *American Jewish Yearbook*'s observation in 1946 that "a larger number of new organizations have been formed during the past five years than in any previous five-year period."
8. Personal interview.

Chapter 3. The Lure of Mass Media

1. Harvey Zorbaugh, *The Gold Coast and the Slum* (Chicago: University of Chicago Press, 1929).

Chapter 4. Big Business

1. Adolf A. Berle and Gardiner C. Means, *The Modern Corporation and Private Property* (New York: Social Science Research Council, 1932).
2. Ida M. Tarbell, *The History of the Standard Oil Company* (New York: McClure, Phillips, 1909).
3. R. W. Hidy and M. E. Hidy, *History of the Standard Oil Company (New Jersey)* (New York: Harper, 1955).
4. Paul F. Lazarsfeld, Bernard Berelson, and Hazel Gaudet, *The People's Choice: How the Voter Makes Up His Mind* (New York: Columbia University Press, 1941).
5. *Television* magazine, November 1959.
6. The complete paper was originally published in the *Public Opinion Quarterly*, Fall 1949.
7. "The Spread of News on a Local Event," *Public Opinion Quarterly*, Winter 1950–1951.
8. This process was described by Lazarsfeld, Berelson, and Gaudet as the "two-step flow" of information.
9. *Herrliche Zeiten.*
10. Leo Bogart, ed., *Project Clear: Social Research and the Desegregation of the U.S. Army* (New Brunswick: Transaction, 1992).

Chapter 5. The Profession

1. This followed in a tradition begun years earlier in a classic study of the Western Electric bank wiring room. Cf. Fritz Roethlisberger and William Dickson, *Management and the Worker* (Cambridge: Harvard University Press, 1939).
2. "Is There a World Public Opinion?" *Polls*, I, No. 3 (Spring 1966), 1. My later exposé of Noelle's past was "The Pollster and the Nazis," *Commentary*, August 1991, 47–49. See also her response and my rejoinder (Letters, *Commentary*, January 1992) and the *Chronicle of Higher Education*, August 8, 1997.

Chapter 6. Immigration, as Immigrants See It

1. The complete study which this paper summarizes was originally published as *Les Algériens en France: Adaptation Réussie et Non Réussie*, in Alfred Sauvy, ed., *Français et Immigrés*, II (Paris: Presses Universitaires de France, 1953).

Chapter 7. On the Edge of the Cold War

1. Gunnar Myrdal, *An American Dilemma: The Negro Problem and Modern Democracy* (New York: Harper, 1944).
2. Cf. Edward W. Barrett, *Truth Is Our Weapon* (New York: Funk and Wagnalls, 1953). As assistant secretary of state, Barrett had been in charge of the Voice of America before becoming dean of the Columbia University School of Journalism.

Chapter 8. The Ad Business

1. Sloan Wilson, *The Man in the Grey Flannel Suit* (Mattituck, N.Y.: Amereon House, 1999).
2. Mark Zborowski and Elizabeth Herzog, *Life Is with People: The Jewish Little-Town of Eastern Europe* (New York: International Universities Press, 1952).
3. Vance Packard, *The Hidden Persuaders* (New York: McKay, 1957).
4. Review of Leo Bogart, ed., *Current Controversies in Marketing Research*, in *Journal of the Market Research Society*, XII, No. 3, 204–205.
5. Charles Winick refreshed my memory on this point.
6. Summarized from my article "Measuring the Effects of an Overseas Information Campaign: A Case History," *Public Opinion Quarterly*, XXI, No. 1 (January 1962).
7. Wilbur L. Schramm, *The Process and Effects of Mass Communication* (Urbana: University of Illinois Press, 1961).

Chapter 9. Beauty and the Beasts

1. The appeal of the quiz show format was studied in radio days by Herta Herzog: "Why People Like the Professor Quiz Program," in Paul Lazarsfeld, ed., *Radio and the Printed Page* (New York: Duell, Sloan and Pearce, 1940).
2. Robert Foreman, *The Hot Half Hour* (London: Angus and Robertson, 1959).

Chapter 10. From Radio to Television

1. Leo Bogart, *The Age of Television* (New York: Frederick Ungar, 1956, 1958, 1972).
2. John P. Murray, Eli A. Rubenstein, and George A. Comstock, eds., *Television and Social Behavior: Reports and Papers* (Rockville, Md.: National Institute of Mental Health, 1972). For a summary and commentary, cf. Leo Bogart, "Warning: The Surgeon General Has Determined That TV Violence Is Moderately Dangerous to Your Child's Mental Health," *Public Opinion Quarterly*, XXXVI, No. 4 (Winter 1972–1973).
3. R. K. Baker and S. J. Ball, eds., *Violence and the Media* (Washington, D.C.: U.S. Government Printing Office, 1969).

Chapter 11. Selling Newspapers

1. This and the following three paragraphs are taken from *Preserving the Press* (New York: Columbia University Press, 1991), p. 27.
2. John B. Stewart, *Repetitive Advertising in Newspapers* (Boston: Harvard University, Graduate School of Business Administration, 1964).

Afterword

1. According to David Poltrack, CBS Television's executive vice president.

INDEX

A NOTE ON THE AUTHOR

As a sociologist, Leo Bogart has specialized in mass media and communication for more than fifty years. After receiving a Ph.D. from the University of Chicago, he directed public opinion research for the Standard Oil Company (New Jersey), marketing research for Revlon, and account research service for McCann-Erickson advertising, and was for many years executive vice president of the Newspaper Advertising Bureau. He has also taught at New York University, Columbia University, and the Illinois Institute of Technology, and has been a senior fellow at the Center for Media Studies at Columbia and a Fulbright research fellow. He has received distinguished achievement awards and citations from the American Marketing Association, the American Association for Public Opinion Research, and the American Society of Newspaper Editors. He and George Gallup were the first persons elected to the Market Research Council's Hall of Fame. His books include *Strategy in Advertising, Silent Politics, Premises for Propaganda, Preserving the Press,* and *Commercial Culture.* He now writes a column for *Presstime* and is a director of the Innovation International Media consulting group. He lives in New York City.